Universal Basic Income (UBI)
from Apes to Humanity

Jingwei (景維)
jjingwei11@gmail.com
Singapore
13 November 2022
This is a self-published monograph.

Jingwei Publishing (self-publisher)
Title Availability:
Worldwide (order online)
Print-on-demand (POD) by Lightning Source, UK
Distribution through Ingram International
Espresso Book Machine
Amazon.com
The Book Depository.co.uk *(with free delivery worldwide)*

Publication Data
Disclaimer:
Every precaution has been taken in the preparation of this monograph.
The publisher and author apologize for any errors or omissions that may remain.
The publisher and author assume no liability whatsoever, for damages suffer from its usage.
Copyright © 2022
All rights reserved.
Copying is allowed for individual private use.
Copying is *not* allowed for commercial trade.

Self-Published by Jingwei (景維)
email: jjingwei11@gmail.com
Title Availability:
Worldwide (order online)
Print-on-demand (POD) by Lightning Source, UK
Distribution through Ingram International
The Book Depository.co.uk (with free delivery worldwide)
Espresso Book Machine
Amazon.com
List price: SGD$20.00

National Library Board, Singapore Cataloguing in Publication Data

Name(s): Jingwei, 1945-
Title: Universal basic income (UBI) : from apes to humanity / Jingwei.
Description: [Singapore] : Jingwei Publishing, [2023]
Identifier(s): ISBN 978-981-18-5995-3 (paperback)
Subject(s): LCSH: Basic income. | Income distribution--Social aspects.
Classification: DDC 331.23--dc23

Jingwei Publishing (self-publisher)
Book cover:
Thousand miles of rivers and mountains landscape (Wang Ximeng, Northern Song)
千里江山圖 (王希孟, 北宋, c.1113 AD. 青綠山水,12 m.長卷)
Photo: to be purchased online from ~ALAMY.com, usd19.99.
Printer: Ultra Supplies, Singapore
First Print: 10 copies, November 2022
Print-on-demand (POD) by Lightning Source UK Ltd.
Paperback: B&W 156 x 234mm
Page Count: 187
Weight: 300g (approx.)

Dedicated to:

Total Implementation of the UBI Concept

Thus

Honoring our BirthRight to a Universal Basic Value

Leading to Complete Eradication of Poverty on Earth

That is Conducive to Harmony among all Races and Nations

Thereby Uplifting the Naked Apes

from the Uncivilized state

to the Civilized state

Mother Nature leaves no one hungry

Synopsis

"...The most affluent and the most miserable of the human race are to be found in the countries that are called *civilized*... Poverty therefore, is a thing created by that which is called *civilized* life. It exists not in the natural state. ..The life of an Indian is a continual holiday, compared with the poor of Europe;.." Thomas Paine has first called out the 'UNCIVILIZED' state of modern society in his *Agrarian Justice (1817)*. In the election campaign for president in 2020, Andrew Yang promised if elected, to establish a Universal Basic Income (UBI); that is to give *unconditionally* to *every* American $1000/- *cash per month for life*. This money only supports the individual's basic needs for food and lodging, so that he is 'freed' and has energy to work for a better life.

Many pilot studies into the desirability and feasibility of the Universal Basic Income (UBI) have been initiated the world over; in Africa, America, Brazil, Canada, Europe, India, Iran, … Even with a modest UBI, results are positive with recipients happier and in better health. Children are better nourished and stay in school longer. Certainly there is no evidence of recipients working less as feared. Or abused the use of UBI cash on alcohol/drugs. In fact they turned entrepreneurial, starting new businesses and making better use of their limited cash than welfare workers with relief funds.

In our world today, great advances in technologies have created enormous wealth, enough to make the majority of us wealthy and to eliminate poverty on earth. But instead selfish governments have allowed wealth loss through cronyism, enriching only the top 1% of the population, and the gap between the Have and the Have-nots to close not but widened!!! The *uncivilized* state of society that Paine described has persisted to this day. The solution has to be the simple UBI that he proposed, fair to everyone and easily administered by any government who honestly cares for its citizens. Just put the cash into the hands of citizens and their self-help effort is certain to make a happier world for themselves.

Firstly, we reviewed our World of Miseries like Poverty, Homelessness, Suicides, ..
Then we examined the World of Capitalism, the root causes of these miseries.
Next we appreciated the compelling positivity of the pilot Studies on UBI, worldwide.
Lastly, we discussed 35 topical issues around the concept of UBI as basic Human Right.

Conclusion:

Miseries of the human race can find relief with a minimum UBI in place.

Every morning, I see birds foraging/fighting to fill their stomachs, to live for the day.

Hopefully the UBI will lift all humanity above the animal level of subsistence.

A simple UBI Index of happiness is proposed, UBI cash paid as % of the poverty line.

PREFACE

Since retirement from bio-research in 2007, I have researched 3 ancient Chinese texts.
Laozi: Quest for the Ultimate Reality (ISBN 978-981-07-3758-0), nonfiction, Oct 2012.
Yijing: Wisdom of 4 Sages (ISBN 978-981-14-0204-3), nonfiction, March 2019.
Liezi: World of Delusions (ISBN 978-981-14-8572-5), nonfiction, February, 2021.
Laozi is listed among "Indie Books Worth Discovering", 15 May 2017, *Kirkus Reviews*.
All books are set to print-on-demand by Lightning Source UK, and offered only online.

Yijing teaches self cultivation of a gentleman (君子) for love/justice/public service.
The *Laozi* teaches primal virtues like honesty/humility/non-violence/unselfish/respect.
The *Liezi* rejects transcendence, helps us with revelation of pride/prejudice/Delusions.
This trilogy all happened to expound the core values and teachings in natural Daoism.
They are guiding the caring/sharing actions of leaders in the peaceful rise of China.
To build a world of equal nations with common destiny and sharing prosperity.
Mutual respect, non-violence, unselfish; building trust and harmony among nations.
To promote awareness of natural Daoism, I offered free books to University Libraries.
To date I donated > 350 copies to individuals and institutional libraries, worldwide.
The National Library of China, Congress Library, Diet Library, British Library, ..
University libraries of Yale, Cambridge, Amsterdam, Barcelona, Macau, Wuhan, ..

Universal Basic Income (UBI)

In 2020, a presidential candidate, Andrew Yang revitalized this idea of UBI in America.
Adults reaching age 18, are to be given $1000/mth, cash for life with no string attached.
Such similar plan to alleviate poverty was first proposed by Thomas Paine (1817).
Today, automation increasingly made jobs redundant, pushing more people out of work.
To help the masses, urgency of a UBI scheme is acutely felt by many around the world.
I feel this is the greatest idea for alleviating poverty on earth and in any human society.
It can be easily implemented, placing cash directly into the hands of individuals.
The problem is getting finance, cash needed which one estimate puts at 10% GDP!
Citizens born to the land inherit the land, and Paine proposes taxing for land usage.
Citizens have the right to automation-gains, and Yang proposes a Goods & Service Tax.

Aims of Study:

In 1817, Paine said, "The present state of civilization is as odious as it is unjust."
I propose to examine this UBI concept as a solution and write my findings here.
To argue fairness in the UBI concept, to give everyone a universal basic value (UBV).
To argue inherent rights to a UBV that will lift us from animal existence to Humanity.

The title chosen for this work is:
Universal Basic Income (UBI): from Uncivilized to Civilized

<u>Contents</u>

Introduction

AGRARIAN JUSTICE

OPPOSED TO

Agrarian Law,

AND TO

AGRARIAN MONOPOLY;

BEING A PLAN FOR

MELIORATING THE CONDITION OF MAN,

BY CREATING IN EVERY NATION A

NATIONAL FUND,

To pay to every Person, when arrived at the Age of Twenty-one Years, the Sum of Fifteen Pounds Sterling, to enable him, or her, to begin the World;

AND ALSO,

Ten pounds Sterling per Annum during Life to every Person now living, of the Age of Fifty Years, and to all Others when they shall arrive at that Age, to enable them to live in Old Age without Wretchedness, and go decently out of the World.

BY THOMAS PAINE.

LONDON:

PRINTED BY W. T. SHERWIN, 183, FLEET STREET.

1817.

Thomas Paine's Dedication, 1817.

Introduction

Problem

Laozi has called the ruling class 'Chiefs of robbers' some 2500 years ago.

09 服文采	Cloth in finery (Lords and Kings)
10 帶利剑	Carry sharp swords
11 厌饮食	Over-indulge in food and wine
12 财货有余	Wealth and goods possession in excess
13 是谓盗夸	They are chiefs of robbers *(ch.53, Jingwei 2012)*

Liezi says the elite class who want ever more are 'Termites of nature'.

01 杨朱曰：	Yangzhu Said:
02 "丰屋美服，	"Luxurious House Beautiful Clothes,
03 厚味姣色，	Rich Taste (food) Pretty Color (sex)
04 有此四者，	Having These 4 Things,
05 何求于外？	What Else To Request ?
06 有此而求外者，	People Having These And still Request More,
07 无厌之性。	Always Greedy This Character.
08 无厌之性，	Wanting Ever-more This Character,
09 阴阳之蠹也。	The Termites of Yin Yang (Nature). *(ch.7.16, Jingwei 2021)*

Since ancient times, oppression of the masses by the ruling class has been reprimanded.
In our world today, we still see the wealth of nations concentrating in the top 1%.
Whereas the large majority live from paycheck to paycheck, if not already in poverty.
Oppressive nature of the ruling elite has persisted to this day, with increased intensity.

Solution

Thomas Paine (1817) saw the wretchedness of the masses that landlords had exploited.
He proposed to pay adults aged 21, the sum of 15 pound Sterling to start Life with.
And 10 pounds/annum for life, to all persons aged 50, to live without wretchedness.
And to exit this world with some degree of grace at least (see *Agrarian Justice*).

Andrew Yang (2018) sees the coming of automation and mass displacement of workers.
He proposes a Freedom Dividend of $1000/- a month for all aged 18 & above, till death.
Putting Cash directly into the hands of the people, with no whatsoever string attached.
Funding plan with a Goods and Service Tax (GST), taxing every business transaction.
The money needed is huge but not formidable, estimated to be about 10% of the GDP.
The money stimulates the local market, a trickle-up economy that increases the GDP !
Funding can also be had from savings with cut-back from the many costly aid-schemes.
Thomas Paine's idea of a National Fund may be added, a ground-rent on land usage.
Paying out a Universal Basic Income (UBI) is certainly feasible *without* increased tax
on the 'rich'.

Universal Basic Income (UBI)

This concept to alleviate poverty is rather refreshing, unlike traditional aid schemes.
Giving *money* directly to the people, with *no string attached* as to how they may use it.
Guaranteed basic income provides economic security to everyone from age 18 till death.

At the turn of the 21 century, people were excited over the idea in talks and in seminars.
UBI pilot studies have been initiated the world over, in Brazil, Germany, Iran, India, ...
Results are positive, less stress/quarrels, more healthier/children learning better, ...
United States Congress had passed a bill for such a scheme in the Nixon administration.
Democrats in the Senate wanted the amount increased, resulting in endless debates.
The state of Alaska has struck oil, and is wondering what to do with tax revenue from it.
The governor has decided to distribute it (~1000 usd/annum), and Alaskans are happy.

UBI: A Panacea for Miseries of the World !

It hurts to see beggars/homeless on the streets, especially in first world countries.
Thomas Paine saw no such misery among Indian tribes but only in 'civilized' states.
Pondering the truth of the universe, I also look-out for a panacea for human sufferings.
It strikes me that the UBI Index can alleviate many human miseries, all at the same time.
Studies have shown monetary security, even for a limited period, has positive effects.
People are happier, healthier, less violent, children are better nourished/better at school.
Thus if UBI is fully implemented for life, the true human spirit will be fully liberated.
With financial security, people have more children and the aging population is resolved.
Financing a UBI monthly is formidable, and one estimates it at 10% of the GDP.
Thomas Paine proposes a National Fund from collecting ground-rent from proprietors.
Andrew Yang proposed a Goods and Service Tax (GST) for every business transaction.
UBI cash stimulates the local market, a trickle-up economy that helps increase the GDP.
Automation kills jobs but at the same time does generate an abundance of resources.
Enough to pay everyone a subsistence UBI if the wealth is not stolen by 'billionaires'.
Really there is no question of increased taxation of businesses and 'rich' individuals !
*Government should harvest A.I. generated resources for a UBI **before** the billionaires.*
"UBI can be financed with the abolition of tax cuts, tax credit, increased VAT rate..
There is money for saving corporations in the pandemic, there is money to pay for UBI.
 With so much spent on sponsoring wars, paying for such an endeavor is a breeze."
(Nwanazia, 2021)
Implementing the UBI is simplicity itself, putting money directly into people's hands.
In this electronic-age, transferring cash into people's accounts can be done in seconds.
".. that the earth, in its natural uncultivated state was the common property of the human
race. In that state every man would have been born to property. He would have been a
joint life proprietor with the rest in the property of the soil, and in all its natural
productions, vegetable and animal." *(Paine, 1817)*
Thus every one (rich or poor) have inherent, equal rights to the Universal Basic Income.

Design of this study

Introduction
World of Miseries (problem)
World of Capitalism (cause)
Studies of UBI (solution)
Discussions
Conclusions
Bibliography and References
Appendices

Methodology
The Internet is googled for Facts/Figures that are freely available from open sources.
Selected articles that are relevant to the study are read to extract the precise information.
To avoid errors in paraphrasing, it deems better to present authors in their own words.
Hence redundant sections and words are cut out, often reducing an article to 5% or less.
All chosen texts remaining are presented, enclosed in double quotation marks (" ").
Where sections are cut off, the discontinuity is indicated with (..) at the front or back.
Authors' names and publication addresses on the internet are documented for reference.
Facts/Figures from reputed researchers/institutions are presumed fair and accurate.
Whether acceptable or not, they are from open sources and so are open for discussion.

Shorter/simpler English words are favored when meaning/spirit are not compromised.
Chinese style construct of sentences is adopted, short phrases separated with commas.
All sentences are constructed so as to confine to a single line for easy reading.
Over 2 years, different words/phrases are used in various sections for the same purpose.
No attempt is made for uniformity as the differences may give a broader perspective.
Like the initial title chosen is left in place, *"UBI: from Uncivilized to Civilized."*

Aim of study
In 1817, Paine said, "The present state of civilization is as odious as it is unjust."
I propose to examine this UBI concept as a solution and write my findings here.
To argue fairness in the UBI concept, to give everyone a universal basic value (UBV).
To gather facts/figures and information freely available in the internet, on:
World of Miseries, the prevalence of poverty, homelessness, crimes rates and suicide.
World of Capitalism, the 'privileged' few who stole billions, making the majority suffer.
UBI Studies, that offers compelling evidence of the many benefits of the concept.

Every morning, I saw early birds furiously forage/contest for food, to live for the day.
Supported with an UBI, society can lift humanity above the level of animal subsistence.
Thus the title chosen: **Universal Basic Income (UBI): from Apes to Humanity.**

World of Miseries

City Slum

17   World of Miseries (25 articles)

Thomas Paine

Agrarian Justice
By Thomas Paine (1737-1809). (http://piketty.pse.ens.fr/files/Paine1795.pdf)
grundskyld.dk Digital edition 1999 by www.grundskyld.dk

"*...The most affluent and the most miserable of the human race are to be found in the countries that are called civilized...* Poverty therefore, is a thing created by that which is called civilized life. It exists not in the natural state. *..The life of an Indian is a continual holiday, compared with the poor of Europe;* and, on the other hand it appears to be abject when compared to the rich. Civilization therefore, .. has operated two ways to make one part of society more affluent, and the other more wretched...the first principle of civilization ought to have been, ..that the condition of every person born into the world, after a state of civilization commences, ought not to be worse than if he had been born before that period. But the fact is, that the condition of millions, in every country in Europe, is far worse than if they had been born before civilization began, or had been born among the Indians of North America at the present day.

...that the earth, in its natural uncultivated state was the common property of the human race. In that state every man would have been born to property. He would have been a joint life proprietor with the rest in the property of the soil, and in all its natural productions, vegetable and animal.

...Cultivation is at least one of the greatest natural improvements ever made by human invention. It has given to created earth a tenfold value. *But the landed monopoly that began with it has produced the greatest evil. It has dispossessed more than half the inhabitants of every nation of their natural inheritance, without providing for them, as ought to have been done, an indemnification for that loss, and has thereby created a species of poverty and wretchedness that did not exist before...*In advocating the case of the persons thus dispossessed, it is a right, and not a charity, that I am pleading for. Every proprietor of cultivated land, owes to the community a ground-rent...To create a National Fund, out of which there shall be paid to *every person*, when arrived at the age of twenty-one years, the sum of fifteen pounds sterling, as a compensation in part, for the loss of his or her natural inheritance, by the introduction of the system of landed property: And also, the sum of ten pounds per annum, during life, to every person now living, of the age of fifty years, and to all others as they shall arrive at that age.

...The fault, however, is not in the present possessors. No complaint is intended, or ought to be alleged against them, unless they adopt the crime by opposing justice. The fault is in the system, and it has stolen imperceptibly upon the world, aided afterwards by the agrarian law of the sword.

...It is proposed that the payments, as already stated, be made to every person, rich or poor. It is best to make it so, to prevent invidious distinctions. It is also right it should be so, because it is in lieu of the natural inheritance, which, as a right, belongs to every man, over and above the property he may have created, or inherited from those who did. ..taking twenty-one years as the epoch of maturity, all the property of a nation, real and personal, is always in the possession of persons above that age. It is then necessary to know, as a datum of calculation, the average of years which persons above that age will live. I take this average to be about thirty years, for though many persons will live forty, fifty, or sixty years after the age of twenty-one years, others will die much sooner, and some in every year of that time...I have no idea it would be accepted by many persons who had a yearly income of two or three hundred pounds sterling. But we see instances of rich people falling into sudden poverty, even at the age of sixty, ...

...*It is not charity but a right, not bounty but justice,* that I am pleading for. The present state of *civilization* is as odious as it is unjust. It is absolutely the opposite of what it should be, and it is necessary that a revolution should be made in it. The contrast of affluence and wretchedness continually meeting and offending the eye, is like dead and living bodies chained together... I care not how affluent some may be, provided that none be miserable in consequence of it. But it is impossible to enjoy affluence with the felicity it is capable of being enjoyed, whilst so much misery is mingled in the scene.

...It is, however, but little that any individual can do, when the whole extent of the misery to be relieved is considered. He may satisfy his conscience but not his heart. He may give all that he has, and that all will relieve but little. It is only by organizing civilization upon such principles as to act like a system of pulleys, that the whole weight of misery can be removed. The plan here proposed will reach the whole. It will immediately relieve and take out of view three classes of wretchedness--the blind, the lame, and the aged poor; and it will furnish the rising generation with means to prevent their becoming poor; and it will do this without deranging or interfering with any national measures.

...The rugged face of society, chequered with the extremes of affluence and want, proves that some extraordinary violence has been committed upon it, and calls on *justice* for redress. The great mass of the poor in all countries are become an hereditary race, and it is next to impossible for them to get out of that state of themselves. It ought also to be observed that this mass increases in all countries that are called *civilized*.

...for if we examine the case minutely it will be found that the accumulation of personal property is, in many instances, the effect of paying too little for the labor that produced it; the consequence of which is, that the working hand perishes in old age, and the employer abounds in affluence.

...The superstitious awe, the enslaving reverence, that formerly surrounded affluence, is passing away in all countries and leaving the possessor of property to the convulsion of accidents. When wealth and splendour, instead of fascinating the multitude, excite emotions of disgust; ...when the more riches a man acquires, the better it shall be for the general mass; it is then that antipathies will cease, and property be placed on the permanent basis of national interest and protection."

Comments:

Thomas Paine found the most miserable human race in 'civilized' countries in Europe
In contrast the life of an Indian is a continual holiday compared to the poor of Europe.
He correctly said the landed monopoly dispossessed more than half of the inhabitants.
Thereby producing the greatest of evil, the poverty and wretchedness among the poor.
Fairly, he stated that the earth and all therein are common property of the human race.
And *every man* is a joint life proprietor with the rest in the common property of the soil.
Paine therefore advocates a National Fund to be created from collecting ground-rent.
To pay every person, rich or poor, starting life at the age of 21 years, 15 pounds sterling.
Also 10 pounds yearly for life, to every person now living, upon retirement at age fifty.
Universal Basic Income in lieu of natural inheritance, is a right, not a charity.

Crime. World

Crime Rate By Country 2021
https://worldpopulationreview.com/country-rankings/crime-rate-by-country

Overall crime rate is calculated by dividing the total number of reported crimes of any kind by the total population, then multiplying the result by 100,000 (because crime rate is typically reported as X number of crimes per 100,000 people).

Crime rates vary greatly from country to country and are influenced by many factors. For example, high poverty levels and unemployment tend to inflate a country's crime rate. Conversely, strict police enforcement and severe sentences tend to reduce crime rates. There is also a strong correlation between age and crime, with most crimes, especially violent crimes, being committed by those ages 20-30 years old.
The overall crime rate in the United States is 47.70. The violent crime rate in the United States has decreased sharply over the past 25 years. Crime rates vary significantly between the states, with states such as Alaska, New Mexico, and Tennessee experiencing much higher crime rates than states such as Maine, New Hampshire, and Vermont.

Some of the world's lowest crime rates are seen in Switzerland, Denmark, Norway, Japan, and New Zealand. Each of these countries has very effective law enforcement, and Denmark, Norway, and Japan have some of the most restrictive gun laws in the world.

The countries with the ten highest crime rates in the world are:
Venezuela (83.76): corrupt authorities, a flawed judiciary system, and poor gun control.
Papua New Guinea (80.79): violent crime, gangs, corruption, drug, human trafficking.
South Africa (76.86): assaults, rape, homicides,..inequality,.. normalization of violence.
Afghanistan (76.31): corruption, assassinations/contract killings, drug trafficking, ..
Honduras (74.54): 2012, 20 homicides per day, gun-toting gangs..a major drug route..
Trinidad and Tobago (71.63): gangs, drugs, weapons..drug..assault, theft, and fraud.
Guyana (68.74): murder..firearms..domestic violence..Armed robberies..hotel break-ins..
El Salvador (67.79): Organized gangs..drug traffickers..robbery, vehicle thefts common.
Brazil (67.49): corruption, organized crime, homicide, drugs, domestic violence,..
Jamaica (67.42): government corruption, gang activity, violent crime, sexual assault.
Comments:
Inequality and corruption create poverty that breeds misery, violence, high crime rates.
The solution is relatively simple; quickly establishes a guaranteed UBI for all citizens.
As Paine says, "..take out of view the wretchedness of the blind, lame and aged poor".
A full UBI is truly expensive, but even a sub-UBI can start to have beneficial effects.
A sub-UBI at 20% subsistence level may be built up gradually over 5 years to 100%.
UBI is equality, and its establishment is proof of a just and incorrupt government.

Crime. Prison

Prison
From Wikipedia, the free encyclopedia (//en.wikipedia.org/ wiki/Prison)

..In simplest terms, a prison can also be described as a building in which people are legally held as a punishment for a crime they have committed.
Prisons can also be used as a tool of political repression by authoritarian regimes. ..In times of war, prisoners of war..may be detained in military prisons and large groups of civilians might be imprisoned in internment camps.

History: ..Plato, began to develop ideas of using punishment to reform offenders instead of simply using it for its own sake. The Romans were among the first to use prisons as a form of punishment, rather than simply for detention. A variety of existing structures were used to house prisoners, such as metal cages, basements of public buildings, and quarries. ..Forced labor on public works projects was also a common form of punishment. In many cases, citizens were sentenced to slavery, often in ergastula (a primitive form of prison where unruly slaves were chained to workbenches and performed hard labor). ..Another common punishment was sentencing people to galley slavery, which involved chaining prisoners together in the bottoms of ships and forcing them to row on naval or merchant vessels.

Modern era: ..From the late 17th century and during the 18th century, popular resistance to public execution and torture became more widespread both in Europe and in the United States. ..Particularly under the Bloody Code, with few sentencing alternatives, imposition of the death penalty for petty crimes, such as theft, was proving increasingly unpopular with the public; ..They developed systems of mass incarceration, often with hard labor, as a solution. ..The concept of the modern prison was imported to Europe in the early 19th-century. Punishment usually consisted of physical forms of punishment, including capital punishment, mutilation, flagellation (whipping), branding, and non-physical punishments, such as public shaming rituals (like the stocks).

England used penal transportation of convicted criminals (and others generally young and poor) for a term of indentured servitude within the general population of British America between the 1610s and 1776. ..Britain would resume transportation to specifically planned penal colonies in Australia between 1788 and 1868. ...Jails at the time were run as business ventures, and contained both felons and debtors; the latter were often housed with their wives and younger children. The jailers made their money by charging the inmates for food, drink, and other services, and the system was generally corruptible.

In 2010, the International Centre for Prison Studies found that at least 10.1 million people were imprisoned worldwide. As of 2012 the United States of America had the world's largest prison population, with over 2.3 million people in American prisons or jails—up from 744,000 in 1985—making 1 in every 100 American adults a prisoner. ..Not all countries have a rise in prison population: Sweden closed four prisons in 2013 due to a significant drop in the number of inmates.

In the United States alone, more than $74 billion per year is spent on prisons, with over 800,000 people employed in the prison industry. As the prison population grows, revenues increase for a variety of small and large businesses that construct facilities, and provide equipment (security systems, furniture, clothing), and services (transportation, communications, healthcare, food) for prisons. These parties have a strong interest in the expansion of the prison system since their development and prosperity directly depends on the number of inmates. The prison industry also includes private businesses that benefit from the exploitation of the prison labor. Some scholars, using the term prison-industrial complex, have argued that the trend of "hiring out prisoners" is a continuation of the slavery tradition, pointing out that the Thirteenth Amendment to the United States Constitution freed slaves but allowed forced labor for people convicted of crimes.

..Evaluation: Prisoners are at risk of being drawn further into crime, as they may become acquainted with other criminals, trained in further criminal activity, exposed to further abuse (both from staff and other prisoners) and left with criminal records that make it difficult to find legal employment after release. All of these things can result in a higher likelihood of reoffending upon release. ..This has resulted in a series of studies that are skeptical towards the idea that prison can rehabilitate offenders.

..The National Institute of Justice argues that offenders can be deterred by the fear of being caught but are unlikely to be deterred by the fear or experience of the punishment. ..The argument that prisons can reduce crime through incapacitation is more widely accepted, even among academics who doubt that prisons can rehabilitate or deter offenders. ..some prison abolitionists arguing that imprisoning people for actions the state designates as crimes is not only inexpedient but also immoral.

Comments:

In 2010, studies found that at least 10.1 million people were imprisoned worldwide.
As of 2012 the United States of America had over 2.3 million people in prisons.
Prisons are costly, and the United States spends more than $74 billion per year.
Discrimination, inequality and poverty are grounds for breeding miseries and crimes.
Prisons seldom deter offenders but are often places for 'schooling' hard-core criminals.
A UBI is excellent for removing discrimination, inequality and poverty all at one 'go'.
As Prevention is Better than Cure, UBI is a Priority to Deter Crime before Prison !

Homeless. Worldwide

Homelessness

Wikipedia, last edited on 17 November 2021 (///en.wikipedia.org/wiki/Homelessness)

..In 2005, an estimated 100 million people worldwide were homeless and as many as one billion people (one in 6.5 at the time) lived as squatters, refugees or in temporary shelter, all lacking adequate housing. Historically in the Western countries, the majority of homeless have been men (50–80%), with single males in particular..

..When compared to the general population, people who are homeless experience higher rates of adverse physical and mental health outcomes. Chronic disease severity, respiratory conditions, rates of mental health illnesses and substance use are all often greater in homeless populations than the general population. Homelessness is also associated with a high risk of suicide attempts.

..Article 25 of the Universal Declaration of Human Rights, adopted 10 December 1948 by the UN General Assembly, contains this text regarding housing and quality of living: Everyone has the right to a standard of living adequate for the health and well-being of himself and of his family, including food, clothing, housing, and medical care and necessary social services, and the right to security in the event of unemployment, sickness, disability, widowhood, old age or other lack of livelihood in circumstances beyond his control.

..In 2013, a Central Florida Commission on Homelessness study indicated that the region spends $31,000 a year per homeless person to cover "salaries of law enforcement officers to arrest and transport homeless individuals – largely for nonviolent offenses such as trespassing, public intoxication or sleeping in parks – as well as the cost of jail stays, emergency room visits and hospitalization for medical and psychiatric issues. This did not include "money spent by nonprofit agencies to feed, clothe and sometimes shelter these individuals". In contrast, the report estimated the cost of permanent supportive housing at "$10,051 per person per year" and concluded that "housing even half of the region's chronically homeless population would save taxpayers $149 million over the next decade – even allowing for 10 percent to end up back on the streets again." This particular study followed 107 long-term-homeless residents living in Orange, Osceola or Seminole Counties. There are similar studies showing large financial savings in Charlotte and Southeastern Colorado from focusing on simply housing the homeless."

Comments:

In 2005, an estimated 100 million people were homeless, worldwide.

And 1 billion people (1 in 6.5) lived as squatters, refugees or in temporary shelter.

This is a violation of Article 25 of the Universal Declaration of Human Rights, UN.

In 2013 Florida said, $10K can house a homeless person instead of $31K to police him.

Give the man his birthright, a UBI of $1K/month, and he will solve his own problems.

Homeless. Canada

Homelessness in Canada

Wikipedia, 28 November 2021 (///en.wikipedia.org/wiki/Homelessness_in_Canada)

Homelessness in Canada has grown in hugeness and complexity since 1997. ..In dealing with homelessness in Canada, the government focus is on the Housing First model. Thus, private or public organizations across Canada are eligible to receive HPS subsidies to implement *Housing First programs*. Canada spends more than 30 billion annually on social service programs for the homeless. ..By 2008 the annual homeless count was considered to be a politically charged and methodologically contentious issue. The federal estimate of the core number of homeless people in Canada was 200,000 in 2005, or about 1 percent of the population. Homeless advocates estimated it to be closer to 20,000 annually, or 30,000 on any given night plus those in the hidden homeless category. This includes 6,000 youth nightly and 30,000 youth annually. ..Based on the more conservative figure, the annual cost of homelessness in Canada in 2008 was approximately $5.5 to $7 billion in emergency services, organizations, ..

..Homelessness is a chronic problem for only a small minority of people; the vast majority of individuals are "one-time only" shelter users or experience episodic homelessness. However, this distinctly different subgroup of individuals who are "chronically homeless" consume about half of shelter beds and available resources at any given time. ..In 1999, 2.8 million Canadian households (about 26%) fell below the minimum amount required to afford a basic home, gauged at $25,920. Five years later, this number rose to 3.2 million households (remaining about 26%).

..Lack of low-income housing: While in 1966 30,000 new low-income housing units had been built across Canada, this had fallen to 7,000 in 1999. In the city of Calgary, with one of the most acute housing shortages, only 16 new units of rental housing were built in 1996.

..deinstitutionalization of the mentally ill, moving them out of asylums and other facilities, and releasing them into the community. ..While some of those discharged did integrate with the community, a significant number, estimated at around 75%, did not. Many of these individuals became homeless. Today up to 40% of homeless have some sort of mental illness.

..prisoners who are sentenced or who are awaiting trial often lose their jobs and housing, and without support, wind up in homeless shelters and drop-ins upon release ... When prisoners become homeless, their chances of reoffending increase..

..Poverty remains prevalent with certain groups in Canada. The measurement of poverty has been a challenge as there is no official government measure. Some groups, like the Canadian Council on Social Development and the National Anti-Poverty Organization, believe the low-income cut off published by Statistics Canada is applicable as a poverty measure regardless of whether its intent or designation is to be one. They have argued that as it stands, the LICO is the best measure available that accurately measures a relative poverty rate. The LICO fell to a near-record low of 9.5% in 2006, down from a recent high of 16.7% in 1994. ..In the 2005 census, 702,650 Canadians were considered to be at-risk for homelessness in that they spent more than 50 per cent of their household income on shelter. Lack of income security combined with the lack of affordable housing creates the problem of "hidden" homelessness.

..Cuts to Social Assistance: In 2002, B.C. 's newly elected Liberal government introduced welfare reforms which in the coming years removed tens of thousands from that province's welfare rolls. All of this has had the effect of leaving thousands of people without the means to pay for even the most modest accommodation, resulting in many Canadians having no home and thus relying on homeless shelters or.. sleeping outside.

..1 in 15 Indigenous Peoples in urban centers experience homelessness, compared to 1 in 128 for the general population. First Nation women have the lowest income rate of any group in Canada, and have the highest rate of experience violence. They also have a lack of mobility, due in part to reserve laws, and inability to own property. Indigenous youth are overrepresented in the homeless population of Canada. Systematic discrimination has contributed to this.. There was also a loss of culture when the colonizing populations took over indigenous land and subjected them to European ways of life. ..Survivors of residential schools faced physical, sexual, and emotional trauma. The European settlers used these schools as a tool to assimilate indigenous youth, which has resulted in decades of trauma that can still be seen in indigenous communities today.

..Housing has been declared a fundamental human right. Canada helped to draft the 1948 UN Declaration of Human Rights that includes a right to access housing in Article 25. ..Pathways to Housing Canada uses the *Housing First model, a* "*client-driven strategy* that provides immediate access to an apartment without requiring initial participation in psychiatric treatment or treatment for sobriety."..*Fortune reported* that the Housing First approach resulted in a 66 percent decline in days hospitalized (from one year prior to intake compared to one year in the program), a 38 percent decline in times in emergency room, a 41 percent decline in EMS events, a 79 percent decline in days in jail and a 30 percent decline in police interactions. ..In 2001, in *British Columbia the service and shelter costs* of homeless people ranged from $30,000 to $40,000 annually versus $22,000 to $28,000 per year for formerly homeless persons housed in social housing.

Comments:

Canada's problem, 1% of its population is homeless, especially with indigenous people. *Housing First* is a client-driven strategy with immediate housing, and producing results. Fortune reported 66% decline in hospitalization, 41% less EMS.. 79% less days in jail .. Social housing is more cost effective than providing service/shelter in British Columbia. ***Like a guaranteed UBI being more effective than running welfare services for people.***

Homelessness in China

Wikipedia. 6 September 2021 (///en.wikipedia.org/wiki/Homelessness_in_China)
In 2011, there were approximately 2.41 million homeless adults and 179,000 homeless children living in the country. However, one publication estimated that there were one million homeless children in China in 2012.

Housing in China is highly regulated by the Hukou system. This gives rise to a large number of migrant workers, numbering at 290.77 million in 2019. These migrant workers have rural Hukou, but they move to the cities in order to find better jobs, though due to their rural Hukou they are entitled to fewer privileges than those with urban Hukou. According to Huili et al., these migrant workers "live in overcrowded and unsanitary conditions" and are always at risk of displacement to make way for new real estate developments. In 2017, the government responded to a deadly fire in a crowded building in Beijing by cracking down on dense illegal shared accommodations and evicting the residents, leaving many migrant laborers homeless. This comes in the context of larger attempts by the government to limit the population increase in Beijing, often targeting migrant laborers.

..Several natural disasters have led to homelessness in China. The 2000 Yunnan earthquake left 92,479 homeless and destroyed over 41,000 homes. Homelessness among people with mental health problems is 'much less common' in China than in high-income countries, due to stronger family ties, but is increasing due to migration within families and as a result of the one-child policy. ..It was found that "homelessness was more common in individuals from rural communities, among those who wander away from their communities, and among those with limited education. Homelessness was also associated with greater age;

..During the Cultural Revolution a large part of child welfare homes were closed down, leaving their inhabitants homeless. By the late 1990s, many new homes were set up to accommodate abandoned children. In 1999, the Ministry of Civil Affairs estimated the number of abandoned children in welfare homes to be 66,000.

According to the Ministry of Civil Affairs, China had approximately 2,000 shelters and 20,000 social workers to aid approximately 3 million homeless people in 2014. From 2017 to 2019, the government of Guangdong Province assisted 5,388 homeless people in reuniting with relatives elsewhere in China.

..In 2020, in the wake of the COVID-19 pandemic, ..The Wuhan Civil Affairs Bureau set up 69 shelters in the city to house 4,843 people.

Comments:

One report estimated that there were one million homeless children in China in 2012. In 2020, the government announced alleviating abject poverty in the whole country. The UN and countries around the world are impressed with China for its achievements. ***Western YouTubers are surprised to find no homeless on the city streets of China !***

Homeless. Finland's Mandate

Homelessness in Finland

From Wikipedia, 22 Nov. 2021 (///en.wikipedia.org/wiki/Homelessness_in_Finland)
Homelessness in Finland affected approximately 4 300 people at the end of 2020.
Finland is the only European Union country where homelessness is currently falling.
The country has adopted a Housing First policy, whereby social services assign
homeless individuals rental homes first, and issues like mental health and substance
abuse are treated second. Since its launch in 2008, the number of homeless people in
Finland has decreased by roughly 30%, and the number of long-term homeless people
has fallen by more than 35%. "Sleeping rough", the practice of sleeping outside, has
been largely eradicated in Helsinki, where only one 50-bed night shelter remains.[3]

..The Constitution of Finland *mandates* that public authorities "promote the
right of everyone to housing". In addition, the constitution grants Finnish citizens "the
right to receive indispensable subsistence and care", if needed. Since 2002, the Night of
the Homeless event has been hosted throughout the country. The events include
demonstrations, food distribution, and movie screenings, among other activities.

A "night café" in Helsinki, Kalkkers (run by the non-governmental
organisation Vailla vakinaista asuntoa ry), operates as a temporary overnight resting
place for approximately 15 people each night. Here showers, a meal and place to be
with no questions asked is provided.

Since 1987, the Housing Finance and Development Center of Finland (Finnish:
Asumisen rahoitus- ja kehittämiskeskus; ARA) has been publishing annual statistics
related to homelessness. The figures are collected independently by the municipalities of
Finland, leading to minor inconsistencies in reporting. ARA publishes data on homeless
families and homeless people living alone separately.

The majority of homeless people reside in larger cities, notably in the capital
region. Over 60 percent of Finland's homeless population resides in the Greater Helsinki
area. Homelessness disproportionately affects men, although this gap has been reduced
due to recent efforts. Roughly three out of four homeless individuals are male.
Some key figures for homeless people in Finland (2019) include the following:

- 21% of the homeless are considered long-term homeless
- 26% of the homeless are female
- 18% of the homeless are young (under 25 years old)
- 24% of the homeless are immigrants

Comments:

Finland, the only EU country that has achieved reduction of homelessness recently.
The Constitution of Finland mandates, "promote the right of everyone to housing".
It is time for all governments to mandate "the right of everyone to a guaranteed UBI".
To focus efforts in setting up a UBI for everyone, so as to relieve all human miseries.

Homeless. Hong Kong

What's stopping Hong Kong from fixing its housing crisis?
Zhou Wenmin and Wang Duan. Caixin Global. 09 Jul 2021(thinkchina.sg/whats-)
Hong Kong, home to 7.5 million people, has the world's least affordable housing market with the average price for commercial housing hovering around HK$200,000 (US$25,764.50) per square meter. Meanwhile, the average waiting time for subsidized public housing has climbed to 5.8 years. ..it would take an ordinary family nearly 21 years to buy a home in Hong Kong, and that doesn't even take into account spending on daily necessities.

..The dearth of new land is the fundamental cause of Hong Kong's awkward housing issue, characterized by being expensive, small and crowded. But does Hong Kong truly lack land? ..According to 2019 data from the government planning department, Hong Kong covers a total of 111,100 hectares (429 square miles). Of that, the downtown area or land used for construction and development accounts for 27,500 hectares, or 25%, and the area of country parks accounts for 42%. But the area of land for building houses accounts for only 7%, which has remained almost unchanged for the past 15 years.

..After Leung Chun-ying took office in 2012, he stressed increasing the housing supply, mainly by diverting some non-residential land for housing development. ..However, the Hong Kong government recently slowed the land redevelopment program, partly due to complicated administrative approval procedures. An application for redevelopment usually takes at least six years, and the subsequent construction work takes an additional four to five years. In addition, some projects may face opposition from the public, forcing a lengthy judicial review. *..a major factor slowing the redevelopment work was opposition from neighborhood residents, who often raise concerns over the projects' impacts on local traffic, the environment and other issues.* .."Redevelopment to provide housing supply in the short to medium term will be difficult, but we must be determined and courageous, without fear of litigation," one government official said.

..Hong Kong has largely depended on reclamation for land. According to official statistics, as of 2016, about 7,000 hectares of Hong Kong's land was reclaimed from the sea, accounting for a quarter of its developed land area. This land is where about 30% of Hong Kong's people live and 70% of its commercial activities take place.

Vested interests: "The sheer size of interest groups in Hong Kong is the root of the problem," ..Property tycoons have deep influence over Hong Kong's political and business arenas, ..Tactics like filibuster — action designed to prolong debate and delay or prevent a vote on a bill — are often used in Hong Kong's Legislative Council to block decision-making related to housing policies. ..In June 2018, the Hong Kong government proposed a new housing policy — *levying a vacancy tax on new private residential units* — to encourage real estate developers to bring completed residential properties to the market as early as possible. However, the draft was aborted in June 2020. ..Some government insiders expressed disappointment, citing interference from stakeholders in real estate development.

..Hong Kong depends heavily on property sales for revenue, giving the industry great sway over the city's politics. In the 2020–21 fiscal year, Hong Kong's overall fiscal revenue fell 8% to HK$543.5 billion, mainly due to a drop in land revenue, which accounted for 16% of the government's total revenue. .."To ensure high land revenue, the government prevents the housing prices from falling so that real estate developers are willing to pay high prices for land," Chan said. "This creates a vicious circle."

Time for change: "Hong Kong's land problem is a political problem, not an economic one," .."Who was responsible for Hong Kong's land insufficiency more than two decades ago?" Chan said. "I think politicians should bear the brunt. Every time the government introduced a land policy, it was blocked by opposition politicians in the Legislative Council.

..In March, the central government revised Hong Kong's electoral system, *mitigating the Legislative Council's filibuster.* The new system expanded the number of Election Committee members from 1,200 to 1,500, representing broad industries. It resumed the Election Committee's function of electing some members of the Legislative Council and increased its role in the nomination of candidates for Legislative Council seats. ..The OHKF recommended that the government accelerate all major land development projects, including new development areas, land rezoning, properties above subway stations and urban renewal, as well as streamlining the administrative procedures for land and housing development.

..It has been 24 years since Hong Kong's reunification with China in 1997, and housing and land supply have been the common administrative priorities of Hong Kong's five administrations. ..In 1997, the first chief executive, Tung Chee-hwa, pledged to build 85,000 new flats every year to meet citizens' housing demands. The campaign led to a quick rise in housing supply. But the Asian financial crisis dampened the city's real estate market and Tung's plan ground to a halt. ..After the 2003 SARS outbreak, Hong Kong's real estate market crashed again. To bolster the market, the government stopped selling land until 2010. ..Construction of subsidized public housing was suspended for eight years. ..It wasn't until the final years of the tenure of Sir Donald Tsang Yam-kuen, chief executive from 2005 to 2012, that the government revived efforts to increase Hong Kong's land supply to meet public housing demand.

Comments:

Privileged citizens' opposition to redevelopment to preserve their property's high value. Property tycoons influence opposition politicians to block government housing policy. To ensure high land revenue, the government prevents the housing prices from falling. Thus all the minority privileged forces combine to exploit the underprivileged majority. ***Self-help, the hapless majority must combine to vote in a pro-UBI government !***

Homeless. India

Homelessness in India

From Wikipedia, 2 August 2021 (///en.wikipedia.org/wiki/Homelessness_in_India)

Homelessness is a major issue in India. The Universal Declaration of Human Rights defines 'homeless' as those who do not live in a regular residence due to lack of adequate housing, safety, and availability. ..It is about protection from forced eviction and displacement, fighting homelessness, poverty and exclusion. India defines 'homeless' as those who do not live in Census houses, but rather stay on pavements, roadsides, railway platforms, staircases, temples, streets, in pipes, or other open spaces. There are 1.77 million homeless people in India, or 0.15% of the country's total population, according to the 2011 census consisting of single men, women, mothers, the elderly, and the disabled. However, it is argued that the numbers are far greater than accounted by the point in time method. For example, while the Census of 2011 counted 46.724 homeless individuals in Delhi, the Indo-Global Social Service Society counted them to be 88,410, and another organization called the Delhi Development Authority counted them to be 150,000.

..Furthermore, there is a high proportion of mentally ill and street children in the homeless population. There are 18 million street children in India, the largest number of any country in the world, with 11 million being urban. Finally, more than three million men and women are homeless in India's capital city of New Delhi;

..There is a shortage of 18.78 million houses in the country. Total number of houses has increased from 52.06 million to 78.48 million (as per 2011 census). However, the country still ranks as the 124th wealthiest country in the world as of 2003. More than 90 million people in India make less than US$1 per day, thus setting them below the global poverty threshold. The ability of the Government of India to tackle urban homelessness and poverty may be affected in the future by both external and internal factors. The number of people living in slums in India has more than doubled in the past two decades and now exceeds the entire population of Britain, the Indian Government has announced. About 78 million people in India live in slums and tenements. 17% of the world's slum dwellers reside in India. Subsequent to the release of Slumdog Millionaire in 2008, Mumbai was a slum tourist destination for slumming where homeless people and slum dwellers alike could be openly viewed by tourists.

Comments:

A major issue in India with 1.77 million homeless (2011), or 0.15% of the population.
There are 18 million street children in India, the largest of any country in the world.
90 million people in India make less than US$1 per day, below global poverty threshold.
About 78 million in India live in slums and tenements, 17% of world's slum dwellers.
SEWA's Basic Income project produced very positive results in Indian villages (2013).
With a modest UBI, the government can simply allow the people to help themselves !

Homeless. Japan

HOMELESSNESS IN JAPAN: THE COUNTRY WITH THE SMALLEST
PERCENTAGE OF HOMELESS PEOPLE
Eduardo Bravo, AUGUST 03, 2021 (///tomorrow.city/a/homelessness-in-japan)

..homeless people are those who simply live and sleep on the street. For others, the definition also includes individuals who find themselves sleeping in shelters and care centers.

..Although the homeless people in Japan today are victims of the financial crisis of 2008, the problem with the homeless in this country dates back to the real estate bubble collapse of 1990. ..the Japanese government, ..between 2018 and 2020 it did take action, resulting in the number of homeless people in the country dropping by 12%, going from 4,555 to 3,992 people, with a population of over 125 million. In other words, 0% (rounded off) of Japanese people.

..one of the reasons behind this important drop was not just the assistance programs designed specifically to solve the problem, but the outbreak of the COVID-19 pandemic, ..The closure of cybercafes in the country's major cities.. left homeless people without key areas in which to live their lives.. Far from merely being places in which to connect to the internet, Japanese cybercafes tend to be open 24 hours a day.. offer a wide range of services, including computer games, television, food and even showers.
To ensure that these homeless people were not even more vulnerable, the authorities of Tokyo, the city with the highest number of homeless.. offer them accommodation in vacant hotels due to the cancellation of holidays as a result of the pandemic. In other cities, ..they also housed the homeless in municipal buildings including sports centers.

..According to Japanese laws, begging is not allowed in the country and may constitute a criminal offense. Together with this situation of illegality, is the socially extended prejudice that considers homeless people to be solely responsible for their misfortune. ..and no solutions being provided for a situation which, given that social stigma, even the homeless considered to be shameful. To such an extent that many of those affected would reject what little help was offered as they considered it to be offensive. ..However, after the financial crisis of 2008.. the perception changed and authorities had to implement social assistance programs.. included training courses for these citizens, many of whom were around fifty years of age, incentives to encourage businesses to hire these employees and subsidized rent options for housing, together with direct food aid for the most deprived people.

Comments:
Lowest among OECD countries, Japan's homeless rate is near 0% (~5K in 125 million).
Begging is an offense and the homeless are held responsible for their own misfortune.
And those affected would reject what little help offered as they consider it offensive.
Guaranteed UBI is the solution these people can accept without a stigma, long-term.

Homeless. US

State of Homelessness: 2021 Edition
(///endhomelessness.org/homelessness-in-america/homelessness-statistics/)
..In January 2020, there were 580,466 people experiencing homelessness in America. Most were individuals (70 percent), and the rest were people living in families with children. ..Chronically homeless individuals are currently 19 percent of the homeless population. ..veterans ..They represent only six percent of people experiencing homelessness. ..Risk is significantly tied to gender, race, and ethnicity.

..Males are far more likely to experience homelessness than their female counterparts. Out of every 10,000 males, 22 are homeless. For women and girls, that number is 13. ..Numerically, white people are the largest racial group within homelessness, accounting for more than a quarter-million people. However, historically marginalized racial groups are far more likely to experience homelessness as a result of segregation and discrimination in employment and housing, among other things. ..Native Hawaiians and other Pacific Islanders have the highest rate of homelessness (109 out of every 10,000 people). Groups such as Native Americans (45 out of every 10,000) and Black or African Americans (52 out of every 10,000) also experience elevated rates. Importantly, these rates are much higher than the nation's overall rate of homelessness (18 out of every 10,000).

..A national-level snapshot of the reach of homeless services systems is informative. Individual community circumstances vary. However, in the aggregate, *systems were able to offer a year-round bed to only 50 percent of individuals, but to 100 percent of families (with a surplus of nearly 18,000 beds).*

..Many Americans live in poverty, amounting to nearly 34 million people or 10.5 percent of the U.S. population. ..In 2019, 6.3 million American households experienced severe housing cost burden, which means they spent more than 50 percent of their income on housing. ..severely cost-burdened American households are still 10 percent higher than they were in 2007,

.."Doubling up" (or sharing the housing of others for economic reasons) is another measure of housing hardship. In 2019, an estimated 3.7 million people were in these situations. ..over that same time period, the number of people doubled up expanded by 102 percent in Idaho and 65 percent in Florida.

..COVID-19-related health concerns disrupted counts of unsheltered people in 2021. ..leaving a significant hole in available knowledge on homeless

Comments:
There were 580,466 people experiencing homelessness in America in January 2020. And 6.3 million households are at risk, with housing burden at >50% of income. Another housing hardship, an estimated 3.7M people are 'doubling up' with others. Homeless services mis-managed, housing only 50% of individuals, surplus for families.
It seems easier and fair to reach everyone with distribution of a subsistence UBI.

Poverty. China

Has China lifted 100 million people out of poverty?
By Jack Goodman. 28 February 2021 (https://www.bbc.com/news/56213271)

Chinese President Xi Jinping says his country has reached the ambitious goal set when he assumed office in 2012 of lifting 100 million people out of poverty. ..Poverty is defined by China as anyone in rural areas earning less than about $2.30 a day (adjusted for inflation). It was fixed in 2010 and looks at income but also living conditions, healthcare and education.

Provinces have been racing to reach the goal. Jiangsu, for example, announced in January last year that only 17 of its 80 million residents still lived in poverty. The national benchmark used by the Chinese government is slightly higher than the $1.90 a day poverty line used by the World Bank to look at poverty globally. Using these figures gives us a better standard measurement used by the World Bank across all countries.

In 1990 there were more than 750 million people in China living below the international poverty line - about two-thirds of the population. By 2012, that had fallen to fewer than 90 million, and by 2016 - the most recent year for which World Bank figures are available - it had fallen to 7.2 million people (0.5% of the population). So clearly, even in 2016 China was well on the way to reaching its target. This suggests that overall, 745 million fewer people were living in extreme poverty in China than were 30 years ago.

..China's rapid reduction in poverty went hand in hand with a long period of sustained economic growth. Much of the focus has been on the poorest rural areas. The government has relocated millions of people from remote villages into apartment complexes. Sometimes these were built in towns and cities, but sometimes new villages were built near the old ones.

..the World Bank draws a higher poverty line for upper-middle-income countries, which tries to reflect economic conditions. It sets this at $5.50 a day. China is now an upper-middle-income country, says the bank. About a quarter of China's population is in poverty, according to this metric.

..Chinese Premier Li Keqiang said China still had 600 million people whose monthly income was barely 1,000 yuan ($154). ..by any measure China has made huge strides to lift millions out of the toughest standards of living over the last few decades.

Comments:
End of 2020, China had declared success in lifting 100 million people out of poverty. China still had 600 million people whose income was barely 1,000 yuan/mth ($154). And the government adopts 'common prosperity' policies to reduce the wealth gap.
Thus establishing a guaranteed Universal Basic Income is equally valid in China !

Poverty. South Africa

1 in 5 South Africans Are Living in Extreme Poverty: UN Report
- Khanyi Mlaba December 23, 2020 (//www.globalcitizen.org/en/content/)
..Last year, the World Bank determined that South Africa is the most unequal country in the world — and the recently released 2020 UN Human Development Index (HDI) and Human Development Report (HDR) show that the country has made little to no progress in eradicating its inequalities.

The HDR — which looks at a range of socioeconomic indicators such as average life expectancy, education, and income inequality — provides a detailed look of the progression of the world. The HDI is a measurement of equality developed by the UN that ranks countries by analysing their quality of life against the backdrop of their industrial development.

South Africa has been ranked 114 out of 189 countries assessed in the index due to its declining standards of living and worsening income inequality. Since 2014, the country has dropped two ranks lower on the index, and as the COVID-19 pandemic has resulted in the loss of more than 2 million job losses, the case of South Africa's inequality is expected to get worse.

The country's wealthiest 10%, meanwhile, possesses more than half the nation's income, while the poorest 40% shares just 7.2%. According to Business Insider, this level of income inequality is the largest anomaly observed by the UN's HDI. The country's inequality in life expectancy and education also rank as some of the highest deviations in the world.

The HDR also indicates that there are a number of South African citizens living below the international poverty line. The report notes that 18.9% of the population — about 11 million South Africans — live on less than R28 ($1.90) a day, which is around R800 ($55) per month.

The report also looks at different forms of poverty which it categorises as "multidimensional poverty." This looks at poor health, malnutrition, a lack of clean water, inadequate access to health care services and poor, if any, housing conditions. According to the report, nearly 4 million South Africans are in a state of multidimensional poverty.

South Africa also ranked lower on the HDI as a result of planetary pressure monitoring, which adjusts the overall HDI score by measuring the level of carbon dioxide emissions and material footprint per capita. This is an area in which South Africa has not progressed.

Comments:
South Africa is the most unequal country with a fifth of its population in abject poverty. HDR index (for life expectancy, education, income equality, ..) is 114 of 189 countries. The vast majority of blacks in South Africa were not enfranchised until 1994.
UBI is equality, is best suited to fight inequality and abject poverty in South Africa.

Poverty. South Korea

South Korea's inequality paradox: long life, good health and ...
Justin McCurry in Seoul, Wed 2 Aug 2017 (//www.theguardian.com › inequality ›)
..The survey found that 48.6% of South Korea's elderly were in poverty (defined as earning 50% or less of median household income) in 2011, the highest level among the 34 OECD countries. About a quarter of them live alone, and high levels of isolation and depression have led to a dramatic rise in elderly suicide, from 34 per 100,000 people in 2000 to 72 in 2010. Anecdotal evidence suggests many decide to take their own lives to avoid becoming a burden to their families.

..Ironically, part of the reason for their plight may be the cost of supporting their own offspring. "While they were still working," says Shin, "many elderly people were unable to put aside enough savings for later in life because they spent too much on their children's education." ..A woman in her late 70s says she can't afford to feed herself on her pension. "I come here for free meals," says the woman, who declines to give her name. "My children can't help me because they are struggling financially themselves. *I don't want much, but a bit more money every month would be a great help."*

..The traditional expectation that children will perform their filial duty and look after their parents in old age has stifled the emergence of a welfare state able to cope with South Korea's rapidly ageing society, ..And the increasing polarisation of South Korean society means it is getting harder for adult children to support their parents financially."..Outside the cafe, ..Every now and then, an old man or woman passes by pulling rickety wooden hand carts loaded with piles of collected cardboard and paper they can sell for a few thousand won a day.

..Like Japan, South Korea is expected to undergo rapid demographic change in the coming decades – with the proportion of over-65s predicted to increase dramatically to 40% of the population by 2060, compared to 13% today, according to Statistics Korea.

..Those over 65 years old today belong to a generation with very low obesity prevalence – one of the lowest worldwide – and low levels of smoking. .."The elderly poverty rate in South Korea is not absolute poverty," says Yang. "It refers to relative poverty, or below 50% of the median income. That's why it is possible for poor elderly people to live longer, even though they are in relative poverty. *In addition, healthcare is universal and treatment for the poor is paid for by the state."*

Comments:
South Korea: a developed country of 51 million, with half living in the Seoul area.
The elder generation has low obesity and with universal healthcare, enjoy longevity.
However 49% of them live in relative poverty recycling cardboard; suicide rate is high.
Woman: *"I don't want much, but a bit more money every month would be a great help."*
Certainly a small UBI is going a long way to help the elderly poor in South Korea.

Poverty. Syria

https://en.wikipedia.org/wiki/Syria

Since March 2011, Syria has been embroiled in a multi-sided civil war, with a number of countries in the region and beyond involved militarily or otherwise. As a result, a number of self-proclaimed political entities have emerged on Syrian territory, including the Syrian opposition, Rojava, Tahrir al-Sham and Islamic State of Iraq and the Levant. ..The conflict has killed more than 570,000 people, caused 7.6 million internally displaced people (July 2015 UNHCR estimate) and over 5 million refugees (July 2017 registered by UNHCR), making population assessment difficult in recent years.

10 Facts About Poverty in Syria

Elise Ghitman, APRIL 24, 2020 (https://borgenproject.org/poverty-in-syria-2/)

Before the Syrian civil war, the Syrian economy was flourishing. In 2010, right before the start of the Syrian civil war, the World Bank listed Syria as a rapidly-growing middle-income country. In addition, farming, oil, industry and tourism formed the major economic base. Meanwhile, primary and secondary education and health care received state funding. Until 2011, nearly 80 percent of the Syrian economy relied upon small to medium-sized businesses. In 2010, the GDP per capita in Syria was $2,807. Today, the GDP per capita is a mere $870.

Today,.. Over 80 percent of people in Syria live below the world poverty line, which means that they make less than $1 per day. The economic impact of ongoing conflict has resulted in an unemployment rate of 55 percent or more. ..Corruption is prevalent in Syria. Syria ranks fourth on the list of countries with the most corruption in the world. ..The Syrian civil war interferes with education. ..Around 1.3 million children are at a high chance of withdrawing from school. ..The Syrian civil war has impeded health care. Bombing damaged or destroyed many medical facilities. ..There is extreme wealth inequality in Syria. ..A few big business owners have established a monopoly over approximately 75 percent of the economy,.. average Syrian person lives in poverty.

Inflation has greatly affected the Syrian population. ..The value of the Syrian pound has gone down over 90 percent since 2010. ..Many Syrians flee the country. There are 3.6 million Syrian refugees in Turkey, a neighboring country. In Lebanon, around 70 percent of Syrian people live below the poverty line. In Jordan, around 93 percent of Syrian refugees live below the poverty line.

Comments:

In 2010, the World Bank listed Syria as a rapidly-growing middle-income country. Since 2011, multi-sided civil war brought death, destruction and poverty to the nation. Over 80% of its people now live below the poverty line, both at home and as refugees. Among the dispossessed, poverty breeds hatred and willingness to join armed conflict. ***Global UBI for eradicating global poverty will contribute to building peace on earth.***

Poverty. USA

"Contempt for the poor in US drives cruel policies,"
says UN expert. Sep, 2019 (https:web.archive.org/web/)
GENEVA (4 June 2018) – The United States' principal strategy for dealing with extreme poverty is to criminalise and stigmatise those in need of assistance,.. *"For one of the world's wealthiest countries to have 40 million people living in poverty and over five million living in 'Third World' conditions is cruel and inhuman,"* the UN Special Rapporteur on extreme poverty and human rights, Philip Alston, said in a new report.

"The Trump Administration has brought in massive tax breaks for corporations and the very wealthy, while orchestrating a systematic assault on the welfare system," he said. .."Locking up the poor precisely because they are poor, greatly exaggerating the amount of fraud in the system, shaming those who need assistance, and devising ever more obstacles to prevent people from getting needed benefits, is not a strategy to reduce or eliminate poverty.

"It seems driven primarily by contempt, and sometimes even by hatred for the poor, along with a 'winner takes all' mentality", said the independent human rights expert.. "The evidence is everywhere. On Skid Row in Los Angeles, *14,000 homeless persons were arrested in 2016*, including for urinating in public and other "quality of life" offences, while overall arrests in the city were declining. ..one public toilet per 200 individuals would not even meet the minimum standards the UN sets for Syrian refugee camps.

..The legal system is used to raise revenue for states, not to promote justice, .. judges set large bail amounts for defendants awaiting trial, allowing the rich to pay their way to freedom, while the poor sit in jail unable to work or provide for their families. Some 11 million people are admitted to local jails annually, and on any given day more than *730,000 people are being held, of whom almost two thirds are awaiting trial and therefore presumed to be innocent.*

.."Several political appointees with whom I spoke were completely sold on the narrative that the poor are scammers living high on welfare. .. the evidence is that welfare fraud is not widespread and that most welfare recipients already work.. The United States now has the highest income inequality in the Western world, the highest incarceration rate in the entire world, and *one of the lowest turnout rates in elections* among developed countries. It is no coincidence that high inequality coincides with the overt and covert disenfranchisement of millions and millions of American voters.

Comments:
The United States, a superpower nation, still has 40 million people living in poverty. Philip Alston says this is due to *contempt for the poor and cruel government policies.* Poverty wouldn't be a problem if a UBI is in place, empowering the masses to self-help. Thus voters should unite and turnout in full force instead of giving-up voting !
To vote out governments that fail to support a UBI, put cash in their hands.

Poverty. World

Poverty Rate By Country 2021
(https://worldpopulationreview.com/country-rankings/poverty-rate-by-country)
..The poverty rate is the number of people (usually expressed as a percentage) in a given demographic group whose income falls below the poverty line. ..Poverty has a wide range of possible causes, from the amount of fresh water and arable land in a region to government policies or ongoing armed conflict. Additionally, natural disasters such as the COVID pandemic or the 2020 earthquakes in Puerto Rico..

..Country-wide poverty is typically measured in one of two ways. The first is to determine the percentage of people whose daily income falls below specific baseline amounts, such as $10 per day. These baselines remain the same for every country, enabling a slightly different perspective on country-to-country comparisons...The second way to measure a country's poverty level is to determine the percentage of people or families who earn less than the "national poverty line", or poverty threshold.. The national poverty line is calculated independently for each country because each country's economy is different. For example, a person earning $25,000 a year in the United States would have different opportunities than a person who earned $25,000 a year in Somalia. ..The majority of countries in the world,.. set the national poverty line at 50% of a given year's median income. For instance, the median income in the United States was $67,521 in 2020 so the national poverty line according to the United Nations would be $33,761.

..Globally speaking, the number of people living in extreme poverty has been on the decline for several decades, from 1.94 billion in 1982 to 696 million in 2017. This decrease is particularly encouraging because the Earth's population rose considerably.. from roughly 4.5 billion people in 1981 to more than 7.8 billion in 2021. ..people still live in extreme poverty, surviving on less than $1.90 (INT) per day. More than 430 million of these people live in Sub-Saharan Africa, the poorest region in the world, where more than 40% of people lived in extreme poverty as of 2018. Many countries in which poverty is rising have been plagued by political instability or conflict. Others are hampered by frequent natural disasters or ongoing environmental stresses (increased drought in particular) caused by climate change.

.. According to the U.S. Census Bureau, the official 2017 poverty rate in the U.S. was 12.3%. ..the largest economy..U.S. also has a significant wealth inequality gap. ..World Bank, poverty rates: S. Sudan ~82%, Eq. Guinea ~76%, Madagascar ~70%...

Comments:
Extreme poverty hit 430 million in sub-Saharan Africa; even the USA has 12% poverty.
The causes of poverty may be natural disasters or man-made exploitation and inequality.
On city streets or in the sub-Sahara deserts, the misery of poverty is equally inhuman.
Only the government can prevent the privileged from bullying the underprivileged.
It is simple to set up a survival UBI to help the underprivileged to help themselves.

Suicide. Children

Syrian children turn to suicide, self-harm to escape horrors of war: report
By Lin Taylor, MARCH 7, 2017 (//www.reuters.com/article/us-mideast-)
..Children living in war-torn Syria, some as young as 12, are self-harming, taking drugs, and attempting suicide to escape the horrors they have endured after six years of conflict, ..One in four children, around 2.5 million, are on the brink of developing a mental health disorder, ..Nearly five million Syrians have fled the country since the war began in 2011, but 13.5 million people remain in need of aid in Syria and almost half are children, ..Nightmares, bedwetting, anger, suicidal thoughts and depression are a few of the symptoms plaguing Syrian children, who suffer from an endless barrage of trauma from bombings, death and destruction, Most of the children interviewed for the report were too fearful to play outside, have dropped out of school, or have witnessed the death of a friend or relative. ..More and more children were self-harming, taking drugs and attempting suicide, Brophy told the Thomson Reuters Foundation, and they were doing so at an increasingly younger age.

North West Syria: Number of suicide attempts and deaths rise sharply
Source: Save the Children 29 Apr 2021 (//reliefweb.int/report/syrian-arab-republic/)
..Almost one in five of all recorded suicide attempts and deaths in North West Syria are children, with a total of 246 suicides and 1,748 attempts recorded in just the last three months of 2020, ..The number of suicides in the area has been rising sharply over the past year, jumping by 86% from the first three months of 2020. ..Of those who attempted suicide, at least 42 are 15 years old or younger, while 18% are adolescents and young people between the ages of 16 and 20. ..These figures emerge among constantly deteriorating conditions for people in North West Syria including poverty, a lack of education and employment, domestic violence, child marriage, broken relationships and bullying, in communities that have been reeling from ten years of conflict. ..Almost 15% of adult patients have suicidal thoughts. Children meanwhile express [their -emotional struggles] through behaviour. They become aggressive, isolated or vengeful."..It is incredibly sad that children are reaching a point where they see no other way out from a life where they cannot get an education, enough food or adequate shelter. ..The majority of deaths by suicide recorded, 187, were among people who have been displaced from their homes.

Comments:
Suicide, a desperate attemp to leave this world of miseries, where there is no hope !
Almost 1/5 of all recorded suicide attempts and deaths in North West Syria are children.
Surviving a war and being displaced from their homes, refugees suffer extreme distress.
Children are most affected and trauma suffered is carried into the adult life of survivors.
Thus, UBI inclusive of children is important, to help them grow into healthy adults.

Suicide. China

Suicide in China

From Wikipedia, 10 November 2021, (///en.wikipedia.org/wiki/Suicide_in_China#)
China's suicide rates were one of the highest in the world in the 1990s; however, by 2011, China had one of the lowest suicide rates in the world. According to the World Health Organization, the suicide rate in China was 9.7 per 100,000 as of 2016. As a comparison, the suicide rate in the U.S. in 2016 was 15.3. Generally speaking, China seems to have a lower suicide rate than neighboring Korea, Russia and Japan, and it is more common among women than men and more common in the Yangtze Basin than elsewhere.

..Between 1990 and 2016, suicide rates in China fell by 64%, making China the #1 country in the world in suicide reduction. ..Family conflicts are the number one cause of suicide in China, other common causes include poverty, and disease of the body and mind. ..For 2009–2011, 44% of all suicides occurred among those aged 65 or above and 79% among rural residents. ..By 2016, suicide rates among Chinese men and women were almost the same—9.1 for men and 10.3 for women. A 2008 study—which was based on data from the 1990s—found that: female suicides outnumbered male suicides by a 3:1 ratio; rural suicides outnumbered urban suicides by a 3:1 ratio; a large upsurge of young adult and older adult suicides had occurred; a comparatively high national suicide rate two to three times the global average was evident; and a low rate of psychiatric illness, particularly clinical depression, existed in suicide victims.

..Ritual suicide was long practiced in traditional Chinese culture, owing both to the power of the state to enforce collective punishment against the families of disgraced ministers and to Confucian values that held that certain failures of virtue were worse than death, making suicide morally permissible or even praiseworthy in some altruistic contexts. ..the preferred methods -as recorded in for instance the Book of Han- appear to have been those that did not leave the corpse significantly disfigured, notably hanging/strangulation.

..the Han had a practice of women committing suicide to preserve their chastity, while the Manchus had a practice of wives committing suicide to follow their husbands into death. The loss of a woman's chastity was viewed as shameful to the family so the act of suicide to preserve chastity was seen as a heroic act. The Qing dynasty tried to reduce female suicide by creating preventative laws. One of the laws made making lewd comments towards a woman equivalent to rape if she later committed suicide due to these comments.

Comments:
The economy greatly improved between 1990 and 2016, creating prosperity in China. With reduction of poverty and hunger, suicide rate fell by 64% to 9.7 per 100,000. This rate is lower than neighbors like Korea, Japan, and Russia; male:female is 1:1.
Thus to lower suicidal stress, lower financial pressure with a UBI for everyone.

Suicide. EU

Health at a Glance: Europe 2020 : State of Health in the EU Cycle
OECD/EU (2018), (//www.oecd-ilibrary.org/sites/89109c81-en/)
Good mental health is vital for people to be able to lead healthy and productive lives.
Living with a mental health problem can have a significant impact on daily life,
contributing to worse educational outcomes, higher rates of unemployment, and poorer
physical health. ..As of 2020, the COVID-19 crisis is also having a negative impact on
mental wellbeing, especially amongst young people and people with lower
socio-economic status.

..Without effective treatment and support, mental health problems can have a
devastating effect on people's lives, ..In 2017, over 48 000 people died of suicide across
EU countries. The most frequent number of suicides were amongst men aged 45 and
over. ..men represent over three-quarters of suicides in EU countries, ..In Lithuania, the
suicide rate among men was more than five times higher than that for women.

..On average, there were 11 deaths by suicide per 100 000 population across
EU countries in 2017. ..Suicide rates were lowest in Cyprus, Greece, Italy and Malta,
where there were fewer than six suicides per 100 000 population in 2017. Lithuania and
Slovenia had the highest suicide rate, with 26 and 20 deaths per 100 000 population, ..

..Suicide rates have decreased in almost all EU countries, falling by 50%
between 2000 and 2017. ..including in Hungary, the Slovak Republic and Bulgaria,
where deaths by suicide have fallen by more than 50%.

..Effective approaches to reducing death by suicide include good access to
support and mental health care; suicide prevention training for gatekeepers such as
health workers and community leaders; reducing access to lethal means such as firearms
and pharmaceuticals; responsible media reporting around suicide; and awareness and
anti-stigma campaigns. ..and training for persons in contact with identified high-risk
groups such as agencies working *with debt relief, unemployment support* workers, ..

..In Switzerland, the suicide rate has decreased by 64% since 2000. While rates
of 'assisted suicide' are rising, mainly in older people, since 2009 assisted suicides have
been excluded from overall suicide data, explaining the sharp decline the year the
reporting changed. ..The registration of suicide is a complex procedure, affected by
factors such as how intent is ascertained, who is responsible for completing the death
certificate, and cultural dimensions including stigma. Caution is therefore needed when
comparing rates between countries.

Comments:
Between 2000 and 2017, suicide rates have decreased 50% in almost all EU countries.
Excluding 'assisted suicide', suicide rate deceased in Switzerland by 64% since 2000.
EU stresses on support and treatment with mental health care to reduce suicide rates.
However high risk groups identified include people in debt and unemployed workers.
Mental health aside, economic assistance in having the rightful UBI is important.

Suicide. Lithuania

Latvia and Lithuania begin to tackle a chronic scourge: suicide
By Gordon F. Sander, 11 Feb. 2020 (///www.csmonitor.com/World/Europe/)

Latvia and Lithuania are two of the most westernized of the fifteen former Soviet republics, with robust economies and relatively sound democratic political systems. Unfortunately, both countries share a less happy distinction when it comes to suicide. While they have made considerable progress in overcoming their global-high rates of suicide, significant obstacles remain. Perhaps the most stubborn is the stigma attached to mental illness and seeking help for it, a vestige of the Soviet era.

..Lithuania had 24.4 deaths by suicide per 100,000 population in 2017, the world's highest rate, with Latvia not far behind with 18.1 per 100,000, according to the Organization for Economic Cooperation and Development.This is a marked improvement for Lithuania in just a handful of years. In 2013, the country had a suicide rate of 31.9 per 100,000. "Somehow suicide has become part of the Lithuanian story," Vaiva Klimaitė, a psychologist at Vilnius City Mental Health Center told the Monitor in 2015.

Inflation at 30-year high. Where it goes next is (partly) up to you. ..That year, several hundred Lithuanians lay down in the capital's Cathedral Square in a widely publicized protest over the lack of progress fighting suicide. As in Lithuania, the tight-knit community of suicidologists and suicide prevention professionals in Latvia say the biggest obstacle to improving the country's mental health and bringing the suicide rate further down are the persistent, regressive Soviet-era attitudes regarding suicide and mental health in general.

"During the Soviet time, people who opposed the system were often put in psychiatric clinics," says Zane Avotiņa, director of Skalbes, a suicide prevention clinic and help line based in Riga. "That's one of the reasons why people at risk are still reluctant to seek help." Another problematic legacy of the Soviet era, says Ms. Avotiņa, "is that many people can't accept that depression is actually an illness. They think that people who are depressed are just lazy. ... There is a belief that adults should deal with their emotions and feelings by themselves."

Comments:
Latvia & Lithuania are 2 of the most westernized of the fifteen former Soviet republics. During the Soviet era, people who opposed the system were put in psychiatric clinics. Since the break-up of the Soviet Union in the 1990s, *inflation was at a 30-year high.* Combined with people's reluctance to seek help, the suicide rate was 32/100k in 2013. Besides measures to destigmatize psychotherapy, economic support is equally needed. ***UBI has no stigma, a plus with suicidal people who fear of being stigmatized.***

Suicide. South Africa

Suicide crisis soars in South Africa
Charlotte Motsoari. 5 Oct 2021 (///mg.co.za/opinion/2021-10-05-suicide-)
The South African Depression and Anxiety Group reports that there are 23 known cases of suicide in South Africa every day, and for every person that commits suicide, 10 have attempted it. Before Covid-19, the organisation fielded 600 calls a day. As of September 2021, that number had risen to 2 200 calls a day — an increase of nearly 40%.

We live in a stressful society. The recent lootings and their aftermath point to the socioeconomic challenges, violence and fragmented homes and communities we live in. ..It is important that we seek to understand the reasons for the increased suicide rates, and, more devastatingly, the extent of these rates among young people.

..University of Cape Town research has shown that during the pandemic, "isolation, uncertainty, economic strain, bereavement and loss have resulted in heightened anxiety, particularly for school-going young South Africans". ..The prevalence of suicidality in our community points to the mental health crisis we are facing as a society. ..The lifetime prevalence of depression in South Africa is 9.7% or 4.5 million, and 70% of people who attempt suicide have a mental health illness. ..While Covid-19 may have exacerbated mental distress, mental illnesses such as depression are not new phenomena. ..This means we need to seriously question why many people find themselves backed against the wall, to the point where suicide becomes the only way to deal with life's challenges.

..Where options are few in times of crisis, most people, particularly young people, may feel as though suicide may relieve their pain or distress. ..With the scarcity of school and community-based programmes that deal with issues of mental health, ..these cycles then go on for generations, with devastating impacts on the entire community. ..It is important to understand some of the contextual and historical factors that contribute to the prevalence of mental health issues in our society.

..Poverty and continuous stressful environments: a driver of depression.
South Africa has the most unequal society in the world, with a Gini coefficient of 63.0. ..Living through that economic disparity and trying to survive a pandemic may lead to continuous traumatic stress. ..Poverty goes beyond a lack of food and access to other basic needs. ..It referred to the inevitable exposure to continuous stressful environments. Under such conditions, people may experience feelings of helplessness and feel stuck in situations that may never change.

Comments:
The vast majority of blacks in South Africa were not enfranchised until 1994.
It's apparent the pandemic exacerbates the endemic poverty to suicidal level for many.
South Africa remains the most unequal society on earth with a Gini coefficient of 63%.
The Mail & Guardian's motto "Keep the powerful accountable" can be applied here.
Government can direct the nation's wealth into a UBI to reduced the suicide rate.

Suicide. South Korea

Suicide in South Korea
From Wikipedia, the free encyclopedia (///en.wikipedia.org/wiki/Suicide_)
..Suicide in South Korea is the 12th highest in the world as of 2019 according to the World Health Organization, as well as the highest suicide rate in the OECD. In 2012, suicide was the fourth-highest cause of death among South Koreans.

..An extremely high suicide rate among the elderly is a major contributing factor to South Korea's overall suicide rate. As people age, certain sociopsychological factors such as income decline due to retirement, increased medical costs, physical deterioration or disabilities, loss of spouse or friends and no sense of purpose increases the risk of suicide. Many impoverished elderly people kill themselves as to not be a burden on their families, since the South Korean welfare system is poorly funded and the tradition of children caring for their parents in old age has largely disappeared in the 21st century.

..Although lower than the rate for the elderly, grade school and college students in Korea have a higher than average suicide rate. ..Over the past 5 years, the number of suicide or self-inflicted injuries has increased from 4,947 in 2015 to 9,828 in 2019, and most cases involved people aged between 9 and 24.

..On average, men have a suicide rate that is twice as high as women. However, the suicide attempt rate is higher for women than men.. The study of divorce, separated or widowed statuses showed that individuals dissatisfied with family relationships were at a higher risk of depression, thoughts of suicide and low self-esteem.

..The Mapo Bridge in Seoul, South Korea has been nicknamed "Suicide Bridge" .. due to its frequent usage as a suicide hotspot amidst South Korea's ongoing suicide epidemic. ..Poisoning is the most commonly used method for South Korean women, with pesticides accounting for half of suicide deaths among that population. ..a major reason for the general upward trend in the South Korean suicide rate from 2000 to 2011 was the increase in suicides by hanging. ..In recent years amid South Korea's suicide epidemic, yeontan burning has been used as a method of suicide by carbon monoxide poisoning.

Comments:
Suicide is the fourth-highest cause of death in South Korea, highest in the OECD.
When government is 'no doing', the elderly choose suicide so as 'not to burden others'.
Similarly Confucian 'self-blaming' tradition pervades among the youths and mid-aged.
And it remains the responsibility of government to solve this 'suicide epidemic'.
The common problem among all 3 levels of society is financial difficulty and insecurity.
Even a little money from a modest UBI will be a great help in improving the situation.
Korea's advanced economy has achieved great development and has made huge profits.
A rich nation, government has allowed corporations to steal the 'gains' of technology.
The enormous wealth created by technology is social property that ought be shared.

Suicide. US

Suicide in the United States

From Wikipedia, 6 November 2021 (///en.wikipedia.org/wiki/Suicide_in_United_States)
Suicide is a major national public health issue in the United States. The country has one of the highest suicide rates among wealthy nations. In 2018, there were 48,344 recorded suicides, up from 42,773 in 2014, according to the CDC's National Center for Health Statistics (NCHS). On average, adjusted for age, the annual U.S. suicide rate increased 24% between 1999 and 2014, from 10.5 to 13.0 suicides per 100,000 people, the highest rate recorded in 28 years. Due to the stigma surrounding suicide, it is suspected that suicide generally is underreported. In April 2016, the CDC released data showing that the suicide rate in the United States had hit a 30-year high, and later in June 2018, released further data showing that the rate has continued to increase and has increased in every U.S. state except Nevada since 1999. Surging death rates from suicide, drug overdoses and alcoholism, what researchers refer to as "deaths of despair", are largely responsible for a consecutive three year decline of life expectancy in the U.S. This constitutes the first three-year drop in life expectancy in the U.S. since 1915–1918.

..In 2015, suicide was the seventh leading cause of death for males and the 14th leading cause of death for females Additionally, it was the second leading cause of death for young people aged 10 to 34. ..In 2008, it was observed that U.S. suicide rates, particularly among middle-aged white women, had increased, although the causes were unclear. As of 2018, about 1.7 percent of all deaths were suicides.

..The American Foundation for Suicide Prevention reported that in 2016 suicide was the 10th leading cause of death in the U.S., imposing a cost of $69 billion to the US annually. Other statistics reported are: The annual age-adjusted suicide rate is 13.42 per 100,000 individuals.

1. Men die by suicide 3.53x more often than women.
2. On average, there are 132 suicides per day.
3. White males accounted for 7 of 10 suicides in 2016.
4. A firearm is used in almost 50% of all suicides.
5. The rate of suicide is highest in middle age—among white men in particular.

..The spike in suicide rates in the United States during the 21st century has gained public and clinical attention. Studies have found that despite all efforts to minimize suicide rates, rates have steadily increased by approximately 2% per year from 2006 to 2014. ..It was found that suicide attempts impact "younger adults with less formal education and those with antisocial personality disorder, anxiety disorders, depressive disorders, and a history of violence" at disproportional rates.

..As of 2019, suicide prevention is being recognized as a public health responsibility rather than within clinical settings due to the trend in increasing suicide rates. ..While suicide is often thought of as an individual problem, suicides may impact families, communities, and society in general. The responsibility of public health would be to develop policies to reduce people's risk of suicidal behavior through addressing factors at the individual to societal levels. ..A 2019 study by ..National Bureau of Economic Research says there is *a direct causal link between worker's wages and suicide.., ..raising the minimum wage would result in a quick drop in the suicide rate.*

..The NVDRS 2015 data showed that, among men of all races, *men over 65 were the most likely to die of suicides (27.67 suicides per 100,000),* closely followed by men 40–64 (27.10 suicides per 100,000). Men 20–39 (23.41 per 100,000) and 15–19 (13.81 per 100,000) were less likely to die of suicides.

..For college students, suicide is the second highest cause of death. ..The suicide rate for male students is about three times higher than that of female students. ..From 1990 to 2004, about 1,404 college students died by suicide. This is about 6.5 percent of those who died by suicide nationwide. ..Students who do not go to counseling services are at 18 times more at risk of suicide compared to those who do. If a college student has any suicidal thoughts, it is always critical to let others, such as members of the school, family, or friends know.

..A 2009 U.S. Army report indicates military veterans have double the suicide rate of non-veterans, and more active-duty soldiers have died from suicide than in combat in the Iraq War (2003–2011) and War in Afghanistan (2001–2021). ..According to a June 2021 study published by Brown University's Cost of War Project, deaths from suicide among active U.S. military personnel and veterans of the post-9/11 conflicts outnumber combat deaths for those same conflicts by four times, with the numbers being 30,177 and 7,057 respectively.

Attempted suicide rates for lesbian, gay, bisexual, transgender and questioning (LGBTQ) youth and adults in the U.S. are elevated in comparison to national rates. ..Suicide rates among veterinarians are a growing problem: suicide rates among male veterinarians are twice the national average, and among female veterinarians the suicide rate is 3.5 times the national average. ..Patients with chronic pain are twice as likely to attempt suicide compared with those without chronic pain. ..Studies have found very high rates of suicide in people with autism spectrum disorders, ..White men account for nearly 70% of suicides in the United States. Native Americans and White Americans have the highest suicide rate in the United States. There have been many high-profile incidents ..of individuals thought to be attempting "suicide by cop" or killing others before killing themselves. ..include the 1999 Columbine High School massacre, ..

Comments:

High rates of suicide in the US are results of stresses of wars, drugs and gun violence. Men over 65 were the mostly likely to die of suicides, suggesting financial insecurity. Hence, of the many risk factors of suicide behavior, first to remove financial insecurity. A 2019 study says, raising the minimum wage would result in a quick drop in suicide. ***UBI certainly helps everyone, the elderly, the debt-ridden students and the veterans.***

Suicide. World

Suicide Rate By Country 2021

© 2021 World Population Review (//worldpopulationreview.com/country-rankings/)
Suicide occurs throughout the world, affecting individuals of all nations, cultures, religions, genders, and classes. Other innate factors, such as disorders of the mind and abnormalities at birth, can heighten someone's propensity for experiencing depression,..

..In 2019, the ten countries with the highest suicide rates (suicides per 100k) were: Lesotho 72.4; Guyana 40.3; Eswatini 29.4; S.Korea 28.6; Kiribati 28.3; Federated States of Micronesia 28.2; Lithuania 26.1; Suriname 25.4; Russia 25.1; S. Africa 23.5.

..surprisingly,.. the most troubled nations in the world have comparatively low suicide rates. Afghanistan has 4.1 suicides per 100k; Iraq has 3.6, and Syria has just 2.0. The world's lowest suicide rates are in the following countries: Antigua and Barbuda 0.4; Barbados 0.6; Grenada 0.7; Saint Vincent and the Grenadines 1.0; Sao Tome and Principe 1.5; Jordan 1.6; Syria 2.0; Venezuela 2.1; Honduras 2.1; Philippines 2.2

..South Korea is the fourth highest in the world. One factor in its high suicide rate is suicides among the elderly. ..many older adults commit suicide, rather than feel like they are a financial burden on their families. ..In addition to the elderly, students have higher-than-average suicide rates, at least partly because they feel high levels of pressure to succeed academically.

..Japan's total numbers.. outside the top 10, but suicide is nonetheless a serious concern there. Suicide is the leading cause of death in men between the ages of 20-44 and women between the ages of 15-34. Japanese men are twice as likely to commit suicide.., particularly after a divorce. ..Of particular concern is suicide among men who have recently lost their jobs..Aokigahara Forest at Mount Fuji is a hotspot for suicides,..

In 2019, Sweden had 14.7 suicides per 100,000 people. Historically, Sweden has had a high suicide rate,.. The government responded to the crisis with *social welfare* and mental health services, and the numbers have dropped dramatically. Today, Scandinavian countries – Norway, Sweden, Denmark, and Finland – have very high happiness rates and relatively low suicide rates.

In China, suicide is the fifth leading cause of death.. In contrast with many Western countries, in which men are more likely to commit suicide, most suicide victims in China are women. China's economic boom has led to greater independence for women,.. more able to get divorced as a means of dealing with domestic violence. ..strain of divor*ce* means that they must work long hours while raising their children,..

Comments:

Individual's crisis of suicide is buried under the mass refugees crisis in Iraq and Syria. South Korea's elderly and Japanese men who lost their jobs suffer personal insecurity. Divorced Chinese women raising children, Swedish suicides down with social welfare. All boil down to financial stress / insecurity among suicidal people around the world.
UBI will emormously help these people in distress, reducing suicide rates worldwide.

World of Miseries

Summary

Thomas Paine (1737-1809) noted the wretchedness of the dispossessed majority.
And advocates paying every person a UBI in lieu of his right to a natural inheritance.

Prison: In 2010, studies found 10 million people imprisoned worldwide.
The US spends > $74 billion/yr on prison; that can support a UBI for crime prevention.

Crime: Inequality and corruption create poverty, breed misery/violence/high crime rates.
UBI is Equality itself and its establishment is proof of a Just and Incorrupt government.

Homeless.Canada: misery of 1% of its population, especially among indigenous people.
Housing First produces results, 66% less hospitalization, less EMS, 79% less jail days.

Homeless in China: In 2020, abolition of poverty in the whole country was achieved.
Western YouTubers are surprised to find no homeless on the city streets of China today !

Homeless. Finland: The constitution mandates *'the right of everyone to housing'*.
With 'Housing First', Finland is the only EU country where homelessness is only 4300.

Homeless. Hong Kong: Country has 42% of land area for parks, only 7% for housing.
Vested interests had made citizens suffer the misery of crammed quarters for 100 years.

Homeless. India: with 1.7 million homeless (2011) and 17% of world slum dwellers.
UBI project gives positive results in Indian villages (2013); let people help themselves.

Homeless. Japan: Lowest among OECD countries, Japan's homeless rate is near 0%.
Begging is an offense and help offered is offensive to receive; only UBI has no stigma.

Homeless, USA: Half a million homeless, 6.3 million households with housing burden.
Reliefs reach 50% of individuals and surplus for families; fairer UBI reaches everyone.

Homeless: 2005, worldwide, 100 million homeless, 1 billion were squatters, refugees, ..
$10K to house but $30K to police a homeless person; it's simpler, give the man his UBI.

Poverty. China: still had 600 million people with income barely 1,000 yuan/mth ($154).
Among policies for promoting 'common prosperity', the UBI is both simple and doable.

Poverty. South Africa: a most unequal country with a fifth of citizens in abject poverty.
The UBI is equality, best suited to fight inequality and abject poverty in South Africa.

Poverty. South Korea: healthy elders with universal healthcare, enjoy longevity.
However 49% live in relative poverty, "just needing a bit more money every month".

Poverty. Syria: war has brought destruction and poverty to this middle-income nation.
Poverty breeds hatred and more armed conflict; a global UBI is needed for world peace.

Poverty. USA: the superpower nation still has 40 million people living in poverty.
Low election turnout! The majority of voters who need UBI ought to unite to vote for it.

Poverty. World: in 2017 the poverty rate in the U.S. was 12%, S.Sudan ~82%, …
On city streets or in the sub-Sahara deserts, the misery of poverty is equally inhuman.

Suicide. Children: 1/5 of suicide attempts/deaths in North West Syria are children.
Surviving a war and suffering extreme distress as refugees, children are most affected.

Suicide. China: by 2016, improved economy reduced suicide to 9.7 per 100,000.
This rate is lower than neighbors like Korea, Japan, and Russia; with male:female at 1:1.

Suicide. EU: developed countries stress the importance for mental healthcare.
But people in debt / unemployed are at high risk, highlighting the economic aspect.

Suicide. Lithuania: people opposing the Soviet system were put in psychiatric clinics.
People are reluctant to seek help, but the 2013 high rate was also due to high inflation.

Sucide. South Africa: the Covid-19 pandemic raised endemic poverty to suicidal level.
"Keep the powerful accountable", the nation's wealth in a UBI for the underprivileged.

Suicide. South Korea: suicide is the fourth-highest cause of death, highest in the OECD.
A rich nation, the wealth created by technology has been 'stolen' by a privileged few.

Suicide. US: suicide is a major national public health issue, 48,344 recorded in 2018.
A 2019 study says raising the minimum wage would result in a quick drop in suicide.

Suicide. World: Divorced Chinese raising children, Swede suicides down with welfare.
Truly it is all about financial stress / insecurity among suicidal people around the world.

World of Miseries

Conclusions:

The wretchedness that Paine lamented centuries ago still exists today in our world.
Born into poverty that breeds crime, vulnerable millions are jailed for petty crimes.
They are the homeless millions on the streets, the billions who live in slum conditions.
They are the discriminated indigenous people in Canada, the slum dwellers in India.
They are citizens living in cramped quarters in Hong Kong, victims of vested interest.
They are the millions of households, daily stressed with a housing burden in the U.S.
Homelessness is estimated at 100m people worldwide, and a billion living as squatters.

China has eliminated abject poverty, but 600m people still earn < 1,000 yuan monthly.
South Africa still suffers extreme inequality with a fifth of its people in abject poverty.
South Korea, rich, has universal healthcare, yet 49% of its elders are in relative poverty.
Syria, a middle-income nation, is reduced to a state of refugees and poverty by wars.
U.S.A., the only superpower on earth, has 40m people living in poverty amidst plenty !
Poverty seems endemic the world over, be it in undeveloped or developed countries.

War, destruction, displacement, alarmingly increase suicide rate of children, in Syria.
Economic growth has reduced suicide rate below that of neighboring states, in China.
Mental Healthcare finds suicides among the unemployed /people in debt, in the EU.
Inflation at 30-year high (2013) inflated the suicide rate to 31.9 per 10,000 in Lithuania.
And Covid pandemic recently raised endemic poverty to suicidal level in South Africa.
Suicide is the fourth highest cause of death in South Korea, highest amongst the OECD.
Suicide is also a major national public health issue in the USA, 48,344 recorded in 2018.
Suicide, the ultimate loss of hope for the individual, is largely financial insecurity.

The miserable world of Poverty is not limited to the visible homeless and slum dwellers.
It is a known fact that millions more live crammed in cubicles above and cellars below.
Many households pay up to 50% of income just for housing, a huge burden indeed.
Thus the prevalence of World Miseries is much more than what meets the eye.
Like for every suicide reported, there are 10 times more people who have attempted.

The problem with the homeless/slum dwellers/others is needing a little financial help.
The average family just needed a few hundred dollars for an occasional emergence.
An elder woman recycling cardboard said, "I just need a bit more money every month".
Just a modest UBI monthly will certainly be a great relief to our World of Miseries.

World of Capitalism

Mother Nature leaves no one behind

52   World of Capitalism (25 articles)

Inequality: Wealth per Adult

List of countries by wealth per adult
From Wikipedia, the free encyclopedia (https://en.wikipedia.org/wiki/)
Countries by mean wealth (US$) per adult. From 2021 publication of Credit Suisse.
Countries by median wealth (US$) per adult. From 2021 publication of Credit Suisse.
..Wealth includes both financial and non-financial assets. Credit Suisse publishes various statistics relevant for calculating net wealth. These figures are influenced by real estate prices, equity market prices, exchange rates, liabilities, debts, adult percentage of the population, human resources, natural resources and capital and technological advancements, which may create new assets or render others worthless in the future.

..During periods of equity market growth, the relative national and per capita wealth of countries where people are more exposed to those markets, such as the United States and the United Kingdom, tends to rise. But when equity markets are down, the relative wealth of countries where people invest more in real estate or bonds, such as France and Italy, tends to rise instead.

..Mean wealth is the amount obtained by dividing the total aggregate wealth by the number of adults. Median wealth is the amount that divides the population into two equal groups: half the adults have wealth above the median, and the other half below. In nations where wealth is highly concentrated in a small percentage of people, the mean can be much higher than the median (e.g. the United States).

Region	Median	Mean	Adults	Total Wealth
Northern America	82,539	486,930	279,950,000	136,316,000
Europe	26,423	174,836	590,343,000	103,213,000
China *	25,067	67,771	1,104,956,000	74,884,000
World	7,522	79,952	5,232,383,000	418,342,000
Asia-Pacific (excl. China and India)	4,793	60,790	1,238,316,000	75,277,000
Latin America	4,466	24,301	447,376,000	10,872,000
India *	3,194	14,252	900,443,000	12,833,000
Africa	1,068	7,371	671,000,000	4,946,000

Comments:
All mean values are way above the median values signifing immense *inequality*.
It exists similarly in first world countries (Europe) and third world countries (Africa).
And World's mean value (79,952) is more than 10x the World's median value (7,522).
This means more than 50% of the world population is living in poverty, in misery daily !
Hopefully 'benevalent' Capitalism allows a Universal Basic Income for everyone.

Inequality: World Report

World Inequality Report. 2018 Executive Summary
Coordinated by: Facundo Alvaredo, et al. (//wir2018.wid.world/files/...)

"In 2016, the share of total national income accounted for by just that nation's top 10% earners (top 10% income share) was 37% in Europe, 41% in China, 46% in Russia, 47% in US-Canada, and around 55% in sub-Saharan Africa, Brazil, and India. In the Middle East, the world's most unequal region according to our estimates, the top 10% capture 61% of national income.

.. The rise in inequality was particularly abrupt in Russia, moderate in China, and relatively gradual in India, reflecting different types of deregulation and opening-up policies pursued over the past decades in these countries.

.. The divergence in inequality levels has been particularly extreme between Western Europe and the United States, which had similar levels of inequality in 1980 but today are in radically different situations. While the top 1% income share was close to 10% in both regions in 1980, it rose only slightly to 12% in 2016 in Western Europe while it shot up to 20% in the United States. Meanwhile, in the United States, the bottom 50% income share decreased from more than 20% in 1980 to 13% in 2016.

.. However, because of high and rising inequality within countries, the top 1% richest individuals in the world captured twice as much growth as the bottom 50% individuals since 1980.

.. Over the past decades, countries have become richer but governments have become poor." "In China and Russia, public wealth declined from 60–70% of national wealth to 20–30%. Net public wealth has even become negative in recent years in the United States and the UK, and is only slightly positive in Japan, Germany, and France. This arguably limits the government ability to regulate the economy, redistribute income, and mitigate rising inequality.

.. Wealth inequality among individuals has increased at different speeds across countries since 1980. ..The rise in wealth inequality has nonetheless been very large in the United States, where the top 1% wealth share rose from 22% in 1980 to 39% in 2014. ..The top 1% wealth share doubled in both China and Russia between 1995 and 2015, from 15% to 30% and from 22% to 43%, respectively.

.. Although the tax system is a crucial tool for tackling inequality, it faces potential obstacles. Tax evasion ranks high as illustrated by the Paradise Papers revelations. The wealth held in tax havens has increased considerably since the 1970s and currently represents more than 10% of global GDP." " It is also worth noting that inheritance taxes are nonexistent or near zero in high-inequality emerging countries, leaving space for important tax reforms in these countries."

Comments:

The top 1% richest individuals capture twice the growth as the bottom 50% individuals! This is unsustainable, and politicians have not been able to reverse it on their own.

It seems a guaranteed monthly subsistence UBI can help and be the simple answer.

The bottom 50% individuals and plus can help by demanding for a UBI constitutionally.

By numbers, they can vote the incumbents out when the cash is not put into their hands.

That is, no second term for any incumbent who fails to deliver a UBI to the voters !

Inequality: A Political Issue

Can universal basic income solve global inequalities?
Erik Olin Wright 14 Feb 2017 (///en.unesco.org/inclusivepolicylab/news/)
"What if this idea, suggesting a flat income given to every citizen regardless of employment or social status, was part of the solution to today's *inequalities*? ..
The idea of an unconditional basic income (UBI) is quite simple: every legal resident in a country receives a monthly stipend sufficient to live above the poverty line. Let's call this the 'no frills culturally respectable standard of living'. The grant is unconditional on the performance of any labour or other form of contribution, and it is universal – everyone receives the grant, rich and poor alike. Grants go to individuals, not families. Parents are the custodians of under-age children's grants which may be smaller. Universalistic programmes such as public education and healthcare, that provide services to people rather than cash, continue alongside UBI, but most other redistributive transfers are eliminated since the UBI provides everyone with a decent subsistence. ... The net increase in cost represented by UBI is not large. Special needs subsidies of various sorts continue – for example, for people with disabilities. Minimum wage rules are relaxed, since all earnings in effect generate discretionary income. ..

"UBI has potentially profound ramifications for inequality. Poverty is eliminated, the labour contract becomes more nearly voluntary, and the power relations between workers and employers become less unequal since workers have the option of exit. The possibility of people forming cooperative associations to produce goods and services to serve human needs outside the market increases."

"Sceptics of basic income raise two main objections: that UBI would reduce incentives to work and that the tax rates needed to fund UBI would be prohibitively high. First, means-tested income support programmes are plagued by poverty traps in which people lose their benefits when their earned income crosses some threshold. By contrast, a UBI creates no disincentive to work. ... In the United States and Canada in the 1970s there were a number of randomized controlled trials. More recently, in India in 2011, eight villages were selected in which all residents were given a basic income. In all of these experiments, receiving a UBI significantly improved the lives of people while having at most a modest effect on labour force participation."

"The level of taxation needed to pay for a basic income is, of course, an important issue. But the sustainable level of taxation in any country is not mainly an economic issue. It is a political issue that depends on the administrative capacity to extract taxes and the political will to do so."

Comments:
Erik Olin Wright is all positive about UBI not being a disincentive to work.
He correctly concludes that financing a UBI is not an economic but a political issue.
It depends on the administrative capacity to extract taxes and the political will to do so.
UBI solves inequalities, provides basic economic security, albeit at subsistence level.

Inequality: Gini Index

Gini Coefficient by Country 2021
https://worldpopulationreview.com/country-rankings/gini-coefficient-by-country

The Gini coefficient, also called the Gini index or Gini ratio, is the most commonly used measure of income distribution—simply put, the higher the Gini coefficient, the greater the gap between the incomes of a country's richest and poorest people. A country's Gini coefficient is important because it helps identify high levels of income inequality, which can have several undesirable political and economic impacts. These include slower GDP growth, reduced income mobility, greater household debt, political polarization, and higher poverty rates.

Developed by Italian statistician Corrado Gini in 1912, the Gini coefficient ranges from 0 to 1, but is often written as a percentage. ..if a nation were to have absolute income equality, with every person earning the same amount, its Gini score would be 0 (0%). On the other hand, if one person earned all the income in a nation and the rest earned zero, the Gini coefficient would be 1 (100%). ..the Gini coefficient is defined based on the Lorenz curve. The Lorenz curve plots the percentiles of the population on the graph's horizontal axis according to income or wealth, ..The cumulative income or wealth of the population is plotted on the vertical axis. While the Gini coefficient is a useful tool for analyzing the wealth or income distribution in a country, it does not indicate that country's overall wealth or income.

South Africa ranks as the country with the lowest level of income equality in the world, thanks to a Gini coefficient of 63.0 when last measured in 2014. ..In South Africa, the richest 10% hold 71% of the wealth, while the poorest 60% hold just 7% of the wealth. Additionally, more than half of South Africa's population lives in poverty.

Top 10 Countries with the Highest Gini Coefficients (%) - World Bank: South Africa, Namibia, Suriname, Zambia, Sao Tome and Principe, Central African Republic, Eswatini, Mozambique, Brazil, Belize. Top 10 Countries with the Lowest Gini Coefficients (%) - World Bank: Slovenia, Czech Republic, Slovakia, Belarus, Moldova, United Arab Emirates, Iceland, Azerbaijan, Ukraine, Belgium. ..Inequality is generally lower in Europe than elsewhere in the world,

..The United States has a Gini coefficient of 41.1. In 2015, the top 1% of earners in the United States averaged 40 times more income than the bottom 90%. In the U.S., poverty is a growing issue, where an estimated 12.3-17.8 percent below the poverty level.. Many of these low-wage workers live paycheck-to-paycheck and have no sick days, pension, or health insurance.

Comments:
Rich and poor nations with high wealth inequality have similarly high Gini Coefficients. ***Rich and poor nations similarly needed a guaranteed UBI to reduce inequality.***

Fraud: Evergrande Crisis

How China handled 3 high-profile corporate meltdowns, including companies considered too big to fail — and what that could tell us about Evergrande's future
Huileng Tan. Nov 24, 2021 (https://www.businessinsider.com/evergrande-crisis-)

..China Evergrande's debt crisis has investors on edge. If the property developer defaults, it could send the world's second-largest economy — and the rest of the world — into a financial crisis. ..To get a sense of how the rest of Evergrande's debt drama could play out, we took a look at how the Chinese Community Party has managed the collapse of three too-big-to-fail private companies in the last five years.

..*Anbang: Car insurance turned conglomerate.* ..Anbang started as a regional car insurer in 2004 but — thanks to an aggressive debt-fueled shopping spree — grew so much in a decade that it managed to snap up the storied Waldorf Astoria hotel in New York for about $2 billion in 2014. ..By 2018, Anbang claimed to have about two trillion Chinese yuan ($313 billion) in assets, ..Anbang's downfall was swift and sudden. Wu was taken away by the police from his office in 2017. ..he was sentenced to 18 years in jail for suspected economic crimes, including fundraising, fraud, and embezzlement.

..By the time Wu was sentenced, Chinese regulators had already taken over Anbang and started a state-led restructuring of the technically insolvent insurer. ..Anbang's core insurance and asset management businesses were transferred to a new state-owned company, Dajia, in 2019. Some other assets were sold off to raise cash. Last year, the Chinese insurance regulator ended its two-year takeover. ..the troubled insurer managed to pay short- and medium-term financial insurance issued on time with no defaults, ..The Chinese government is now trying to sell its stakes in Dajia, ..It hasn't found a buyer yet, and for what it's worth, it's holding onto the Waldorf Astoria.

..*Baoshang Bank:* ..was a small, obscure Chinese bank based in Inner Mongolia with conglomerate Tomorrow Group as its major shareholder. The bank had assets of 576 billion Chinese yuan ($90 billion) in 2017, when it published its last annual report. The collapse: In May 2019, the Chinese government took over the small lender suddenly, citing serious credit risks. ..and the move sent shockwaves across the country's banking system. Regulators said Tomorrow Group had made improper and illegal use of significant bank funds.

..Under a government-led restructuring, parts of Baoshang Bank's assets, liabilities, and businesses were taken over by a newly formed bank — Mengshang Bank — and Hong Kong-listed Huishang Bank. State investors such as a national deposit insurance fund and the Inner Mongolia government entered the restructuring process, injecting funds into the new entity through a facility that provided liquidity. This allowed 90% of debts owed to large creditors to be repaid, Reuters reported, citing the People's Bank of China. Without the injection of public funds, the average repayment rate for creditors would be less than 60%, according to the central bank. In August 2020,

Baoshang was finally allowed to file for bankruptcy and to liquidate its remaining assets. The new Mengshang Bank is still operating.

HNA Group: ..Starting out as an airline in 1993 in the southern China region of Hainan, HNA Group grew to become an aggressive dealmaker snapping up trophy businesses around the world using ultra-loose credit available in the 2010s. At the end of June 2017, HNA had assets of 1.2 trillion Chinese yuan ($187.7 billion.) ..Many of its acquisitions were made at a high premium, ..At its peak, HNA employed 400,000 people around the world, according to The New York Times. ..*HNA's debt-fueled acquisitions* started to come under the microscope of the Chinese government. Its unravelling came in a similar fashion to Evergrande's — *by way of government measures introduced in 2017 that aimed to minimize private domestic companies' risk exposure.* ..HNA started selling off most of its assets unrelated to its original businesses, saying in 2018 it would focus on aviation, logistics, and tourism — but the pandemic hit last year, impacting those sectors. This prompted HNA to seek help from the Hainan provincial government, which took over the company.

..HNA was placed in bankruptcy administration in February 2021 and just last month, creditors of the company voted to approve the company's restructuring plan involving 1.1 trillion Chinese yuan ($172 billion) worth of debt. It has also been broken into four independent units focusing on aviation, airport, financial, and commercial.

..Evergrande, China's second-biggest property developer, has $300 billion in debt. The Chinese government is likely to manage a controlled implosion of the company, keeping the fallout as minimal as possible, ..Chinese officials have sought to calm nerves about the debt crisis. They have publicly chided Evergrande, telling the company to resolve its debt problems and instructing the country's real-estate developers to pay their overseas bondholders.

..Evergrande will likely go the way of HNA, having to sell down assets and managing risks step by step, eventually resulting in "a smaller Evergrande," Warut told Insider. ..Authorities have already asked government-owned firms and state-backed property developers to buy some of Evergrande's assets, Reuters reported. It has also dropped instructions to Evergrande to contain the fallout. Bloomberg, citing people familiar with the matter, reported that Beijing has told Evergrande's billionaire founder, Hui Ka Yan, to use his own money to pay the company's debt. He seems to be complying with the directive, reportedly pumping in $1.1 billion from fire sales of assets including art and two Hong Kong apartments to pay down some of the debt.

Comments:

In 2017, China introduced measures aimed at minimizing companies' risk exposure. Thus unraveling and exposing Evergrande and HNA, their debt-fueled acquisitions. There is no lack of dishonest, selfish 'entrepreneurs' scheming only for personal gains. While hard-working employees suffer exploitation, living from paycheck to paycheck. We cannot depend on charity acts from companies that are out to maximize profits. ***Only a strong government can protect the honest majority with a UBI for everyone !***

Fraud: Lenovo.China

Why Chinese netizens are attacking PC giant Lenovo and its founder Liu Chuanzhi
By Yu Zeyuan. 13 Dec 2021 (Translated by Grace Chong, Candice Chan)
(//www.thinkchina.sg/why-chinese-netizens-are-attacking-pc-giant-lenovo-)

..Caught in a whirlpool of public opinion, Lenovo released a brief statement on its intranet on 10 December, stressing that its equity transfer in 2009 did not result in the loss of state-owned assets but instead achieved the preservation and appreciation of state-owned assets. This is the first time that Lenovo has made a public response following Chinese internet personality Sima Nan's repeated accusations against Lenovo last month which caused widespread public concern.

..But Lenovo's response has not quelled netizens' doubts. This is not surprising, given that two camps have formed on the Chinese internet over Lenovo's controversy. ..Xiang Ligang, ..claimed that there was nothing wrong with Lenovo's sky-high salaries and that Lenovo did not cause the loss of state-owned assets but instead created huge benefits for the country. As a result, netizens also targeted and attacked Xiang's comments section, with some netizens alleging that he was colluding with Lenovo. ..On 1 December, Hu (Global Times editor Hu Xijin) ..said that the high salaries — ranging in the tens to hundreds of millions of dollars — of Lenovo's senior executives were unreasonable and should be adjusted. He noted that the public's questioning of Lenovo's loss of state-owned assets was simple and straightforward and in line with the trend of public opinion which Lenovo must face up to. Hu also pointed out that an authoritative pronouncement on the Lenovo incident must be given by state-owned institution Chinese Academy of Sciences (CAS) or even a higher-level department in charge of the supervision and administration of state-owned assets, which points to Lenovo's lack of credibility in its own response.

..In its statement on 10 December, Lenovo said it had confirmed with the CAS that the CAS's divestment in 2009 of its 29% equity stake in Lenovo via the Beijing Equity Exchange was legal and in line with regulations on state-owned asset property right transactions with rigorous auditing, appraisal and bookkeeping. And no objections were raised following audits and checks by China's disciplinary watchdog and state auditors. ..However, the statement did not address issues such as the details of the transfer of shares, the high salaries of senior management, and a disproportionate number of foreigners among the senior management.

..Lenovo's transaction was the epitome of reforming state-owned enterprises and assets. ..Lenovo's plight and helplessness reflects netizens' frustration over the outflow of state-owned assets, and especially the growing rich-poor gap.

Comments:
Lenovo's transaction was the epitome of reforming state-owned enterprises and assets. Indeed, strong government control is needed to stop theft by 'pseudo-entrepreneurs'.
A strong government can easily close the growing rich-poor gap with a UBI !

Fraud: in Welfare

She Ran a Bronx Homeless Shelter. Here's What She Spent Millions On.
By Andy Newman Nov. 23, 2021 (//www.nytimes.com/-millennium-care-fraud.)

During the mid-2010s, New York City paid a nonprofit in the Bronx more than $10 million to house, feed and provide social services to families at a 100-room homeless shelter. According to the nonprofit's executive director, Ethel Denise Perry, here is where much of the money went: Her gym membership. Her car payments. Shopping sprees at Bergdorf Goodman, Bloomingdale's, Ferragamo, Neiman Marcus, Manolo Blahnik, Tiffany's and other luxury retailers. Her brother and nephew, whom she put on the payroll of the nonprofit, Millennium Care. All together, Ms. Perry, 66, admitted using money the city paid Millennium Care to cover over $1 million in personal credit card bills, according to a plea agreement with the state attorney general's office she signed on Friday. She took $2,394,169 from Millennium Care beyond her official salary.

..And so Ms. Perry, who owns two houses in the Bronx and also runs a dance studio, becomes the latest city homeless shelter operator found to have committed fiscal wrongdoing. ..Ms. Perry was sentenced to five years' probation and must pay $1.1 million in taxes and penalties. Millennium Care will pay a fine of $2,394,169 — the exact amount that Ms. Perry overpaid herself — and will be dissolved.

..The nonprofits that the city contracts with to run shelters have been so rife with self-dealing, nepotism and conflicts of interest that Mayor Bill de Blasio has ordered an audit of every nonprofit group in the system. Nine of the 62 groups that run shelters are on an internal city "watch list."

..Earlier this year, for example, the former head of one of the city's biggest shelter networks, Victor Rivera, was charged with pocketing hundreds of thousands of dollars in kickbacks from contractors. ..Last year, the city filed a suit accusing a nonprofit called Childrens Community Services, which operated 28 shelters, of defrauding it by funneling payments to subcontractors that did not provide the supplies and services they were paid for. On Monday, the city cut ties with another of its biggest shelter operators, CORE Services Group, after a New York Times investigation found that CORE's chief executive, Jack A. Brown III, steered millions of dollars from the city to for-profit companies he controlled and paid himself more than $1 million a year.

Comments:
Frauds exposed in any field, anywhere in the world are possibly tips of icebergs.
When people think they have a reasonable chance of getting away with it, they do it.
In the name of charity, many even steal from the 'begging bowl', so to speak.
It is a wonder that half the aids allocated can reach the people originally intended !
UBI for everyone, a birthright that leaves no stigma, eliminates all welfare wastage.

Welfare: Lacking

World Social Protection Report 2020-22
News | 01 September 2021 (//www.ilo.org/global/about-the-ilo/newsroom/news/)
GENEVA (ILO News) – Despite the unprecedented worldwide expansion of social protection during the COVID-19 crisis, more than 4 billion people around the world remain entirely unprotected, a new International Labour Organization (ILO) report says. It finds that the pandemic response was uneven and insufficient, ..and failing to afford the much-needed *social protection that all human beings deserve*...Social protection includes access to health care and income security, particularly in relation to old age, unemployment, sickness, disability, work injury, maternity or loss of a main income earner, as well as for families with children.

The World Social Protection Report 2020-22: Social protection at the crossroads – in pursuit of a better future gives a global overview of recent developments in social protection systems, including social protection floors, and covers the impact of the COVID-19 pandemic. ..Currently, only 47 per cent of the global population are effectively covered by at least one social protection benefit, while 4.1 billion people (53 per cent) obtain no income security at all from their national social protection system.

..There are significant regional inequalities in social protection. Europe and Central Asia have the highest rates of coverage, with 84 percent of people being covered by at least one benefit. The Americas are also above the global average, with 64.3 per cent. Asia and the Pacific (44 per cent), the Arab States (40 per cent) and Africa (17.4 percent) have marked coverage gaps.

..To guarantee at least basic social protection coverage, low-income countries would need to invest an additional US$77.9 billion per year, lower-middle-income countries an additional US$362.9 billion per year and upper-middle-income countries a further US$750.8 billion per year. That's equivalent to 15.9, 5.1 and 3.1 percent of their GDP, respectively.

"Social protection is an important tool that can create wide-ranging social and economic benefits for countries at all levels of development. It can underpin better health and education, greater equality, more sustainable economic systems, better managed migration and the observance of core rights. Building the systems that can deliver these positive outcomes will require a mix of financing sources and greater international solidarity, particularly with support for poorer countries. But the benefits of success will reach beyond national borders to benefit us all", said Shahra Razavi, Director, ILO Social Protection Department.

Comments:
ILO report says more than 4 billion people worldwide are left out of social protection. Social protection is important for underpinning better health, education, equality, ... Building the systems to deliver these outcomes is complicated, requiring lots of effort !
Put UBI cash in the hands of people, and let them do the rest to help themselves.

Welfare: Stigmatized

UNIVERSAL BASIC INCOME: KEY TO REDUCING FOOD INSECURITY AND
IMPROVING HEALTH - Overview 2021
(//drexel.edu/hunger-free-centre/research/briefs-and-reports/universal-basic-income)

"INADEQUATE AND OUTDATED PUBLIC ASSISTANCE PROGRAMS
For the past five decades, the U.S. relied on a patchwork of public assistance programs, such as SNAP, WIC, and Temporary Assistance for Needy Families (TANF). Each program has their own unique eligibility criteria.The government focus on documentation and surveillance as part of these benefit programs is highly inefficient. Outdated systems and technology also lead to increased labor costs and reduced efficiency in administering programs. For participants, these programs demand a significant amount of time, effort, and documentation, which interferes with seeking work and caring for children. Public assistance programs tied to proof of earned income rely on regular recertification. Public assistance participants must report receiving raises or extra income from one-time odd jobs to maintain compliance. Even a small increase in income could result in having benefits reduced or cut off entirely, leaving families with less available money than before the increase. This is known as the "cliff effect." When this happens, families are more likely to experience hunger and food insecurity, poor health, increased hospitalization, and child development issues. In some states, an increase of just $150 per month for a family of four, or $38 per month for a single person, could mean losing benefits altogether."

STIGMA OF PUBLIC ASSISTANCE: Though public assistance programs are funded by public dollars, participation in these programs has always been stigmatized, creating animosity between people of different socioeconomic classes. From the perspective of people who have wealth and privilege, people receiving public assistance may be perceived as less hardworking or worthy than others. Because of this, individuals receiving assistance often try to hide their participation to avoid further stigmatization. If every person received the same basic income "floor" regardless of income, class, race, location of residence, or other status, the stigma of receiving support could be eliminated.

WHY UNIVERSAL INCOME? A universal, unconditional cash transfer system can address shortcomings in public assistance and other benefits that guaranteed income programs geared to specific income levels cannot.

...Implementing UBI can be slow and would replace the current systems over the course of time. Many progressive proponents argue for a UBI+ approach, which would not immediately replace any existing security-enhancing government programs but instead supplement the existing welfare infrastructure."

Comments:
Focus on surveillance increased labor costs and reduced efficiency in welfare programs.
For participants, documentation demands a significant amount of time and effort.
Reporting a small increase in income could result in having benefits reduced or cut off.
Further, they suffer *stigmatization* by privileged people, as less hardworking or worthy.
A progressive partial UBI+ approach may be ideal with the natural attrition of welfare.
Unconditional UBI for all, does not stigmatize, the simplest for implementation.

Welfare: Diversions

Welfare Money is Paying for a Lot of Things Besides Welfare
By Zach Parolin. June 2019. Columbia University (theatlantic.com/ideas/archive/..)

"What do a Christian overnight camp, abstinence-only sex education, and pro-marriage advertisements all have in common? They've all been funded with money that used to provide *cash assistance to low-income families*."

"In the United States, the federal Temporary Assistance for Needy Families program—often known simply as "welfare"—is administered by the 50 states, which have considerable leeway in how to spend the money. The choices states make are unmistakably correlated with race. The higher the proportion of African Americans in a state, the more likely officials are to try to change the way poor families run their lives, rather than simply help them with basic expenses. *Many know TANF as the nation's primary cash assistance program for low-income families*. But depending on which state you live in, TANF may provide barely any cash assistance at all."

"... In practice, though, the diversion of TANF funds away from cash support and toward programs meant to influence family formation has likely exacerbated racial differences in poverty. A clear pattern emerges: A black family in poverty is more likely than a white family to be offered advice via a "Healthy Marriage Initiative" in place of direct cash support."

"... But Arkansas is hardly alone in spending less on cash support. From the introduction of TANF, in 1997, to 2017, total spending on cash assistance across all states declined from *$14 billion a year to $7 billion*. (In constant dollars, the amount of money spent on cash assistance has fallen by two-thirds.) While cash support has waned, however, states' TANF budgets haven't changed: The federal government provides states the same chunk of money each year to run their TANF programs. Thus, every dollar that a state does not spend on cash assistance should generally be spent on another program or service that, at least in theory, will support low-income families.

"...and as the data on TANF suggest, state governments often function as a source of inequality rather than its cure. Instead of narrowing gaps between the advantaged and disadvantaged, social policy can, when deployed unevenly across the country, act to deepen them instead."

Comments:
TANF ($14B a year), the US primary cash assistance program for low-income families.
Poor black families often get no cash support but programs that advise family planning.
Diversions of money to support capitalist programs like Christian overnight camps.
Like abstinence-only sex education, like pro-marriage advertisements.
The world over, UBI projects have shown very positive effects, even with a little cash.
TANF will have better results reverting to giving out cash support like a UBI !

Welfare: Common Prosperity

What is China's common-prosperity strategy that calls for an even distribution of wealth?

Andrew Mullen, 26 Aug, 2021 (scmp.com/economy/china-economy/article/3146271/)
..The idea of common prosperity was first mentioned in the 1950s, when China was a significantly poorer country, by founding father Mao Zedong. But the phrase was then repeatedly mentioned by former leader Deng Xiaoping in the 1980s when China's private sector began to emerge in some regions, creating disparity. ..In 1985, Deng is quoted as having said that "we will fail if our policies lead to rich-poor polarisation, and we will really be on an evil path if some new bourgeoisie is created [due to the wealth disparity]".

..President Xi Jinping's rhetoric on common prosperity has surged this year – evidence of the Communist Party's commitment to closing the country's yawning wealth gap. .."We can allow some people to get rich first and then guide and help others to get rich together … We can support wealthy entrepreneurs who work hard, operate legally, and have taken risks to start businesses … but we must also do our best to *establish a 'scientific' public policy system that allows for fairer income distribution,"*..

..The speech called for better governance and more balance in the economy, focusing on grass-roots consumption as a key economic multiplier rather than capital-intensive investments, which have been popular in past decades. ..various plans – including those involving favourable changes in taxes and social-security payments for middle-income earners; more policies that increase earnings for those in low-income groups; and *crackdowns on practices, loopholes that may give rise to "illicit income"* ..

Xi also called for the protection of intellectual property rights and property rights, reiterating that the country would stick to promoting the common development of both the private and foreign sectors while *keeping public ownership as the main body of the Chinese economy.* The meeting also placed an emphasis on supporting the development of small and medium-sized enterprises. But common prosperity does not just apply to financial markets, it also applies to society's spiritual and cultural life. It needs to be extended to rural and urban areas – while rural infrastructure and rural living conditions, in particular, need to be improved, Xi said.

..The country should "smooth social mobility to give more people opportunities to get rich and shape a development environment where everyone can take a part in", the meeting said. All levels of government, including local governments, must work together to formulate plans that fit the local conditions to achieve the goal of common prosperity, policymakers at the meeting said. Local governments were called on to fully gauge how long-term, arduous and complex the work could be and act according to their own capability.

The common-prosperity concept also covers access to public services. That means that the privatization of public services such as education, elderly care and medical care will recede, and the government will emphasize the role of inclusiveness and affordability among these service providers, and be strict in monitoring prices, according to Yue Su, principal economist with The Economist Intelligence Unit. Leaders have asked for better financial supervision, while also taking steps to punish financial corruption in line with market principles and the rule of law.

..The common-prosperity system also encourages "third distribution", referring to creating opportunities for high-income groups and enterprises to give back to society, including through voluntary gifts and charitable donations. ..Decades of economic liberalization have delivered tremendous wealth, creating a middle class of 340 million people earning between US$15,000 and US$75,000 per year, according to a report by HSBC. That number is projected to reach 500 million by 2025. China also had 5.28 million US dollar millionaires – households with wealth in excess of US$1 million – by the end of last year. In 2020, the wealthiest 1 percent of Chinese people held 30.6 percent of the country's wealth, up from 20.9 per cent two decades ago, according to a Credit Suisse report. That has resulted in a widening income divide in the country. China's Gini coefficient – a measure of inequality from 0 to 1, with 0 being perfect equality – has hovered between 0.46 and 0.49 over the past two decades. A level of 0.40 is usually regarded as a red line for inequality.

..The wealth gap is even starker. The wealth Gini coefficient, which rose from 0.599 in 2000 to 0.711 in 2015, eased to 0.697 in 2019 before rising again to 0.704 last year, according to the report. A country in which every resident has the same wealth would have an income Gini coefficient of 0, meaning in China, the gap has grown over the last two decades. Just last year, Premier Li Keqiang said the nation had 600 million people living on a monthly income of 1,000 yuan (US$154), which is barely enough to cover monthly rent in a mid-sized Chinese city. ..President Xi pledged last year to make "more substantial progress on common prosperity for all" by 2035, and a pilot programme in Zhejiang province is designed to narrow the income gap there by 2025.

Chinese economists were quick to move to ease fears that China's drive for common prosperity signals aggressive policies are afoot that will seize money from the rich to close the country's yawning wealth gap. "Robbing the rich to give to the poor" would only result in "common poverty," said Zhang Jun, ..Li Daokui, a former adviser to China's central bank, .."We must be vigilant against 'common prosperity' becoming a Great Leap Forward, a risky endeavor, or something that drags down economic development and affects efficiency."

Comments:

The wealth gap is stark, with the richest 1% holding 30.6% of the country's wealth. Common-prosperity means a scientific public policy system of fair income distribution. And crackdowns on practices, loopholes that frequently give rise to "illicit income". With poverty eliminated in 2020, China still has 600 million people living on 1,000 yuan monthly. ***Hence, China still needs to establish a guaranteed UBI to ensure common prosperity.***

Monetary: Democracy

Democratic distress in Europe and the USA: a transatlantic malaise?
Saskia Brechenmacher. 24 July 2018 (//www.opendemocracy.net/en/transformation/)

Liberal democracy is floundering in places where it was long thought to be most securely established. In both Western Europe and the United States, polls suggest that many voters have lost confidence in democratic institutions, ..In 2017, for example, only 12 percent of Americans expressed a "great deal" or "quite a lot" of trust in Congress, down from 30 percent in 2004. ..In France, Greece, Italy, and Spain, for example, fewer than ten percent of people expressed trust in their country's political parties in 2014.

..As more and more political discourse shifts online, domestic and foreign actors are also exploiting new platforms to sow distrust and undermine fact-based debate. ..Polarization in today's Congress is higher than at any time since the late 1800s, and the share of Americans with highly negative views of the opposing party has more than doubled since 1994.

..In practice, the result has been persistent legislative gridlock, as well as a greater willingness on both sides to disregard democratic norms, neglect congressional oversight, and play constitutional hardball for political gain. In addition to horizontal polarization between left and right, the US also struggles with exceptionally high levels of vertical polarization caused by deepening *socioeconomic inequality*. Weak institutional safeguards—particularly lax campaign finance and lobbying regulations—enable the highly privileged to exert disproportionate political influence. For example, outside spending on presidential elections has skyrocketed from approximately $339.5 million in 2008 to $1.3 billion in 2016. Costly campaigns perpetuate the overrepresentation of wealthy politicians and corporate interests, while low-income citizens participate in politics at much lower rates. While socioeconomic divides have also deepened in some European countries, the trend is most pronounced in the USA.

..Since 2010, 23 US states have enacted new laws that make it harder to vote, particularly for low-income voters. ..Partisan gerrymandering has become another hotly contested issue, with critics arguing that allowing legislative majorities to redraw districts in their favor has undermined democratic competition and fair representation.

Comments:
Presidential elections funding rocketed from 339m to 1.3b, vested interests take-over.
Wealthy politicians are over represented and low-income citizens' participation declines.
Government is polarized left and right, is ineffective, socioeconomic inequality deepens.
With one simple stroke, a UBI will instantly ameliorate socioeconomic inequality.
The vast majority of people certainly love to have and benefit from a guaranteed UBI.
In countries with democracy, people can help themselves with their sheer numbers!
The hapless majority stand up, unite for the politicians who favor guaranteed UBI.

Monetary: GDP

Gross Domestic Product
From Wikipedia, 11 Dec 2021 (https://en.wikipedia.org/wiki/Gross_domestic_product)

Gross domestic product (GDP) is a monetary measure of the market value of all the final goods and services produced in a specific time period. GDP (nominal) per capita does not, however, reflect differences in the cost of living and the inflation rates of the countries; *therefore, using a basis of GDP per capita at purchasing power parity (PPP) may be more useful when comparing living standards between nations*, while nominal GDP is more useful comparing national economies on the international market. ..The ratio of GDP to the total population of the region is the per capita GDP and the same is called Mean Standard of Living. ..The Organization for Economic Co-operation and Development (OECD) defines GDP as "an aggregate measure of production equal to the sum of the gross values added of all resident and institutional units engaged in production and services (plus any taxes, and minus any subsidies, on products not included in the value of their outputs)". An IMF publication states that, "GDP measures the monetary value of final goods and services—that are bought by the final user—produced in a country in a given period of time (say a quarter or a year)."

..GDP can be determined in three ways, all of which should, theoretically, give the same result. ..The most direct of the three is the production approach, which sums the outputs of every class of enterprise to arrive at the total. The expenditure approach works on the principle that all of the product must be bought by somebody, therefore the value of the total product must be equal to people's total expenditures in buying things. The income approach works on the principle that the incomes of the productive factors ("producers", colloquially) must be equal to the value of their product, and determines GDP by finding the sum of all producers' incomes.

.. *Externalities* – Economic growth may entail an increase in negative externalities that are not directly measured in GDP. Increased industrial output might grow GDP, but any pollution is not counted. *Non-market transactions* – GDP excludes activities that are not provided through the market, such as household production, bartering of goods and services, and volunteer or unpaid services. *Non-monetary economy* – GDP omits economies where no money comes into play.. *Quality improvements and inclusion of new products* – by not fully adjusting for quality improvements and new products, GDP understates true economic growth.. *Sustainability of growth* – GDP is a measurement of economic historic activity and is not necessarily a projection. *Wealth distribution* – GDP does not account for variances in incomes of various demographic groups. ..It can be argued that GDP per capita as an indicator standard of living is correlated with these factors, capturing them indirectly. As a result, GDP per capita as a standard of living is a continued usage because most people have a fairly accurate idea of what it is and know it is tough to come up with quantitative measures for such constructs as happiness, quality of life, and well-being.

..*Economic welfare* cannot be adequately measured unless the personal *distribution of income* is known. And no income measurement undertakes to estimate the reverse side of income, that is, the intensity and unpleasantness of effort going into the earning of income. The welfare of a nation can, therefore, scarcely be inferred from a measurement of national income as defined above.

..Ever since the development of GDP, multiple observers have pointed out limitations of using GDP as the overarching measure of economic and social progress. For example, many environmentalists argue that GDP is a poor measure of social progress because it does not take into account harm to the environment. Furthermore, the GDP does not consider human health nor the educational aspect of a population.

..GDP does not account for the *distribution of income* among the residents of a country, because GDP is merely an aggregate measure. An economy may be highly developed or growing rapidly, but also contain a wide gap between the rich and the poor in a society. These inequalities often occur on the lines of race, ethnicity, gender, religion, or other minority status within countries. This can lead to misleading characterizations of economic well-being if the income distribution is heavily skewed toward the high end, as the poorer residents will not directly benefit from the overall level of wealth and income generated in their country. Even GDP per capita measures may have the same downside if inequality is high.

..*GDP does not take into account the value of household and other unpaid work.* Some, including Martha Nussbaum, argue that this value should be included in measuring GDP, as household labor is largely a substitute for goods and services that would otherwise be purchased for value. Even under conservative estimates, *the value of unpaid labor in Australia has been calculated to be over 50% of the country's GDP.* A later study analyzed this value in other countries, with results ranging from a low of about 15% in Canada (using conservative estimates) to high of nearly 70% in the United Kingdom (using more liberal estimates). For the United States, the value was estimated to be between about 20% on the low end to nearly 50% on the high end, depending on the methodology being used.

..In 2017 Diane Coyle explained that *GDP excludes much unpaid work*, writing that "many people contribute free digital work such as writing open-source software that can substitute for marketed equivalents, and *it clearly has great economic value despite a price of zero"*, which constitutes a common criticism "of the reliance on GDP as the measure of economic success" especially after the emergence of the digital economy.

Comments:

GDP per capita at purchasing power parity is more useful comparing living standards.
GDP doesn't account for externalities like pollution, volunteer unpaid work in society.
GDP doesn't account for domestic work done at home by wives, .. (est. 15-70 % GDP).
GDP not indicative of socioeconomic welfare like income inequality, health, education.
UBI enables people to help themselves improve socio economic welfare all at once.
A UBI index (% of median income paid) may be a good indicator of social wellbeing.

Monetary: Automation

A basic income really could end poverty forever
But to become a reality, it needs to get detailed and stop being oversold.
By Dylan Matthews Jul 17, 2017 (///vox.com/policy-and-politics- automation)

"Basic income, wherein the government gives everyone enough cash to live on with no strings attached, struck me as an idea in that mold: another never-going-to-happen but fun-to-think-about alternative to the unfettered financial capitalism. … And when you take a look under the hood of major plans from basic income advocates, the politics begin to look daunting. "

Basic income is a useful tool for reducing poverty in both poor and rich countries. But a lot of basic income advocates embrace it for other reasons, like responding to automation's threat to jobs, or dismantling the welfare state.
Andy Stern's *Raising the Floor* (2016): The arrival of driverless trucks and taxis and 3D-printed houses and robotic mall cops, he predicts, will cause a wave of joblessness that will lead to mass immiseration and social breakdown — unless a universal basic income lets people out of work still earn enough to get by. Peter Frase's *Four Futures* and Nick Srnicek and Alex Williams's book *Inventing the Future*: feature a future where labor is completely automated, no one needs to work, and a basic income program distributes the dividends of the robots' efforts equally to all citizens.

Whether or not basic income is a good idea depends entirely on how you pay for it. Charles Murray's book *In Our Hands* (2006) laid out a basic income proposal to replace all welfare spendings. Free market advocates see the UBI as a replacement for the existing welfare state. Many call for a UBI as an additional benefit on top of existing programs, funded through new taxes on carbon, natural resources, businesses, 'the rich.' The potential is even greater in countries with great mineral or natural resource wealth. In 2011, Iran introduced basic income providing about 29% of the median household income on average and saw no appreciable effect on labor supply. Thus Oil rich countries in Africa like Nigeria, Angola and Equatorial Guinea can follow Iran's example in this regard. Say, a quarter or a third of revenues are to be distributed as a basic income, you could probably wipe out extreme poverty altogether.

"But we shouldn't let American parochialism blind us to the immense good that basic income, as an idea, can still do in poorer nations. Conditional cash transfers like Brazil's Bolsa Familia or Mexico's Oportunidades already play an important role in poverty alleviation. Basic income is the logical next step. And let's not fall prey to the myth that, in poor countries or rich ones, a basic income is unaffordable, or would discourage work to an excessive degree."

Comments:

Unfettered financial Capitalism sees UBI as a response to automation, loss of jobs.
Unfettered financial Capitalism sees UBI for dismantling the welfare state.
Oil and mineral resources belong to all citizens, hence UBI is the logical step in Africa.
Like Iran, UBI pays 29% of median household income, people have not worked less.
Huge *automation gains* also belong to all citizens, thus UBI is also the logical next step.
Matthews is right: in poor countries or rich ones, that a UBI is unaffordable is a myth.
The masses can vote the government out when a fair-share UBI is not forthcoming.

Monetary: AI funding

Silicon Valley Leaders Think A.I. will one day fund free cash handouts.
Sam Shead Mar 30 2021 (///.cnbc.com/openai-ceo-sam-altman-)
"In as little as 10 years, AI could generate enough wealth to pay every adult in the U.S. $13,500 a year, Altman said in his 2,933 word piece called "Moore's Law for Everything" My work at OpenAI reminds me every day about the magnitude of the socioeconomic change that is coming sooner than most people believe," said Altman, the former president of renowned start-up accelerator Y-Combinator earlier this month. "Software that can think and learn will do more and more of the work that people now do." "We could do something called the American Equity Fund," wrote Altman. "The American Equity Fund would be capitalized by taxing companies above a certain valuation 2.5% of their market value each year, payable in shares transferred to the fund, and by taxing 2.5% of the value of all privately-held land, payable in dollars."
He added: "All citizens over 18 would get an annual distribution, in dollars and company shares, into their accounts. People would be entrusted to use the money however they needed or wanted — for better education, healthcare, housing, starting a company, whatever."

"Founded in San Francisco in 2015 by a group of entrepreneurs including Elon Musk, OpenAI is widely regarded as one of the top AI labs in the world, along with Facebook AI Research, and DeepMind, which was acquired by Google in 2014."

"But critics are concerned that Altman's views could cause more harm than good, and that he's misleading the public on where AI is headed. Glen Weyl, an economist and a principal researcher at Microsoft Research, wrote on Twitter: "This beautifully epitomizes the AI ideology that I believe is the most dangerous force in the world today... One industry source, who asked to remain anonymous due to the nature of the discussion, told CNBC that Altman "envisions a world wherein he and his AI-CEO peers become so immensely powerful that they run every non-AI company (employing people) out of business and every American worker to unemployment. So powerful that a percentage of OpenAI's (and its peers') income could bankroll UBI for every citizen of America... "Acemoglu said algorithms are good at performing some "very, very narrow tasks" and that they can sometimes help businesses to cut costs or improve a product. But they're not that revolutionary, and there's no evidence that any of this is going to be revolutionary," he said, adding that AI leaders are "waxing lyrical about what AI is doing already and how it's revolutionizing things.""

Comments:
Acemoglu correctly says AI algorithms help businesses cut costs, nothing revolutionary. But businesses combined, AI can help generate huge gains of wealth to support a UBI. Altman correctly says AI can generate enough wealth to pay every adult $13,500 yearly. AI is a social property, and all gains ought to be shared among all citizens with a UBI. ***Not be stolen in boardrooms by top management, creating the 'Billionaire' class !***

Monetary: Billionaires

Forbes 400 list of richest Americans
Kerry A Dolan. 5 Oct. 2021 (///forbes.com/sites/kerryadolan/)

The 40th annual Forbes 400 list of the wealthiest Americans: the members' collective fortune rose a massive 40% over the last year to $4.5 trillion, up from $3.2 trillion. The top 20 on the list are worth a stunning $1.8 trillion together.

..The richest person in America, 4 year in a row, is Jeff Bezos. The founder and chairman of online retailer and cloud computing juggernaut Amazon is worth $201 billion. At number two is Elon Musk, worth $190.5 billion—almost triple what he was worth on the 2020 list, due to the huge runup in the price of Tesla's shares.

..Mark Zuckerberg took the third spot, thanks to a 63% jump in Facebook stock since last year's list. Bill Gates is at number four, the first time he hasn't been in one of the top two spots in three decades.

..There were 44 newcomers to the ranking, the richest of whom is 29-year-old cryptocurrency entrepreneur Sam Bankman-Fried, worth $22.5 billion. He's the youngest list member this year and the richest self-made newcomer. In total there are seven cryptocurrency entrepreneurs on the ranks—six more than a year ago. Another newcomer is R.J. Scaringe, founder of privately held Rivian, which is working to produce electric pickup trucks and SUVs and counts Amazon and Ford as investors.

...The minimum net worth needed to gain—or hold onto—a spot on the list this year jumped to $2.9 billion... The number of women on The Forbes 400 is unchanged from a year ago at 56… The richest woman in America, for the seventh year in a row, is Walmart heir Alice Walton, worth an estimated $67.9 billion.

...A total of 282 members of this year's ranking have fortunes that are self-made—defined by Forbes to mean they are entrepreneurs who either started a company (like Jeff Bezos founding Amazon) or were hired by someone to help build one (such as Meg Whitman, who was CEO of Ebay for a decade,..)..Sixty-one on the list inherited their fortune. Another 57 heirs of fortunes, but were active in increasing them.

...California is home to more Forbes 400 members than any other state with 89 ..New York state has the second highest with 67, followed by a tie for third: Texas and Florida each have 37.

Comments
Techno advancements have generated huge profits for companies creating billionaires.
Amazon.com online sales platform is built on innovations that belong to all people.
A 10% Goods and Service Tax on every transaction will bring in billions for a UBI.
Apple Inc. arbitrarily took a 30% cut on cash transactions on its platform for years.
Then rightly, 25% of this ought to be collected for distribution to everyone via a UBI.
Innovation profits should not be stolen in the boardrooms by 'pseudo' entrepreneurs.

Monetary: Corporate Taxes

Why Amazon Pays No Corporate Taxes

Stephanie Denning. Feb 22, 2019 *(//www.forbes.com/sites/ /?sh=6752965c54d5)*

Amazon's recent decision to pull HQ2 out of New York City has reignited an older debate about why the company pays "no taxes." One graphic, for example, produced by data journalist Mona Chalabi and subsequently reshared by House member Alexandria Ocasio-Cortez among many others, shows two superimposed graphs comparing Amazon's quickly growing profit next to its negligible taxes over the last nine years. The comparison is striking. And also misleading. As one of today's most influential economists, Tyler Cowen, wrote on his site Marginal Revolution, "When it comes to the discussion surrounding Amazon and taxes, I can only sigh...."

..First, a quick look at Amazon's financial statements shows it does pay taxes. In 2017, Amazon paid close to $1 billion in income tax. In 2018, the amount jumped to $1.18 billion, accounting for local, state, and international taxes.

..Amazon pays plenty in terms of payroll taxes and also state and local taxes. Nor should you forget the taxes paid by Amazon's employees on their wages. Not only is that direct revenue to various levels of government, but the incidence of those taxes falls somewhat on Amazon, which now must pay higher wages to offset the tax burden faced by their employees," Cowen adds.

..It is true that in the last two years, Amazon did not pay federal taxes. (It's odd to think I paid more federal tax last year than Amazon did.) But before yelling partiality, it is worth understanding why. A more thorough examination of the underlying economics demonstrates that only looking at Amazon's profits versus corporate taxes is too simplistic of a model.

..Instead, a good place to start is understanding economic incentives. Incentives, in layman's terms, sound like free money. Incentives, to an economist, operate as a lever to generate a better result which offset the cost. Taxes are one such lever. But taxes are too often interpreted only by their first-order effect of generating revenue, rather than the second-order effect of stimulating economic activity. If you look at the Internal Revenue Code, as one CPA cites, less than 1% of it is dedicated to revenue generation. The majority, in fact, is on tax deductions. "There are only about 30 pages in the Code that actually raise revenue...[T]here are about 6,000 pages that tell you how to reduce taxes through tax deductions, tax credits and other incentives."

..Tax deductions can be incorrectly categorized as "crony capitalism." But tax deductions, tax credits, and other incentives act as an important driver for organizations to then stimulate economic activity, job creation, and innovation.

There are three main drivers of Amazon's tax breaks:

- Investment in Research & Development. Amazon invests heavily in research and development and therefore benefits from the tax credit. In 2017, as Recode stated, Amazon topped the list of U.S. companies in R&D spend, at $22.6 billion. The next closest was Alphabet at $16.6 billion. Many of Amazon's innovations have been birthed from this investment.
- Investment in Property, Plant, and Equipment. Amazon's investment in property, plant, and equipment also makes it eligible for tax credits. Cities can benefit from Amazon's investment in real estate and job creation (benefits New York City could have enjoyed). Amazon's PPE expenditure has steadily increased over the last five years, netting to approximately $60 billion as of the end of last year.
- Employee Stock Compensation. A move away from cash compensation to stock-based compensation for employees is the third driver of its tax breaks. Tax deductions increase as the stock increases. While this can certainly create adverse incentives, it is important to assess the benefits it creates relative to the cost. While such a tax policy can introduce misaligned management incentives, it also generates incentives for management to drive the best possible return for investors.

..Amazon largely pays no corporate tax precisely because it reinvests those profits into its operations. Under a scenario where Amazon had no corporate tax breaks, it would disincentive the company from reinvesting and thus creating greater opportunity for the businesses and cities in which it operates.

..Raising a pitchfork to fight Amazon's corporate tax breaks is fine if the argument is rooted in strong economic reasoning. The risk is that too often the data is pulled out of context, and inaccurate storylines circling that data gain momentum and undeservedly accelerate.

..The building impetus to tear down existing economic structures without a strong grounding in why the structures even exist could land us in a worse position. The question to address is not why Amazon pays no taxes, but under what tax structure could we be better off?

Comments:

The existing tax structure supports tax breaks for businesses to expand, to earn more.
Top management then claims credit for the increase in profits, and gets huge bonuses.
Employee Stock Compensation is only for top management, not the general employees.
Top management then sells the stock in the market without the need to pay income tax !
This is how the common employees are short-changed, and the rich/poor gap widens.
If all employees can enjoy Employee Stock Compensation, not just top management.
They can also sell their stock without the need to pay income tax, just like the rich !

Monetary: Inheritance Tax

Estate and Inheritance Taxes around the World
Alan Cole. March 17, 2015 (///taxfoundation.org/estate-and-inheritance-taxes-)

Key Findings
- The U.S. has the fourth highest estate or inheritance tax rate in the OECD at 40 percent; the world's highest rate, 55 percent, is in Japan, followed by South Korea (50 percent) and France (45 percent). Fifteen OECD countries levy no taxes on property passed to lineal heirs.
- The U.S. estate tax has a high rate and a large exemption; as a result, it raises very little revenue and applies to very few households.
- U.S. estate tax receipts have declined precipitously over the last fifteen years, from $38 billion (2015 dollars) in 2001 to an estimated $20 billion in 2015.
- As estate taxes become narrow-based, meager revenue sources with high administrative costs, repeal becomes a strong option. Thirteen countries or jurisdictions have repealed their estate or inheritance taxes since 2000.
- Repeal of the U.S. estate tax would gradually increase the U.S. capital stock by 2.2 percent, boost GDP, create 139,000 jobs, and eventually increase federal revenue.

The highest top estate tax rate to lineal heirs can be found in Japan, at 55 percent. South Korea (50 percent) and France (45 percent) also have rates higher than the U.S. At the low end, fifteen of the thirty-four countries in the OECD have no taxes on property passed to lineal heirs. The average estate tax rate across the OECD is 15 percent with a median tax rate of 7 percent.

Eleven countries (including Singapore, 2008) and two tax jurisdictions have repealed their estate or inheritance taxes since the year 2000. The two tax jurisdictions to repeal were Macau and Hong Kong, which brought them in line with the rest of mainland China.

Conclusion: The estate tax is losing ground around the world, not because moral conundrums have been resolved, but rather because it fails at the basic characteristics of being a tax. Its rate is high, causing a substantial drag on growth. Its base is narrow, making it a poor revenue raiser. And lastly, its base is poorly-defined, creating additional economic losses from tax planning. The ultimate purpose of tax collection is revenue generation. Due to the properties described above, the estate tax fails at effectively achieving that end. Eliminating it is the most serious option for reform.

Comments:

I am no economist, cannot understand how repeal of estate tax boosts GDP, creates jobs. That means when nothing is done (no estate taxing), the economy will grow by itself !
The heirs **work not** to inherit their fortunes, just being lucky to have rich forebears.
Children of the land too need **not work** to inherit the nation's wealth through a UBI.
Furthermore 50% inheritance tax distributed in a UBI will grow the home economy.
All estates wealth, 50% to heirs and 50% to the rest of the population, to be fair.

Monetary: MMT

Modern Monetary Theory or Modern Money Theory (MMT)
Wikipedia, the free encyclopedia (wikipedia.org/wiki/Modern_Monetary_Theory)

MMT says that governments create new money by using fiscal policy and that the primary risk once the economy reaches full employment is inflation, which can be addressed by gathering taxes to reduce the spending capacity of the private sector.

MMT's main tenets are that a government that issues its own fiat money:

1. Can pay for goods, services, and financial assets without a need to first collect money in the form of taxes or debt issuance in advance of such purchases;
2. Cannot be forced to default on debt denominated in its own currency;
3. Is limited in its money creation and purchases only by inflation, which accelerates once the real resources (labour, capital and natural resources) of the economy are utilized at full employment;
4. Recommends strengthening automatic stabilisers to control demand-pull inflation rather than relying upon discretionary tax changes;
5. Bond issues are a monetary policy device, not a funding device.

..In sovereign financial systems, banks can create money but these "horizontal" transactions do not increase net financial assets because assets are offset by liabilities. *According to MMT advocates, "The balance sheet of the government does not include any domestic monetary instrument on its asset side; it owns no money. All monetary instruments issued by the government are on its liability side and are created and destroyed with spending and taxing or bond offerings."* In MMT, "vertical money" enters circulation through government spending. Taxation and its legal tender enable power to discharge debt and establish fiat money as currency, giving it value by creating demand for it in the form of a private tax obligation. In addition, fines, fees, and licenses create demand for the currency. This currency can be issued by the domestic government or by using a foreign, accepted currency. An ongoing tax obligation, in concert with private confidence and acceptance of the currency, underpins the value of the currency. Because the government can issue its own currency at will, MMT maintains that the level of taxation relative to government spending (the government's deficit spending or budget surplus) is in reality a policy tool that regulates inflation and unemployment, and not a means of funding the government's activities by itself. The approach of MMT typically reverses theories of governmental austerity. The policy implications of the two are likewise typically opposed.

..MMT labels transactions between the government (public sector) and the non-government (private sector) as a "vertical transaction." The government sector includes the Treasury and Central Bank. The non-government sector includes domestic and foreign private individuals and firms (including the private banking system) and foreign buyers and sellers of the currency.

..MMT is based on an account of the "operational realities" of interactions.. A sovereign government typically has an operating account with the country's central bank. From this account, the government can spend and also receive taxes and other inflows. Each commercial bank also has an account with the central bank, by means of which it manages its reserves.. When a government spends money, its Treasury debits its operating account at its Central Bank and deposits this money into private bank accounts.. This money increases the total deposits in the commercial bank sector. Taxation works oppositely: Private bank accounts are debited; thus, deposits in the commercial banking sector fall.

..The Central Bank buys bonds by simply creating money – it is not financed in any way. ..It is a net injection of reserves into the banking system. If a central bank is to maintain a target interest rate, then it must buy and sell government bonds on the open market in order to maintain the correct amount of reserves in the system.

..MMT economists describe any transactions within the private sector as "horizontal" transactions, including the expansion of the broad money supply through the extension of credit by banks. ..According to MMT, bank credit should be regarded as a "leverage" of the monetary base and should not be regarded as increasing the net financial assets held by an economy: only the government or central bank is able to issue high-powered money with no corresponding liability. ..that bank money is generally accepted in settlement of debt and taxes because of state guarantees, ..

..Imports are an economic benefit to the importing nation because they provide the nation with real goods. Exports, on the other hand, are an economic cost to the exporting nation because it is losing real goods that it could have consumed. *Currency transferred to foreign ownership, ..represents a future claim over goods of that nation.*

..MMT says that "borrowing" is a misnomer when applied to a sovereign government's fiscal operations, because the government is merely accepting its own IOUs, and nobody can borrow back their own debt instruments. Sovereign government goes into debt by issuing its own liabilities that are financial wealth to the private sector. "Private debt is debt, but government debt is financial wealth to the private sector.

..Under MMT, QE – the purchasing of government debt by central banks – is simply an asset swap, exchanging interest-bearing dollars for non-interest-bearing dollars. The net result of this procedure is not to inject new investment into the real economy, but instead to drive up asset prices, shifting money from government bonds into other assets such as equities, which enhances economic inequality. The Bank of England's analysis of QE confirms that it has.. benefited the wealthiest.

Comments:

MMT tenet: state can issue new money to fund spending without first collecting taxes. Make sense, but importantly to spend the money effectively to stimulate the economy. Like Roosevelt's 'new deal', building facilities, bridges and roads, reviving the economy. Unlike 'banana' notes of the Japanese occupation army, leeching Singapore in 1943-45. ***MMT for governments to implement UBI that is guaranteed to boost the economy!***

UBI: Social Solidarity

Social solidarity Requires a Universal Basic Income
James Magnus-Johnston April29, 2020 (///steadystate.org/social-solidarity-)
"Going forward in these uncertain times, a universal basic income could be the best way to maintain social solidarity—whether referring to health, wellbeing, or public order. "Solidarity," writes Eric Klinenberg, "motivates us to promote public health, not just our own personal security. It keeps us from hoarding medicine" and prompts us "to knock on our older neighbor's door." It is a structure and a mindset that breaks down the barriers of inequality and improves trust, maintaining cohesion and stability of society."

"*A basic income is an expression of care and solidarity among members of society* across divides of age and opportunity... Economic stability is essential for strengthening social solidarity as the coronavirus continues to spread. The COVID-19 pandemic drives home the fact that, if everyone's basic needs are met, we can take care of ourselves (and shelter-in-place) with less fear and anxiety. A universal basic income could improve social and health outcomes, as well as avoid a protracted economic crisis for months and even years to come."

"The COVID-caused recession struck at a time when inequality had already reached historic levels. Social solidarity was precarious when the crisis began. Poverty levels in OECD countries were unnecessarily high, at an average of 11.7 percent of the population; 18 percent in the USA… Those who live at the margins worrying how to feed or shelter themselves suffer from poorer health; the understandable worrying exacerbates stress-induced illness and addictions. If everyone received a living wage, individuals would have easier access to medicine and clinics. A "side" benefit—hardly a minor one—would be a reduction in the spread of viruses conducive to pandemics."

"A basic income would help people replace a precarious and anxious work culture with life-affirming, creative, and healthier pursuits... A UBI incentivizes folks to replace tedious jobs with life-affirming, creative pursuits... With an increase in automation over the last 30 years, job productivity is no longer coupled with the production of income, which has been stagnant over roughly the same time period. A basic income would allow folks to devote energy to passions and priorities outside of these redundant and monotonous careers. They could dedicate themselves to family, artistic, or artisanal projects. They might even have more energy to volunteer for causes they care about…"

Comments:
Poverty levels are rather high in OECD countries at 11.7% and in the USA at 18%.
Automation in the last 30 years has increased productivity but not people's income.
Those who live at the margin worrying about food/shelter, suffer from poorer health.
A basic income would help people meet their basic needs with less fear and anxiety.
Magnus-Johnston rightly says 'social solidarity' requires a Universal Basic Income.

UBI: Increases Poverty !

***Commentary: Universal Basic Income May Sound Attractive But, If It Occurred,
Would Likelier Increase Poverty Than Reduce It***
by Robert Greenstein June 2019 (///cbpp.org/research/poverty-and-opportunity/)

" At first blush, universal basic income (UBI) seems a very attractive idea, especially to a progressive. The key issues related to UBI include what it would cost, how it would be paid for, and the risks it poses.

The Cost: There are over 300 million Americans today. Suppose UBI provided everyone with $10,000 a year. That would cost more than $3 trillion a year. This single figure equals more than three-fourths of the entire yearly federal budget. It's also equal to close to 100 percent of all tax revenue the federal government collects... Or, consider UBI that gives everyone $5,000 a year. That would provide income equal to about two-fifths of the poverty line for an individual (which is a projected $12,700 in 2016) and less than the poverty line for a family of four ($24,800).

Paying For It: That it would come mainly or entirely from new taxes isn't plausible. We'll already need substantial new revenues in the coming decades to help keep Social Security and Medicare solvent and avoid large benefit cuts in them. A UBI that's financed primarily by tax increases would require the American people to accept a level of taxation that vastly exceeds anything in U.S. history.

The Risk: They generally propose UBI as a replacement for the current "welfare state." If you take the dollars targeted on people in the bottom fifth or two-fifths of the population and convert them to universal payments to people all the way up the income scale, you're redistributing income upward. That would increase poverty and inequality rather than reduce them.

Universal vs. Means-Tested Programs: Recent decades have witnessed large expansions of SNAP, Medicaid, the EITC, and other programs. Conservatives generally have been more willing to accept expansions of means-tested programs than universal ones, largely due to the substantially lower costs they carry.

Conclusion: UBI has to be financed mainly by raising taxes layered on top of the large tax increases we'll already need to avert large benefit cuts in Social Security and Medicare and meet other needs. Were we starting from scratch — and were our political culture more like Western Europe's — UBI might be a real possibility. But that's not the world we live in."

Comments:
Giving every citizen $100 monthly, 2/3 of the population are happier (ask the Alaskans).
The cost of starting a UBI at 10% is only 0.3 Trillion, then step-up to 100% over 10 yrs,
Paying for it with a GSTax, taps automation's huge profit before losing it to billionaires.
The risk of increased poverty is a no-brainer as the welfare system needs not be touched.
Greenstein is right, "Were we starting from scratch – UBI might be a real possibility."

UBI: Pros & Cons

Universal Basic Income - Top 3 Pros and Cons
Author: ProCon.org Feb.25, 2021 (www.procon.org/headline/universal-basic-income-)

"A universal basic income (UBI) is an unconditional cash payment given at regular intervals by the government to all residents, regardless of their earnings or employment status.

Pro 1. Universal Basic Income (UBI) reduces poverty and income inequality, and improves physical and mental health...Participants in India's UBI trial (2013-2014) said that UBIs helped improve their health by enabling them to afford medicine, improve sanitation, gain access to clean water, eat more regularly, and reduce their anxiety levels.

Pro 2: UBI leads to positive job growth and lower school dropout rates...Since implementation of the Alaska Permanent Fund, the increased purchasing power of UBI recipients has resulted in 10,000 additional jobs for the state.

Pro 3: UBI guarantees income for non-working parents and caregivers, thus empowering important traditionally unpaid roles, especially for women... The Basic Income Grant Coalition trial UBI in Namibia (2007-2012) found that UBI "reduced the dependency of women on men for their survival" and reduced the pressure to engage in transactional sex.

Con 1: Universal Basic Income (UBI) takes money from the poor and gives it to everyone, increasing poverty and depriving the poor of much needed targeted support... It could effectively subsidize employers who pay low wages and – by creating a small cushion for workers on short-term and zero-hours contracts – help to normalise precarity."

Con 2: UBI is too expensive. A 2018 study found that a $1,000 a month stipend to every adult in the United States would cost about $3.81 trillion per year, or about 21% of the 2018 GDP, or about 78% of 2018 tax revenue...UBI at a level which can guarantee an acceptable standard of living is "impossibly expensive… Either the level of basic income is unacceptably low, or the cost of providing it is unacceptably high.

Con 3: UBI removes the incentive to work, adversely affecting the economy and leading to a labor and skills shortage...However "if we pay people, unconditionally, to do nothing… they will do nothing" and this leads to a less effective economy, says Charles Wyplosz PhD, Professor of International Economics at the Graduate Institute in Geneva (Switzerland)."

Comments:
Pro 1: Indian trial, recipients less anxiety, healthier, has clean water and eat regularly.
Pro 2. Alaskan trial, positive results, lower school dropout rates, creates 10,000 jobs.
Pro 3. Namibian trial empowers women in unpaid roles, reducing dependence on men.
Con 1. A false proposition, as it is quite heartless to suggest robbing welfare to pay UBI.
Con 2. A false perception, as automation has created billions to enrich the top 10%.
Con 3. A false preconception, as recipients on the contrary are encouraged, enterprising.
UBI trial-data supports the Pros-, contradicting misconceptions of the Cons-capitalist.

UBI: Who wins ?

Who Really Stands to Win from Universal Basic Income?
Nathan Heller. July 2, 2018 (///newyorker.com/magazine/)

"...Elizabethan Poor Law, divided indigent adults into three groups: those who could work, those who could not, and those—the "idle poor"—who seemed not to want to. *..The idle poor* were forced into labor or rounded up and *beaten for being bums.*

...The magistrates at Speenhamland devised a way of offering families measured help. Household incomes were topped up to cover the cost of living. ..As the Speenhamland system took hold and spread across England, it turned into a parable of caution. The population nearly doubled... David Ricardo complained that the Speenhamland model was a prosperity drain, inviting "imprudence, ...When the Speenhamland system ended in 1834, people were plunged into a labor machine in which they had no role or say. The commission... replaced it with Dickensian workhouses—a corrective, at the opposite extreme,...

...In 1969, Richard Nixon.. the Family Assistance Plan,..He sought to be the President to lift the lower classes. ..The plan died in the Senate, ...and the only thing to survive was,... Speenhamland-inspired fear of being seen to *indulge the idle poor*...A work requirement stuck around, first in the earned-income tax credit,..

...Recently, a resurrection has occurred. ..."Give People Money: How a Universal Basic Income Would End Poverty, Revolutionize Work, and Remake the World" by the economic journalist Annie Lowrey,.. Her conscientiously reported book assesses the widespread effects that money and a bit of hope could buy... supporters generally propose a figure somewhere around a thousand dollars a month: enough to live on ...but not nearly enough to live on well.

..In "Raising the Floor: How a Universal Basic Income Can Renew Our Economy and Rebuild the American Dream" (2016), the labor leader Andy Stern nominates U.B.I. as the right response to technological unemployment...

...Philippe Van Parijs and Yannick Vanderborght's recent "Basic Income: A Radical Proposal for a Free Society and a Sane Economy" ..not a perfect system, but better than anything else...Everybody gets a basic chance.

..Junkies, alcoholics, scam artists: Do we really want to hand these people monthly checks? In 2010, a team of researchers began giving two-hundred-dollar payments to addicts and criminals in Liberian slums. The researchers found that the money, far from being squandered on vice, went largely to subsistence and legitimate enterprise. Such results, echoed in other studies, suggest that some of the most beneficial applications of a U.B.I. may be in struggling economies abroad.

...Charles Murray,...His book "In Our Hands: A Plan to Replace the Welfare State" (2006) called for a U.B.I. of ten thousand dollars a year, plus catastrophic health insurance, to replace existing social programs, including Social Security.

...In "The War on Normal People: The Truth About America's Disappearing Jobs and Why Universal Basic Income Is Our Future", Andrew Yang.. recommends the model as a way to bypass kludgy governmental systems.

...Many of the super-rich are also super-pumped about universal basic income. Elon Musk has said it will be "necessary." Sir Richard Branson speaks of "the sense of self-esteem that universal basic income could provide to people."

...What's the appeal for the plutocracy? For one thing, the system offers a hard budget line: you set the income figure, press start, go home. No new programs, no new rules. It also alleviates moral debt: because there is a floor for everyone, the wealthy can feel less guilt as they gain more wealth... U.B.I. fits with a certain idea of meritocracy. If everybody gets a strong boost off the blocks, the winners of the economic race—the ultra-affluent—can believe that they got there by their industry or acumen.

...Chris Hughes, in "Fair Shot: Rethinking Inequality and How We Earn", seeks to shed the idea that special skills brought him success. .. "In a winner-take-all world, a small group of people get outsized returns as a result of early actions they take," he writes...Hughes searches for points of exception that explain why he, not someone else from another middle-middle-class family, ended up with *half a billion dollars*...Massive tech companies such as Facebook have been possible because of deregulation, financialization, tax cuts, and lowered tariffs rolled out, he thinks, at a cost to ordinary people since the nineteen-seventies...The solution, Hughes has decided, is a modest basic income: five hundred dollars a month for every adult in a household making less than about fifty thousand dollars. He sees it as a boost to the current system,.. the money can be found by closing tax exemptions for the ultra-wealthy —"people like me."

...Rutger Bregman championed universal basic income in his popular book "Utopia for Realists"...he touted it as a matter of both categorical principle and maximized good, and tried to make these virtues square.

Comments:

Elizabethan Poor Law identified the 'idle poor' as bums, rounded up and beaten.
The Speenhamland system offered families measured help and the population doubled.
Ricardo said Speenhamland a 'prosperity drain'; next came Dickensian workhouses.
Nixon 's plan to lift the lower classes failed, but fear of indulging the poor survives.
Lowrey explores the effects that money ($1000/mth generally) and hope could buy.
Andy Stern sees UBI as 'Raising the Floor' security in response to unemployment.
Van Parijs & Vanderborght say UBI is not perfect but 'Everybody gets a basic chance'.
Indeed given $200, recipients in Liberian slums spent on subsistence/legitimate pursuits.
Murray calls out to replace the Welfare State with UBI $10,000/yr cash 'In Our Hands'.
Yang says 'UBI is Our Future', the model way to handle America's disappearing jobs.
The super-rich are also super-pumped about UBI saying it's necessary, it's self-esteem.
Hughes in 'Fair Shot': money can be found closing tax exemptions for the ultra-wealthy.
Bregman championed UBI for maximizing good and touted it 'Utopia for Realists'.
A "winner-take-all" culture only creates a world of billionaires and homelessness today.
UBI is a win-win as it provides a level playing field for everyone, also it is a birthright.

UBI Hurt Poor People

A UNIVERSAL BASIC INCOME MIGHT HURT POOR PEOPLE MORE THAN HELP
Dwyer Gunn. Feb.15, 2019 (///psmag.com/economics/a-universal-basic-income-)

"In recent years, the concept of a universal basic income (UBI)—governments providing every single citizen with a cash transfer sufficient to ensure a minimum standard of living—has gained a diverse following. "One reason we think it may work is that technological improvements should generate an abundance of resources," wrote Y Combinator president Sam Altman in a blog post. "Although basic income seems fiscally challenging today, in a world where technology replaces existing jobs and basic income becomes necessary, technological improvements should generate an abundance of resources and the cost of living should fall dramatically."

In a new working paper, economists Hilary W. Hoynes and Jesse Rothstein, take a look at the costs, distributional effects, and possible labor-market effects of UBI programs in advanced economies with existing social safety nets. They find, in line with many of the most prominent criticisms of the UBI, that such programs, if they were truly universal, would indeed be very expensive and, in comparison to the existing social safety net, would *likely redirect spending to better-off families, potentially leaving low-income families worse off than they currently are.*

The researchers start by calculating the cost of a UBI in the United States. They estimate that providing a $12,000 payment—approximately equivalent to the poverty line for a single adult—to every U.S. adult over the age of 18 would cost about $3 trillion per year. This is, to put it simply, an enormous sum. "This is about 75 percent of current total federal expenditures, including all on- and off-budget items," the researchers conclude. "Thus, implementing this UBI without cuts to other programs would require nearly doubling federal tax revenue."

Hoynes and Rothstein note that even cutting all existing transfer programs—like food stamps, welfare, and the Earned Income Tax Credit—which account for half of federal expenditures, would make only a dent in the cost of a UBI."

Comments:
Altman is correct to say technological improvements create abundance of resources.
Things are made faster and cheaper, and the cost of living should fall dramatically.
However technology replaces existing jobs and basic income becomes necessary.
Hoynes & Rothstein say, paying all adults $1,000/mth would cost $3 trillion a year.
And cutting welfare to finance a UBI would make low-income families worse off.

Technical advancements are social properties, the enormous gains belong to everyone.
Apple Inc. charges 30% for transactions, then 25% ought be diverted to share in a UBI.
A 10% Goods Service Tax on transactions in Amazon.com and others, brings in billions.
These tech resources ought be collected before they slip into the pockets of billionaires.
Citizens inherit all the nation's resources in common, i.e. direct equal share with a UBI.
The rich on demise ought to share his/her fortune equally with heirs and fellow citizens.
Thomas Paine says UBI is not charity, so welfare should not be touched to finance it.
Therefore it is a Fallacy to say UBI will hurt poor people more than help.

UBI: Global

Why UBI should go global
By Guest Contributor. Sep 20, 2021 (///basicincome.org/news/)

New research from World Basic Income finds that more than half of the world's people live in countries where UBI could reach only $5 to $18 per person per month on average, as a result of global inequality and national income constraints. To support UBI activism in lower income countries and ensure that people everywhere can receive a sufficient UBI, the group proposes topping up this amount with a worldwide basic income of $30.

The briefing uses World Bank data to uncover how much money flows through each country every year, and how much of it could be taxed and redistributed as UBI. The analysis shows that UBI could reach a maximum of $12 per person per month in India, $3 in Afghanistan and just over $1 in Burundi, if governments tax and redistribute cash at the average rates for each continent. Even if these countries managed to spend as much as France (the highest-spending country) on cash benefits, UBI could reach only $36, $10 and $5 respectively.

Laura Bannister, World Basic Income's campaign director, explained, "Global inequality is deeply unjust and much more severe than many people think. Gross national income is just $811 per person per year in an average low income country, and in Burundi it is $270. Governments of these countries should still be pushed to implement UBI, but there just isn't enough money flowing through these economies to enable payments at the level people need and deserve." Frank Kamanga, Director of Universal Basic Income Malawi.. said, "I was motivated to join the universal basic income global movement because of the inequality that I observed in the world, especially between the Northern and Southern hemispheres. Currently with our resources it isn't possible to have a universal basic income in Malawi, but with support from development partners we could manage to have such a policy."

The briefing proposes a new mechanism for such support – a worldwide basic income of $30 per person per month, which would underpin national UBI efforts. It would be funded at the global level through taxes and charges on transnational corporations, and would be paid directly to every person worldwide that registered with the scheme. "An extra $30 a month for every adult and child would be hugely significant for at least half of the world's people," said Laura Bannister. "..Today's extreme inequality between North and South is the result of a shameful history that the UBI movement should be aiming to help redress. UBI has incredible potential to reduce inequality and it's time to apply that between countries as well as within them."

Frank Kamanga concluded, "Poverty by its nature is inhumane, it steals away dignity and it denies people opportunities. A radical approach to do away with poverty at the global scale is implementing universal basic income."

Comments:

The extreme inequality seen between North and South is the result of shameful history. The World UBI can help redress this with implementing a worldwide basic income. Global UBI, a great idea when half of the world's people can be helped with $30/month. Estimate cost: 3.5 billions x $30 x 12 month = $1,260 billions or $1.26 trillion per year. *It is 1.3% of the world's 194 economies in 2021, projected at US$93.86 trillion (IMF).*

World of Capitalism

Summary

Inequality
Wealth per Adult: world's mean value (79,952) is 10x the world's median value (7,522).
That is, more than 50% of the world population is living in poverty, in misery daily !

World Report: top richest 1% capture twice the growth as the bottom 50% combined !
This is unsustainable, ought be alleviated with a guaranteed monthly subsistence UBI.

Political Issue: UBI financing depends on government's will, capacity to extract taxes.
Many studies so far are all positive about UBI, and that it is not a disincentive to work.

Gini Index: an index of inequality is similarly high in both rich and poor nations.
Rich/poor nations alike, they all need a guaranteed UBI monthly to reduce inequality.

Fraud
Evergrande Crisis: dishonest, selfish 'entrepreneurs' scheming only for personal gains.
While hard-working employees suffer exploitation, living from paycheck to paycheck.

Lenovo.China: with transactions causing the loss of state-owned enterprises and assets.
The government needs to be more vigilant to stop theft by such 'pseudo-entrepreneurs'.

Nonprofits: frauds exposed in New York and elsewhere are just tips of icebergs.
We wonder that even half the aid allocated can reach the people originally intended !

Welfare
Lacking: worldwide, > 4 billion people worldwide are left out of social protection.
It is said the systems to deliver social protection are complicated, require lots of effort !

Stigmatized: recipients are shamed as less hardworking and unworthy by the privileged.
They waste large amounts of time and effort on endless documents/surveillance needs.

Diversions: of TANF money to programs like overnight camps/pro-marriage advert.
Poor families get no cash support as intended from these primary cash assistance.

Common Prosperity: is missing with 600 million people still living on 1,000 yuan/mth.
China's wealth gap widens with the richest 1% holding 30.6% of the country's wealth.

Monetary

Democracy: with presidential elections fund rocketed to 1.3b, vested interests corrupt.
Government is ineffective, polarized left and right; socioeconomic inequality deepens.

GDP: doesn't account for externalities like pollution, unpaid work (est. 15-70 % GDP).
GDP not indicative of socioeconomic welfare like income inequality, health, education.

Automation: will cause a wave of joblessness, mass immiseration and social breakdown.
Solution, a UBI to distribute the dividends of the robots' efforts equally to all citizens.

AI: can help business efficiency, to generate huge amounts of wealth to support a UBI.
AI is social property and the enormous gains ought to be fairly shared by all citizens.

Billionares: are created by techno advances that generate huge profits for companies.
Discoveries, technology advances are also social properties that belong to all people.

Corporate Taxes: structure unfairly short-changed the majority of common employees.
It is fair that all employees enjoy Employee Stock Compensation with top management.

Inheritance Tax: repeal, the estate's business as usual; how to boost GDP, create jobs.
But taxing 50% of estate, distributed in a UBI is certain to stimulate the home economy.

MMT: make sense for a sovereign state to issue new money to fund its own spending.
If the money is to be spent on stimulating the economy like Roosevelt's 'new deal'.

UBI

Social Solidarity: requires a Universal Basic Income, Magnus-Johnston rightly says.
Those who live at the margin worrying about food/shelter, suffer from poorer health.

Increase Poverty: no risk as the welfare system needs not be touched by starting a UBI.
Taps automation profit with a GSTax, pays $100/mth, everyone happy as the Alaskans.

Pros & Cons: trials show recipients less stressed, healthier, empowered, enterprising.
Contradict misconceptions of recipients' laziness, has billionaires but no funds for UBI.

Who wins ? The super-rich are super-pumped about UBI, it's necessary, it's self-esteem.
A "winner-take-all" culture only creates a world of billionaires and homelessness today.

Hurt Poor People: this is a fallacy if welfare is not touched to finance a UBI.
Techno innovation has created an abundance of resources and wealth to pay for a UBI.

Global: worldwide basic income of $30/month will help half the world's people.
This will redress the extreme inequality seen in the South, the result of shameful history.

World of capitalism
Conclusions:

The world of Capitalism is literally a world of Inequality, Fraud, Corruption, Bullying.
Half the world's people have 7,522 usd wealth, only 10% of the average (79,952 usd).
The top richest 1% captures 2x the growth of the bottom 50% combined.
And the Gini index of inequality is similarly high in both rich and poor countries.
It is not an economic but a political issue that no Government has implemented a UBI.
Inequality is the problem of the World of Capitalism; UBI is Equality, the solution.

Evergrande Crisis in China exposed selfish entrepreneurs scheming for personal gains.
Lenovo top executives unashamedly voted billions of company's profit for themselves.
And nonprofits that run shelters in New York City were found so rife with self-dealings.
Frauds caught are just the tip of the icebergs, 90% are submerged out of sight.

Welfare lacking worldwide with more than 4 billion people left out of social protection.
Recipients are stigmatized and traumatized on endless surveillance and documentation.
Diversion of cash support to capitalist schemes of overnight camps/pro-marriage ads.
China with common prosperity still missing, has 600m people earning 1,000 yuan/mth,
Welfare is lacking or capitalized; Common Prosperity is missing in Capitalism.

Vested interests corrupt the Democracy process when election funds needed billions.
GDP doesn't account for pollution /unpaid work /income inequality /health/education.
Automation will cause a wave of joblessness, mass immiseration and social breakdown.
But A.I. can help better efficiency, generate huge amounts of wealth to support UBI.
Billionaires are people who stole the billions that technology creates for all employees.
Corporate Taxes are unfair, only top executives enjoy Employee Stock Compensation !
Inheritance Tax repealed, estate's business as usual to boost GDP /create jobs, a myth !
MMT: it makes sense for a sovereign state to issue new money to fund its own UBI.
Corruption: seems order of the day in Capitalism; A.I. and MMT: possible to fund UBI.

Magnus-Johnston rightly says Social Solidarity requires a Universal Basic Income.
No risk of Increased Poverty; the welfare system should not be touched for starting UBI.
Pros & Cons: trials show recipients less stressed, healthier, empowered, entrepreneurial.
Who wins? The super-rich are super-pumped about UBI, it's necessary, it's self-esteem.
Hurt Poor People ? A fallacy as existing welfare must not be touched to finance a UBI.
Global basic income of $30/month can help half the world's people; then why not ?
Bullying be replaced with a modest Global UBI of $30, benefitting the North and South.

A strong willing government can protect the honest majority with a UBI for all citizens.
By recovering the A.I. billions for a UBI for everyone, to close the rich/poor gap.
To put UBI cash into the hands of people, and let them do the rest to help themselves.
A new Capitalist indicator of social wellbeing, UBI index (% of median income paid).

UBI studies

All Lives Matter: Mandai wildlife crossing bridge

88   UBI Studies, worldwide (29 articles)

Brazil. Quatinga Velho

Quatinga Velho (wikipedia.org Sep. 2021. UBI around the world)
The project started in 2008, organized by the non-profit organization ReCivitas.
It provided R30 monthly (4.4% of minimum salary, 2013), just sufficient to help people satisfy the most basic material needs. Even with such a small amount of money, when people's most basic needs are met, the positive impacts are huge. Children especially enjoy the benefits and the results indicate that the BI contributed to sustainable development in Quatinga Velho. In informal interviews, coordinators noticed increased self-esteem and social interaction, reduction of social insecurity, and rising hope for the future, especially for the children. And importantly, they observed no increased use of alcohol or illicit drugs.

Brazil: Basic Income in Quatinga Velho celebrates 3-years of operation
By Karl Widerquist, June 2012 (///basicincome.org/news/)
For 3 years now, Recivitas has run a privately funded basic income for a small impoverished rural community. The project pays 30 Brazilian Reals (~US$15) per month to people of Quatinga Velho, São Paulo, Brazil. This amount of money sounds very small, but has a huge impact in rural Brazil. Coordinators have verified gains in nutrition, clothing, health of children, improved living conditions, even new housing. People have more self-esteem and high hopes, especially for their children's future. Coordinators noted no increase in alcohol consumption, or illicit drugs.

The project leaders are already convinced of the benefits of a local basic income (BI). As long as governments are not ready to do BI on a national scale with tax funding, Recivitas intends to continue with this project to show the way on a small scale with private funding.

Google gives $2.5 Million to a Direct Cash Transfer Charity
Karl Widerquist, July 2013 (///basicincome.org/news/)
"Business Press has been praising GiveDirectly, a direct cash transfer charity. .. Google Giving has donated two and a half million dollars to this charity. They cite the efficiency of it. ..ReCivitas has even less administrative costs than those faced by GiveDirecly. ... Also cash aid creates market demand for food and other needs that could be met by entrepreneurs. Some recipients will use the money to start small businesses or pay school fees. … This could beat back the weird perception that a Basic Income Grant (BIG) is 'impossible'."
Comments:
The Quatinga Velho community has shown us the resilience of the human spirit.
Only R30 (4.4% of min.salary) cash in aid, can improve life, raise hope for the future.
Cash aid creates demand for food /basic needs; some recipients start small businesses.
Importantly they observed no increased use of alcohol or illicit drugs.
This is empirical evidence that UBI works !

Brazil. Marica

More than 50,000 people are set to get a basic income in a Brazilian city
By Dylan Matthews Oct, 2019 (dylan@vox.com)
About 52,000 people of Marica (small city of 157,000) in the suburbs of Rio de Janeiro are to receive a basic income set at roughly three-quarters of the national poverty line (set at 178 reais a month). Called Citizens' Basic Income, it is worth 130 reais per person per month (around US$64). For context, a family of 4, each getting 130 reais per month, will be getting over half a minimum salary (minimum salary for a full-time job is 998 reais. Many families living just below the poverty line will be lifted above it.
It is not a pilot program. It is a policy being adopted across the municipality. Everyone who has lived in Marica for at least 3 years and with low-enough income to qualify (well below Brazil's minimum wage) will get the benefit.
The Marica program is indefinite as it will be funded with Marica's share of Brazil's oil royalties. It represents the beginning of the realization of a law passed in 2004 under left-wing president Lula da Silva, that established a basic cash transfer as *a right of all Brazilians.*

An important aspect of the Marica Basic Income is that it distributes *mumbuca*, a local currency issued by the Banco Mumbuca in Marica. You can spend your mumbuca with a card, or use your cell phone to receive and spend them. The city had offered an extremely small basic payment, about 10 mumbucas or 10 reais per month per person, to its poorest residents for a few years now. The new program is a dramatic expansion of that initiative. Mumbucas can only be used in Marica and Banco Mumbuca will have all the data for tracking its usage. The idea is that 'the money' remains there and forms what the broader left movement calls a 'solidarity economy'. The use of mumbucas also allows researchers to easily pinpoint effects on inflation, a constant worry with large-scale cash programs. The Marica program is a much larger cash transfer than the Bolsa Familia program, a wildly successful and incredibly popular conditional cash program in Brazil that pays checks to families that meet certain criteria, like vaccinating kids and putting them in school. As of three years ago the average Bolsa Familia recipient households were getting 160 reais, that's about four people, or 40 reais each. That is, the Marica program is paying 3 times as much.
Comments:
Called Citizens' Basic Income, funded with oil royalities, to pay 130 reais/person/mth.
About 52,000 of 157,000 residents qualified to receive over half the minimum salary.
It is Basic Income (BI) that relieves poverty, paying everyone in low-income families.
It pays with 'Mumbucas' card, a local currency to be used locally, and is tractable.
The data will be good for studying inflation when a large amount of cash is injected.
Marica's BI guarantee has proven its worth in Brazil's corona crisis (Jens Glüsing, 2021).

Canadian. Mincome
The "Manitoba Basic Annual Income Experiment", a $17-million Guaranteed Annual Income (GAI) social experiment in Manitoba, started 1974. The main purpose was to assess if GAI is a disincentive for work by its recipients. It was aborted 1979 and no final Mincome report was issued. In 1984, the Institute for Social and Economic Research at The University of Manitoba completed a machine-readable database of the experiment, for analysis by individual academics (Wikipedia, 2021). Several studies emerged between 1984 and 1991. Importantly Derek Hum and Wayne Simpson found little impact on the work behavior of recipients (Mason, 2017).

Forget (2011, Canadian Public Policy):
This research did not use the Mincome data directly, but revisited the outcome of the study with analysis of the health administration data routinely collected in the province of Manitoba between 1974 and 1979. They found significant reduction in hospitalization, especially admissions for mental health, accidents and injuries, and a greater proportion of students finishing high school. They concluded that a modest Guaranteed Annual Income can improve population health and education. The possibility of savings in the health system was suggested.

Cox, D. (2020). *Canada Forgotten Universal Basic Income Experiment. (///www.bbc.com/worklife/article/20200624-) reported*:
Once it was implemented in the area, it had real results. An average family in Dauphin was guaranteed an annual income of 16,000 Canadian dollars.
"It wasn't a case of getting money to live and do nothing," says Sharon Wallace-Storm, who grew up in Dauphin and was 15 when the experiment began. "They set a level for how much a family of three or four needed to get by. You applied showing how much you were making, and if you didn't meet that threshold they would give you a top up."
"Joy Taylor, who was 18 and newly married when the scheme began, remembers that people had much less to worry about financially during the course of the experiment, which improved their wellbeing. Her husband was suddenly able to get a loan to open a local record store, with banks being more willing to lend money to small businesses because of the guaranteed payments."
But when the experiment ended in 1979, the improvements which had been seen in health and education soon returned to how things had been in 1974. Taylor remembers how many of the small businesses that had sprung up over the preceding four years began to vanish. Her husband was forced to close their shop, and the couple soon left Dauphin for good. "After the programme ended, we moved to Ontario in 1980 because there was nothing to stay for anymore," she says. "It just wasn't doing very well."

Summary:

Derek Hum and Wayne Simpson analysis of the Mincome data answered the main question asked of the experiment. GAI is not a disincentive to work for the recipients.

Forget analysis of the health administration data routinely collected is informative. Improvement of the population's health and education were found, suggesting possible future long-term savings from the health system.

David Cox reporting was more illuminating of real life on the ground with a Guaranteed Annual Income. The reception was all round positive. With a guaranteed basic income, banks were willing to lend and small businesses sprung up all over the place. When the program ended, the prosperity ended !

Comments:

Basic income for a family of 4 was set at 16k C$ annually.
Mincome had not provided the entire Basic income, merely top-up those lacking.
This guarantee top-up produced stability and security for business loans from banks.
Small businesses sprang up producing prosperity for the 4 years while GAI lasted.
So the recipients had not been lazy because of the help but rather more enterprising.
GAI, with a modest 16k C$ guarantee provides security for loans resulting in prosperity.
This Mincome GAI highlights the importance of the guarantee aspect of a UBI.

Notes

-Cox, David. 2020. Canada's forgotten universal basic income experiment. BBC worklife.
-Forget, EL. (2011). The Town with No Poverty: The Health Effects of a Canadian Guaranteed Annual Income Field Experiment. Canadian Public Policy vol. 37, pp.283-305. University of Toronto.
-Mason, G. 2017. Revisiting Manitoba's basic-income experiment. Winnipeg FreePress.

Canada. Ontario

Canada's cancelled basic income trial produces positive results
Rich Haridy March 12, 2020 (///newatlas.com/good-thinking/canada-basic-income-)

"A new report, from researchers at McMaster University and Ryerson University, has surveyed over 200 participants from a prematurely cancelled basic income experiment that took place in Southern Ontario between 2017 and 2019."

"The Ontario Basic Income Experiment: presented a model where participants were guaranteed either 16,989 CAD (US$12,180) per year if they were single, or 24,027 CAD (US$17,230) per year for a couple. For every dollar a participant earns through employment they lose 50 cents from their basic income payment. This means the basic income proposal would only apply to individuals earning less than 34,000 CAD (US$24,380) a year, or couples earning less than 48,000 CAD (US$34,420).
The experiment enrolled 4,000 subjects and was planned to run for three years. Within months of the project commencing a new government was elected in Ontario and the experiment was swiftly cancelled... By the time the project was completely cut off most participants had been receiving the basic income payments for around 17 months... The data gathered survey responses from 217 subjects and conducted in-depth interviews with 40 individuals."

"In terms of physical and mental health the vast majority of the survey subjects reported notable improvements following the roll out of the basic income project. Around half of the subjects reported decreased use of alcohol and tobacco, while 79 percent reported better physical well-being and 83 percent reported better mental well-being... Around a third of all subjects reported reductions in visits to doctors and hospital emergency rooms. This suggests basic income may be a useful general public health strategy resulting in a reduced load on public health services."

"Only 17 percent of those in the pilot leave employment and most significantly, nearly half of those subjects returned to school or university to up-skill for future employment. A 35-year-old man describes how the basic income allowed him to complete a training course which resulted in him getting a security guard license. Many noted improvements in working conditions and job security, often through a sense of being empowered to find better jobs."
"Source: Southern Ontario's Basic Income Experience report."
Comments:
The Ontario trial guaranteed US$12,180 yearly, enrolled 4,000 subjects for 3 years.
When a new government was voted in (2018), it was *cancelled* after 17 months.
Nevertheless, a survey of 217 subjects among the 4,000 enrolled shows *positive* results.
Participants reported better mental wellbeing, reduced use of public health services.
Economic security empowered many to return to school, or up-skill to find better jobs.
Basic Income for better education /health, with savings in public health services.

China. Macau

Wealth Partaking Scheme (Wikipedia, the free encyclopedia. Sep. 2021)
Macau has been distributing cash to its residents, permanent and non-permanent since 2008. The noble aim is to share the gains of the autonomous region with all its citizens. The first distribution was 5,000 and 3,000 patacas respectively. In 2020, the payout is 10,000 and 6,000.

Macau's small UBI (Furui Cheng. July 2017. blog.news.basicincome.org)
The Wealth Partaking Scheme (WPS) 2017 was announced by the government of the Macau Special Administrative Region (SAR) in China. Permanent residents were to receive a small annual unconditional basic income of 9,000 patacas (usd 1,128) and non-permanent residents 5,400 patacas (usd 672). The budget for the WPS 2017 is 6,080 million patacas (usd 757 million) for the 638,600 permanent and 62,000 non-permanent residents. Since 2008, the government of Macau SAR has given an annual state bonus to all its citizens. Payments may be by direct bank transfers or crossed checks to be deposited into the payee's account. For minors below the age of 18, checks are made payable to themselves or their parents.

Quote: "In addition to the WPS state bonus, the Macao SAR government has injected an annual capital into all qualified Provident Fund Individual Accounts since 2010. Provident fund individual accounts are provided to Macao SAR residents of the age of 22, and they are used to receive the "incentive basic fund" and "special allocation from budget surplus". No formalities are required for the individual accounts of those who are already on the list of special allocation from budget surplus, which is 7,000 patacas [US $872] for 2017. Individuals who are entitled to the allocation of funds for the first time will also be allocated the incentive basic fund of 10,000 patacas [US $1,245]."

Newsdesk, April 2021. IAG (inside asian gaming)
The Macau SAR Government has brought forward its Wealth Partaking Scheme in 2021 due the impact of COVID-19 on the people's livelihoods. Permanent residents are entitled to 10,000 paracas (usd 1,250) and non-permanent residents 6,000 paracas (usd 750). The Macau government reported a tax revenues for the gaming industry of 29.81 billion (usd 3.72 billion) in 2020, down from 112.71 billion paracas (usd 14.08 billion) in 2019

Comments:
The Wealth Partaking Scheme (WPS) is a universal bonus as it pays to all its residents.
It is not guaranteed, but the government does pledge to make it an annual affair.
It is not enough as a basic income at about 10% of a cleaner-worker's annual earnings.
This Macau's small UBI is popular, hopefully the beginning of better things to come.

Finland. Experimental UBI

Results of Finland's basic income experiment: small employment effects, better perceived economic security and mental well-being
6 May 2020. (//kela.fi/web/news.archive/)
The Finnish basic income (BI) was the world's first legislated, nationwide, randomized field experiment. The aim was to study how it would be possible to reshape the Finnish social security system. Among those receiving an unemployment benefit from Kela (the Social Insurance Institution of Finland) in November 2016, mandatorily and unconditionally 2,000 were selected and were paid a monthly tax-exempt basic income of 560 euros, starting from January 2017 to December 2018.

In this period, basic income recipients increased employment by 6 days, being employed for 78 days on average. Survey on phone before experiment ended, respondents described their wellbeing more positively than respondents in the control group. They felt more protected financially, more satisfied with their lives with less mental strain, less depression and better ability to concentrate.

Universal basic income seems to improve employment and well-being
by Donna Lu May 2020 (//newscientist.com/article/2242837-)
Finland ran a 2-year UBI study in 2017 and 2018. Government gave 2000 unemployed people aged 25-58 monthly payments of 560 euros with no strings attached. The study was nationwide and selected recipients cannot opt out as the test was written into legislation. The employment and well-being of this recipient group were compared against a control group of 173,000 people who were on unemployment benefits.

During the 2-year period, recipients worked on average 78 days, 6 days more than the control group. This suggests that basic income is not a disincentive for work. When surveyed, recipients reported better financial well-being, better mental health, better cognitive function, and also more confidence for the future than the control group.

Basic income: Finland's final verdict
By Philippe van Parijs May 2020 (//socialeurope.eu/basic-income-positive-)
Nationwide, Finland's means-tested long-term unemployed are recipients of minimum-income benefits of 560 euros a month. In Jan 2017 among them, 2000 were randomly selected and given the same amount unconditionally for 2 years for a comparative study with the unselected as control. Despite the 'activation model' government introduced in 2018, the basic-income recipients worked significantly more. Their subjective perceptions of health and stress and their trust in people, are also better.

Comments:
Finland legislated BI experiment, subsistence UBI at 560 euros/month for 2 year.
On the same amount, unconditional-recipients fare better than the benefits-recipients.
We can safely predict more positive results if the trial can be extended to a longer term.
The liberating effect of unconditional UBI, better health, trust in people, work more.

India. Cash transfers project

Universal basic income around the world. (https://en.wikipedia.org. Aug 2021)
Since January 2011, two basic income pilot projects have been initiated in India. First communication reports positive results. Villages spent more on food and healthcare, children performed better in school, personal savings tripled, new businesses doubled.

Universal basic income in India (From Wikipedia, the free encyclopedia Aug.2021)
The Madhya Pradesh Unconditional Cash Transfers Project (MPUCTP): to address the vulnerabilities of low income Indians. The first pilot lasted 18 months, involving 20 similar villages. Everyone in 8 villages received grants, none in the other 12 villages. The second pilot lasted 12 months, 2 similar tribal villages chosen, one granted and one not granted. In both pilots, the cash is 200 Rupees (about US$3) per adult per month and 100 per child per month for 12 months. Their grants were raised to 300 and 150 respectively for the next 6 months. These amounts accounted for 20 to 30% of the monthly income of these families. In 2013, preliminary findings show recipient villages showing numerous improvements in health, productivity and financial stability. There were improved children's nutrition, lower rates of illness, more school attendance. Labor productivity increased with agricultural investment, having more life-stocks and even opening new businesses. Financial stability was evident with recipient families decreasing their indebtedness and increasing their savings. There was no evidence of higher alcohol consumption.
Yannick Vanderborght, Sep.2013 posted in BIEN News (basicincome.org/news)
"The Self-Employed Women's Association (SEWA) recently completed a large pilot project on Basic Income in India. The association's June Newsletter reports on the methodology and findings of the study. …. Researchers found no increase in alcohol consumption in the treatment villages. Importantly, the study also found that grant recipients worked more than people in the control villages and that they were three times more likely to start a new business."
MPUCTP: Executive Summary.pdf July 2015 (sewabharat.org)
This 20 pages summary combined quantitative study with qualitative case studies show:
"Unconditional cash transfers are beneficial and the benefits build on one another. … Households use cash transfers wisely and do not dissipate it in wasteful ways like spending it on alcohol."
Comments:
Everyone in 8 villages received grant for 18 months and none in the other 12 villages,
The grants amount accounted for 20-39% of the monthly income of these families.
Recipient villages showed better children nutrition /school attendance /less illnesses.
No more use of alcohol but more savings, more life-stocks, even started new businesses.
Here in India the evidence is compelling that UBI works, even in tribal communities.

Iran. Subsidy with cash

Wikipedia, Aug 2021. (https://en.wikipedia.org/wiki/Subsidies_in_Iran#cite_note-40)
For years Iran had been subsidizing its citizens for petrol, fuel and other supplies that benefit the rich more. In 2010 such subsidies were replaced with a cash payment equivalent to 40 USD per person monthly. Thus Iran is among the first countries to introduce a national basic income. Local press responded negatively, saying people will work less with the extra money.

Jeff Ihaza, May 2017 (the online.com/post/1613/Iran-introduces-basic-income)
In 2010, Iran cut oil and bread subsidies and replaced them with a guaranteed citizens cash payment equivalent to 29% of the nation's median income. Now 6 years on, economists found no evidence that people work less with a universal basic income. Instead people in the service industry work more expanding their small businesses, or finding better employment. And young people in their twenties only worked a little less because they were enrolled for higher education.

Casey Geier, Nov. 2018. Blog (The Borgen Project, a NGO for ending world poverty)
In the prior 40 years, the Iran government had been subsidizing the people for bread, water, electricity and fuel. Energy subsidies always benefit the wealthy more than the poor, and also encourage more consumption to the detriment of the environment.
The government changed to the cash transfer program in 2011. Employees remained attached to their jobs in spite of receiving more cash assistance. The impact was positive on the service sector like housekeepers, teachers and deliverymen, small firms who are credit-constrained. Reviewing papers published by Iranian economists, Geier concluded that the Universal Basic Income in Iran is a proven program of the benefits of UBI, and other countries can use it for guidance.

Comments:
In 2010, the Iran government replaced subsidies for bread /water and fuel, with cash transfers that amount to 29% of the nation's median income. Six years on, Iranian economists found that employees remained attached to their jobs, and small businesses like housekeepers, teachers and deliverymen flourished. *Generally people do not work less* and Geier (2018) concluded that the UBI program in Iran is a proven success that other countries can emulate.
Fuel subsidies benefit the rich more; cash is fairer with a positive impact on everyone.

Kenya. Give Directly

Money for nothing: the truth about universal basic income
Carrie Arnold. 30 May 2018 (///nature.com/articles/d41586-018-05259-x)

"Along the shores of Lake Victoria in western Kenya, mobile phones in several hundred villages ding in unison on the first of every month. For more than 21,000 adults, the sound means one thing: 2,250 Kenyan shillings appearing in their bank accounts. The cash equals one-quarter to half of the average income for a two-adult household in Bomet County, one of the poorest in Kenya.

The money (roughly US$22.50) arrives courtesy of the US-based charity GiveDirectly, which is studying the effects of handing people lumps of cash with no strings attached — an idea known as a universal basic income (UBI). The mobile phones in these villages will ding every month for the next 12 years, making this UBI trial the longest and largest ever conducted. It's a poverty-alleviation tool. Participants can invest in riskier things because they have their basic needs taken care of," says Tavneet Suri."

"Proponents of guaranteed income schemes argue that poor people will benefit more from unrestricted funds than from current welfare systems, which tend to have stringent requirements that often leave recipients trapped in poverty."

"Welfare critics have long argued that the administrative costs are huge and provide limited positive results; in some cases, they discourage people from finding jobs."

"Progressive politicians and thinkers have seen the idea as a way to end poverty; conservatives have viewed it as a streamlined welfare system that is easier and cheaper to run."

"The announcement in April that the Finnish UBI trial wouldn't be funded beyond this year provided a sobering reminder that politics — more than data — will determine the fate of such programmes."

"For the participants of the Kenya trial, that minor miracle has already arrived. The knowledge that GiveDirectly will deposit funds into their accounts every month for more than a decade has already begun to shift how some of them think about money. Each text alert means a chance to invest in their own lives or their businesses with the security that they can still put food on the table. And that, they say, is priceless."

Comments:
It is unfortunate that the author has capped the title with a 'Money for nothing'!
Such negative labels can only produce resistance to the advancement of UBI ideas.
UBI is money for alleviating poverty directly, to streamline the welfare systems.
First day of every mobile phone of 21,000 adults in hundreds of villages ding in unison.
Cash (US$22) equal to half the income for a 2-adult household, appears in their account.
Even in poor Kenya villages, cash transfer to recipients is instantaneous, at little cost!

Kenya. Trials

Examining Universal Basic Income in Kenya
Andrew Eckas, March 2021 (///borgenproject.org/UBI-in-kenya/)
Since 2016, non-profit GiveDirectly has been sending direct cash payments to more than 14,000 households in the Siaya and Bomet Counties of Kenya. For long-term recipients, every adult is to receive $0.75 per day for 12-year. This amount is sufficient to cover food, health and schooling basic needs. The short-term recipients are to receive $0.75 per day, but for 2 years.the third group received a lump sum, a lump sum payment of $500. The control group received no payment at all.

Kenyans receiving the UBI experienced less hunger, with best results from the long-term group. General health including mental health improved with reduced hospital utilization thus helping to preserve hospital capacity. Peace of mind that at least one stream of income would remain steady certainly is a factor for the well-being of people facing economic uncertainty, and also during the COVID-19 pandemic.

How a basic income experiment helped these Kenyans weather the Covid-19 crisis
By Kelsey Piper Sep. 2020 (vox.com/future-perfect/)
In 2017, some 6,000 recipients in a 12-year trial received 75 cents a day, not much but enough for people to be less food-insecure and more likely to start a business. Others received payments for just 2 years (ended Dec. 2019), and still others received a lump sum payment. In early 2020, the coronavirus hit and the government of Kenya imposed a harsh lockdown to prevent spread of the virus, though as yet nobody here is positive for the virus. Food insecurity was widespread. The control group reported 68% of households experiencing hunger in the last 30 days, compared to 5-11% of recipient households. UBI measurably improved things even with the group with the last payments in Dec. 2019. Recipients are less likely to be depressed. People getting a UBI were less likely to go hungry as Kenya shut down.

UBI recipients can afford to eat better, rest when they need it and are less likely to get sick. UBI encourages people to get an education, invest in their future. UBI lets people start businesses in a good time. UBI makes people more resilient when business is bad like in a lockdown, they can still eat. UBI doesn't fix everything, it just makes things a little easier.

Comments:
Six thousand recipients 75 cents/day in a 12-year trial, and others for just 2 years.
Not much but the amount is sufficient to cover food, health and schooling basic needs.
Recipients eat better, less likely to get sick, and even start a business in good time.
When business is bad, they are more resilient during covid pandemic lockdown.
UBI improved things even with the 2-year group compared to non-recipients.
UBI encourages people to get an education, invest in their future.
Even a small Basic Income supplement for 2 years measurably improved things.

Mongolia. Resource cash dividend (2010 -)

Mongolia's resource-to-cash transfers
by Meric Yorgun. Sep 15, 2020 (///basicincome.org/news/)

..As a classic example of a mineral-rich developing country, Mongolia has an export-driven economy in which 90% of the exports come from its minerals.

..In 2004, the government started to experiment with universal resource-financed payments for children. In 2010, the child-oriented payments were replaced with the new Human Development Fund (HDF) that was financed from mining dividends to provide a universal basic income that was paid monthly to every citizen. Mongolians monthly received MNT 21 thousand between 2010 and 2012 through the HDF. This experience provided a unique perspective on public ownership and revenue sharing in the mineral sector as citizens got a direct and equal share of their country's wealth as co-owners of their country.

..However, these payments were based on election promises and resulted in a vast deficit in the HDF as the expenditures were exceeding the actual mineral revenues. In 2012, HDF was stopped and child-oriented payments were brought back...In this regard, in 2019 the country passed an Election Law that prohibited the political parties from using the promise of cash transfers for elections.

.. in 2011, through a new scheme, every citizen received 1,072 shares in the ETT. Mongolians could use these shares for different purposes including tuition fees for students, health insurance coverage, or cash through a stock repurchase program by the government. Around 1.08 million Mongolians have kept all their shares and are entitled to a full dividend payout of MNT 96,480 (USD 34).

..With the outbreak of COVID-19 during the winter of 2019-2020, Mongolian citizens were promised a cheque of up to 96,480 tugrugs (USD 34), ..Mongolians who were born before April 11th 2014 are shareholders of a company called Erdenes Tavan Tolgoi (ETT).. these cash payments are dividends distributed by the company to its shareholders. In 2019, the company made USD 1 billion and 30 million from its sales.

..As we can see, the Mongolia experiment contains very important lessons in regard to the resource-to-cash payments. This experience underlines the importance of independent institutions from governments being tasked with the distribution of basic income type payments.

Comments:
Mongolians as co-owners of the country share in its mineral wealth directly and equally. The Human Development Fund paid monthly to every citizen MNT 21,000 bwt 2010-2. However not all citizens keep all their shares, hence individuals' dividends vary greatly. Also dividends vary from year to year, with commodity prices and market competition. Lessons: citizens be given dividends not shares, political parties cannot over-promised.
Government's spirit of sharing the country's wealth with citizems is commendable.

Namibia. Basic Income Grant (2008 -2009)

Universal basic income around the world. (https://en.wikipedia.org. Aug 2021)
The Basic Income Grant (BIG) pilot project was run in the Namibian settlement of
about 1,000 people in the Otjievero-Omitara area over 2 years, from Jan. 2008 to
Dec.2009. The grant was N$100 per person per month (8% of the average income,
around US$12), cash paid unconditionally to all residents below the age of 60 and
registered living there in July 2007, regardless of social or economic status. Besides
improving child nutrition and school attendance, the project produced many economic
activities in the community and also attracted migration into the area. The project
concluded that the BIG was a success, that it should be a universal *national* grant in
order to avoid migration to particular regions, towns or households.

Namibia - UBI success and institutional failure -
by Gery Petrova (BIEN website. basicincome.org/news/2020/07)
"In conclusion, the pilot project had a dramatic overall positive effect on the selected
community. The Basic Income Grant Coalition calculated that the cost for nationwide
implementation of unconditional universal basic income for all would be N$ 1.2 – 1.6
billion (USD 71 – 95 million) per year, equivalent to 2.2 – 3% of Namibia's GDP (2019
– 12.37 USD Billion). In short, UBI in Namibia was and is feasible. The missing
component then and now remains the lack of political will to apply the project on a
national level."

The Pilot Project - an executive summary
Claudia & Haarmann - BIG Coalition, 2020 (http://www.bignam.org/BIG_pilot.html)
Initially, Otjievero-Omitara was a hopeless area of unemployment, hunger and poverty.
Findings 12 months after implementation of Basic Income Grant (BIG) project were:
a. BIG empowered formation of a local committee to advise residents on use of grants.
b. Start of small businesses such as dress-making, bakery and brick-making.
c. Contributed to creation of a local market by increasing household buying power.
d. Resulted in a huge reduction of child malnutrition.
e. Schooling-going children double with parents willing to pay fees (90%) and uniforms.
f. Residents could afford the settlement's clinic that charged N$4 per visit.
g. Reduced household debt and increased savings, reflected in having more lifestocks.
h. Reduced crime significantly as reports to the local police station down by 42%.
i. Reduced dependency of women on men, reflected in less transactional sex activity.
j. The criticism that BIG leads to alcoholism is not supported by the empirical evidence.
It is the sincere hope of the Coalition that this project will encourage others to demand
what is rightfully theirs, namely "A BIG for all"!
Comments:
BIG is N$100-/pax/mth (~8% av. income) to all residents of the settlement <60 of age.
Residents empowered to form committee, started small businesses, dress-making/brick..
Improved child nutrition/schooling, reduced crime by 42%, women dependency on men.
It's huge success attracting migration into the area, prompting calls for a national grant.
Calculation shows the cost of a nationwide BIG would be 95 mil.USD, ~3% of the GDP.
In short, UBI in Namibia is feasible, the missing component is the lack of political will.
Here is compelling empirical evidence that UBI works, even in poor Namibia.

Netherland. Discussion only, Never tried

Universal basic income in the Netherlands: would it work?
Chuka Nwanazia Sept. 2021 (///dutchreview.com/culture/ubi-in-the-netherlands-)
Salient points in summary of this article on Universal Basic Income (UBI):
Evidence amassed UBI is more effective than traditional forms of social security.
UBI is an unconditional income, money you are entitled to, regardless of your status.
Difference between UBI and a benefit is that there are conditions attached to a benefit.
Research shows that people living in poverty lose 14 points of IQ due to stress.
Giving everyone real freedom is by far the most important argument for a basic income.
UBI is the most efficient, effective and actually cheapest way to eradicate poverty.
UBI is an investment, it's just cheaper to eradicate poverty than for it to exist.
UBI can reduce crime, child mortality, malnutrition, and teenage pregnancies.
UBI improves truancy, school performance, and induces higher economic growth.
Arguments against UBI are: people would work less, costs are financially crippling.
Would attract "illegal immigrants"; the Netherlands is well and doesn't need a UBI.
However jobs disappear due to technology and social security becoming expensive.
UBI is the only policy that is guaranteed to reach everyone unlike current schemes.
UBI must be high enough to guarantee a minimum subsistence to the most vulnerable.
In the Netherlands, this could be an amount of approximately 1,500 euros per month.
The FNV projects, switching to a UBI, will cost the treasury 105 billion euros annually.
UBI can be financed with the abolition of tax cuts, tax credit, increased VAT rate, ...
There is money for saving corporations in the pandemic, there is money to pay for UBI.
Women working at home giving care, the value of unpaid work is estimated >50% GDP.
Subsisting on 1,500 euros/month UBI, nobody will spend their whole life on the couch.
Ideally, a UBI in every country on earth reduces poverty, then no "illegal immigrants.
Basic income is a right for all, not a form of charity, so no divide between rich and poor.
A basic income is guaranteed, so it pays to work to have something extra for the family.
Employees' positions improve with a UBI and can say 'no' to poor working conditions.
Employers get more motivated and productive employees who don't just for money.
Women get financial security with a UBI while doing caring duties or no pay work.
The rich get richer, the poor get poorer, this is unsustainable and unchecked capitalism.
UBI helps eradicate poverty, giving us a much fairer, better and more sustainable world.
During the coronavirus lockdown, governments met the challenge with 'free money'.
People now call out for a 'new normal', a Green New Deal or Universal Basic Income.
With so much spent on sponsoring wars, paying for such an endeavor is a breeze.
Rutger Bregman believes that financial freedom is the truest kind of freedom with UBI.
Comments:
The Netherlands has long discussed UBI since the 1970s, but has never tried it.
Studies worldwide produced positive results consistently, UBI can be the 'new normal'.
Chuka Nwanazia says that with so much spent on wars, paying for UBI is a breeze.

Norway. Social Security System

Universal Basic Income Experiments Across The World
Pieter Wijnen 6. May 2018 (///norwaytoday.info/finance/ubi-)

The Norwegian social security system (NSSS) is popular across the world for providing welfare to its citizens. The rating agencies across the Nordic countries have consistently rated NSSS as the best. Taxation which is considered as an evil is a prerequisite for the NSSS. Norwegians are ready to pay the huge taxes because of their faith in their NSSS. But since cutting edge technologies like Robotics and Artificial Intelligence have made manpower redundant, the Norwegian government will have to take more burden in the future to ensure the smooth running of NSSS. At this outset it is better to run a Universal Basic Income Experiment in the country for the future …

.. When I listen to the economists across the world chanting the mantra, 'Universal Basic Income (UBI)', I am reminded of the Chinese proverb- Give a man a fish, and you feed him for a day. Teach a man to fish, and you feed him for a lifetime. But if fish is not available in the river it will be a futile exercise. Nowadays when employment has been taken by cutting edge technologies, giving a man Basic Income (BI) is the only viable alternative.

.. The world is fast moving so are the technologies that are used like Artificial Intelligence (AI) and Robotics which is making man power redundant. The inability to tackle unemployment has in the last decade or so, become a major reason for UBI being mooted throughout the world, particularly in European countries by a growing number of economists and politicians. Basic income (BI) is inevitable to tackle two evils namely poverty and unemployment. Even though the basic intention of the UBI is the same throughout the world, the proposals from different countries differ along lines of source of funding and the size of transfers already executed.

.. Finnish experiments with Basic income started in 2016, when KELA, the Finnish social security agency proposed a UBI package of €800 a month unconditionally to 2000 selected persons at random. The working age citizens between the age group of 25 and 58 were targeted, unfortunately it failed to secure the funding to extend its program. The program, if extended to the whole country, would have exceeded the Finnish government's total revenue. Fortunately the program was not aborted. It was decided to kick start the program with a new trimmed package of €560 per month which will be provided from 1 January 2017 until 31 December 2018. The lower BI €560 is not adequate enough to live in Finland. Basic things like hiring an apartment will cost more than the BI. So the experiments are not applied in the case of unemployed, who are resuscitated by a higher level of government support- at least €32.4 a day for the first 400 days after losing a job. Only the working poor would benefit significantly from this exercise. The objective of this exercise is to find out answers to the twin problems of low employment rate and complex system of housing, child care and other benefits. The solutions expected – the lump sum payments should create incentives for the unemployed citizens to seek employment and the complex system can be replaced. How far the low UBI payments will allow the country to embrace the solutions is debatable.

.. Similar experiments have been conducted by other countries like the USA and Iran with even lower BI packages. USA's Alaska Permanent Fund is a state-owned investment fund established using oil revenues. Since 1982, it has paid out an annual dividend to every individual in Alaska. When oil prices were very high in 2015, the dividend was a whopping $2,072 per person. By 2017 the payment had whittled down to $1100 and could further dip to $800. Research studies done by two Economists, Jones and Marinescu on the impact of Alaska's BI on employment, came to a conclusion that a universal and unconditional cash transfer does not significantly reduce aggregate employment.

Another experiment was conducted by Iran in 2011. The monthly transfer amounted to 29% of median household income, or about $1.50 extra per head of household, per day. Based on the Iran experiment a study was done by two economists Djavad Salehi-Isfahani and Mohammad H. Mostafavi-Dehzooei, the paper finds that individuals who receive cash transfers didn't quit their jobs nor did they decrease their working hours. It was startling to observe that some individuals even extended their working hours. Both studies are likely to buttress and provide an iota of positivity to the ongoing Finnish experiments though the amount of BI is lower.

.. Support for the UBI is gaining momentum across the world. New basic income pilots have been announced in Canada, Finland, and the Netherlands. There have been several attempts from countries as varied as India, Switzerland, France, New Zealand, Namibia, Scotland, and Germany. Even an underdeveloped country like Kenya had dared to start a 12 year experiment with UBI, transferring $22 a month to support the family. ..It is worth pursuing UBI if it accelerates the productive or creative endeavors of citizens.

Comments:

The Norwegian social security system is popular but is supported by high taxation. But Robotics and A.I. make manpower redundant, reducing the employment tax base. Giving a man Basic Income seems the only viable alternative in future development. Finnish trial program proposed to pay euros 560/month from Jan. 2017 to Dec. 2018. US Alaska has paid $1,000 to $2,000 oil dividends to all citizens annually since 1982. This unconditional cash transfer has not significantly reduced aggregate employment. Iran in 2011 replaced fuel/food subsidies with cash transfers up to 29% median income. It was startling to observe that some individuals even extended their working hours !
Support for UBI is gaining momentum with pilot studies announced across the world.

South Korea. Youth Basic Income

Gyeonggi Province sets example for universal basic income
- by Ock Hyun-ju (koreaherald.com August 2020)
The Youth Basic Income was launched in 2019 by governor Lee across the Gyeonggi Province, encompassing 31 counties surrounding Seoul. The area is home to a fourth of the country's population with 13.35 million residents. Under this program, all 24-year-old citizens who have lived in the area for 3 consecutive years or lived in the province for more than 10 years in total are given 250,000 won in the form of 'local currency' every quarter for a total of 1 million won over the course of one year. No conditions such as job-search efforts or parental income levels, are attached. The number of recipients stands at around 150,000 people.

More than 80% of the youth recipients were happy with the program as their quality of lives improved and they had more trust in politics, law and fellow citizens. For Lee, this is more than a welfare policy as his vision is to make Korean society more equal. Also his key policy is to sustain economic growth in the era of Industry 4.0. Hence his 'local currency' can only be used at traditional markets, restaurants and shops, not franchise stores and supermarkets run by conglomerates. This is to help small and medium-sized businesses and in turn boost the local economy. A poll of 1,000 residents showed some 80% of respondents had gone shopping at local shops, not at large supermarkets. In May the central government handed out relief cash to all Koreans and foreign nationals, 100,000 to 400,000 won, depending on household size. Indeed, shops and restaurants that accepted the 'local currency' did report an increase in sales by 53% during the COVID-19 pandemic.

Is Universal Basic Income the Key to Happiness in Asia?
By Fan Li (July 2021, StanfordSocialInnovationReview, https://ssir.org)
The largest UBI trial in Asia to date, the mayor of Seongnam in Gyeonggi Province initiated the Youth Basic Income in 2018. At 24, most young South Koreans graduate from university. Many need to take additional courses to develop skills or qualification to get a job. The 175,000 24-year-olds in Gyeonggi, each receive an equivalent of $220 in a locally negotiable currency per quarter via a credit card for a single year. The amount is small, but the program is popular with young people and local businesses. With the money, they quit their temporary job to focus on self-improvement. Local businesses see a surge in sales as the 'local' currency can only be used within the province and not at international chains like McDonald's. The recipients are happier and the willingness to work among UBI beneficiaries has not wane as some have feared

Comments:
Youth Basic Income is cash, paid universally to all 24-years-olds, quarterly for a year. It is "local currency" in a credit card, to be spent in the province, but no McDonald's. The 175,000 recipients are happier and their willingness to work has not diminished. Quality of lives improved and they had more trust in politics, law and fellow citizens. *The $880 is small but helps youths quit temporary jobs to focus on self-improvement.*

South Korean. Aging Population (2019 -)

The South Korean UBI and Regional Currency Experiment: An Effective Security Net?
By Haanbi Kim, 19 Nov. 2020 (///theeconreview.com/)

..As of June 2019, South Korea had one of the highest youth unemployment rates at 10.4%,.. the decreasing fertility rate, which has hit below one birth per female during 2018, raises concerns of human capital supply.. In response, one province has started experimenting with a Regional Currency and Universal Basic Income (UBI) system in hopes of alleviating poverty and tackling these problems.

Initiated in early 2019, Gyeonggi Local Currency is the said experiment that is operating across 31 counties and cities within Gyeonggi-do, a province of the Seoul Metropolitan Area. According to the program's website, it is defined as an *"alternative currency"* used freely by everyone within their respective city or county of residence.. It is used primarily through a debit card,.. The system has a specialized youth dividend program providing 250,000 KRW (~221 USD) every quarter.. for those who are 24-years-old, and a maternity subsidy program distributing 500,000 (~442 USD) KRW for each newborn in every household to incentivize childbirth..purchases with the currency receiving a 6% discount and additional 30% in income tax deductions later..However, there is one caveat: the money can only be spent on local businesses and traditional markets, an attempt to increase economic circulation throughout Gyeonggi province, while also benefiting small businesses..

..Whether this project is beneficial for the long-term is still up in the air, ..Less than 10% of small businesses accepting local currency transactions experienced an increase in revenue,...Another concern is *unwanted inflation* as local spending balloons and markets overstimulates. These subsidies can be vulnerable to rising inflation rates as seen with Iran's failed UBI program, where inflation eroded the distributed income's purchasing power by two-thirds (Gentilini, 2020, pp. 54-5). Some scholars have also suggested a *negative impact on labor markets*, especially in an *aging population*, ..But, improving the *liquidity of such subsidization* seems like a more important endeavor for now..

Comments:
Gyeonggi Local Currency, like unconditional UBI cash, is used through a debit card.
The system provides 4x$221 for youth dividend, ~$442 for each newborn for incentive.
There are concerns that subsidies may stimulate inflation as local spending ballooned
Subsidies may also negatively *impact labor markets*, especially in an *aging population.*
UBI subsidies as incentive for childbirth /aid for youth, besides for alleviating poverty.

Spain. Pandemic UBI (2020 -)

Pandemic speeds largest test yet of universal basic income
Carrie Arnold 10 July 2020 (https://www.nature.com/articles/d41586-020-01993-3)

"Spain was one of the hardest-hit countries in the early days of the pandemic. The nationwide lockdown curbed the spread of the virus. Millions of people lost their jobs putting many of the most vulnerable citizens at risk."

"Spain's government has started what might just be remembered as the world's biggest economics experiment. On 15 June, it launched a website offering monthly payments of up to €1,015 (US$1,145) to the nation's poorest families. The programme, which will support 850,000 households, is the largest test yet of an idea called universal basic income (UBI) — in which people are given a cash payment each month to spend however they choose."

"The aim is to provide recipients with enough cash to meet their basic needs without trapping them in poverty in the same way as existing welfare programmes that offer support only to those without jobs or other income. The scheme will cost the government at least €3 billion per year. The website where people can apply for grants launched on 15 June and received more than 50,000 applications within the first 4 hours."

"Spain's scheme — which was passed by the Cabinet on 29 May — is the first to be rolled out nationwide. Its budget is limited to 0.2% of gross domestic product. The government will target only those households — amounting to an estimated 850,000 — with the lowest incomes.The funds will be distributed monthly to each household and range from €462 for single adults to €1,015 for larger families. The 8% of households with the lowest incomes received their first payment by late June without needing to apply."

"Spain isn't running the scheme as a trial or research study as such, although there are plans to evaluate the programme continuously to monitor whether the grants are reducing poverty, boosting employment rates and improving livelihoods. The government isn't planning to stop the scheme when the economic threat from the coronavirus eases."

Comments:
Spain was hit hard by Covid-19, risking millions jobless among the most vulnerable.
A BI program was started to aid the poorest families with a monthly *subsistence* grant.
Supporting 850,000 households nationwide, it is the world's biggest economic trial.
Governments are keen to see if it boosts employment rates and improves livelihoods.
Subsistence cash of 462 to 1,015 euros are given monthly to spend as they choose.
The grant is not given to all citizens alike, so is not truly a Universal Basic Income.
Spain shows the way forward, giving aid in cash to the poorest, the most vulnerable.
Covid Pandemic sped up implementation of the concept of Universal Basic Income.

Switzerland. $2800, proposed UBI (2013)

Should the Government Pay Everyone a Basic Income?

Steven Mazie. Nov. 20, 2013 (///bigthink.com/articles//

In 2014, voters in Switzerland will decide whether their country should send a monthly check for $2,800 to every Swiss citizen and legal resident. ..

..In a post at The Economist yesterday, I looked at arguments on both sides: .. Some economists think a UBI would disincentivise work; others argue that it would enhance entrepreneurialism by easing the path to start a small business or switch careers. Philippe Van Parijs, a Belgian philosopher, believes a UBI provides "the real freedom to pursue the realization of one's conception of the good life", whether that means surfing and living small, or trading stocks and living large. Erik Olin Wright, a Marxist sociologist at the University of Wisconsin, posits that a basic income could even hasten a march toward communism (without the messiness of violent revolution) by raising the bargaining power of the proletariat. If you don't need your job to survive, Mr Wright reasons, you can command a higher salary and better benefits from your boss. Ms Lowrey [of the New York Times] points out the opposite is also a possibility: McDonald's has little pressure to pay you a living wage if the government is sending you supplemental checks every month. ..Financing a UBI would not be easy. The first step would be to cancel every anti-poverty measure, including food stamps, the Earned Income Tax Credit and unemployment insurance. (This is why some libertarians salivate at the prospect.) But the money recouped from these programs wouldn't be enough to fund a monthly salary for the 200 million or so Americans over the age of 21, so a progressive tax would likely be necessary as well. This means that while low-income Americans would see a large boost to their yearly income, the monthly income checks sent to the very rich would be balanced against tax increases exceeding their take. So while Bill Gates and a homeless man would receive the same $1000 or so every month from the government, the former would be footing the bill.

..The most robust philosophical defense of a basic income is found in a 1991 article by Van Parjis, "Why Surfers Should Be Fed." He argues that people who prefer to laze on beaches should not be compelled to work in order to feed themselves. The same goes for people who would opt for part-time job, or take up volunteering, or start up a new business. A basic income, in short, could provide everyone with a minimal sum that would support them in living the life they want to live.

Comments:

A living UBI of a monthly check of $2800/- is impossible to finance at the present time. A survival UBI of $1000/- per month is more reasonable, feasible to finance presently. Robotics and A.I. are social properties and huge profits generated be shared with a UBI. The money is sufficient but was 'stolen' by capitalists to produce billionaires like Gates. Thomas Paine argues that a survival UBI is the birthright of every man born to the land.

Yes, the government should pay a survival UBI, the birthright of every citizen.

Switzerland. Rejects plan (2016)

Switzerland rejects plan to pay every citizen at least $2,500 a month
By Ivana Kottasova and Jackie Wattles. June 2016 (///money.cnn.com/)
Swiss votes (77%) rejected a referendum that would pay every citizen a guaranteed income of $2,500 Swiss francs ($2,520) after tax regardless of their employment status or wealth.

"The plan would have allowed those earning less than the minimum to have their pay topped up. Those out of work would have been handed the full amount. The income would have been unconditional and untaxed, and it would have replaced various welfare payments."

Switzerland's voters reject basic income plan
5 June 2016 (///bbc.com/news/world-europe)
The referendum: a guaranteed basic income for all, was rejected by 77% Swiss voters. The proposal: an unconditional monthly income for all adults, whether working or not. Supporters suggested a monthly income of SFr2,500 for an adult, SFr625 for a child. Che Wagner from Basic Income Switzerland argued, it is not money for not working. "In Switzerland over 50% of the total work that is done is unpaid. It's care work, it's at home, it's in different communities, so that work would be more valued with a basic income." Luzi Stamm opposed the idea saying that billions would then try to move into Switzerland

The lessons from the Swiss basic income referendum
By Martin Farley. June 8 2016 (///web.archive.org/web/)
The referendum was lost. Martin Farley summarized the reasons for voters' rejection:

1. It was a risky experiment
2. It was a Utopian fairy tale with no basis in reality
3. It would result in inflation if adopted
4. The Swiss are not poor, so a Basic Income is not really required
5. Switzerland already has a very good and effective system of social welfare, so it does not need to be replaced
6. People should earn their income, not just receive it
7. The proposal was prohibitively expensive, would require a huge increase in tax
8. There was no plan in place to fund it

Comments:
Che Wagner says it is money for work as >50% of work done in Switzerland is unpaid.
Luzi Stamm opposition is unfound as the billions who move in aren't qualified citizens.
To pay monthly SFr2,500 for an adult, SFr625 for a child is prohibitively expensive.
The proposed payout seems too high for a Basic Income to be realistic and fundable!
A subsistence UBI is a birthright; a living UBI of $2500 only encourages dependency.
Likely voters may accept a subsistence UBI of $1,000 per month as proposed in the US.
The Swiss rejection is for fear of high inflation and huge increase in taxation.

USA. Alaska Oil Dividend (1982 -)

Alaska Permanent Fund Dividend (APFD) (apfc.org)

Ten years after Alaska achieved statehood, oil was discovered and Alaskans voted to create a permanent fund to invest the oil proceeds for future generations.The Alaska Permanent Fund (APF) was established in 1976 by Governor Jay Hammond. APF is 25% of oil money put aside each year for investment to earn interest for the current and future generations.

The APF has 2 parts, the Principal and the Earnings Reserve Account (ERA). Both are invested for income by the state-owned corporation, the Alaska Permanent Fund Corporation (APFC). The Principal is permanent saving, only the ERA is available to be spent.

Each year, the ERA is split to pay for operation costs, inflation-proofing, the annual Alaska Permanent Fund Dividend (APFD), and to supplement the state budget. All Alaskan citizens are eligible for the same annual amount of APFD, (young and old, natives and non-natives) who have resided in the state for a year or more, except for those who have been incarcerated for felonies of the state.

The first annual individual payout of PFD in 1982 was $1000 USD. The lowest individual dividend payout was $331.29 in 1984 and the highest was $2,072 in 2015. Alaska has no state income tax but payments from the fund are taxable by the federal administration. As of June 2021, the Principal has grown to $60.1 billion and the ERA total $20.0 Billion. Today, dwindling flow of oil means a decline in oil revenues. To support state services and programs, earnings from the APF are playing an increasing role in the fiscal health of the State besides the annual individual payout of APFD. The APFD is a Basic Income in the form of a resource dividend. Some researchers argue, "It has helped Alaska attain the highest economic equality of any state in the United States... And, seemingly unnoticed, it has provided unconditional cash assistance to needy Alaskans at a time when most states have scaled back aid and increased conditionality (wikipedia.org).

Comments:

The ideal Universal Basic Income (UBI) is:
1. For all legitimate citizens, young and old, rich and poor (universal).
2. Subsistence amount of cash for unconditional usage (basic income).
3. From birth till death.
4. Subsistence amount at least.

The Alaska Permanent Fund Dividend payouts on average, about $1200 USD annually. This is only a tenth of what is needed for survival in the states, i.e.1000 USD per month. Nevertheless most Alaskans are most happy to have it, and have marched to defend it. *Some extra cash or UBI is always welcome by most citizens, save the few 'privileged'.*

USA. California, Santa Clara County. FosterYouth (2020 -)

Santa Clara County rolls out UBI program for youth transitioning out of foster care
by Bay City News Service Jul 28, 2020 (///paloaltoonline.com/news)
..The program, ..provides a monthly stipend of $1,000 for a year to former foster youth
ages 24 and over who are too old to receive foster assistance...Foster youth stop
receiving assistance from the county at 25, .."When you turn 25 you are alone, no one is
helping you. You have to work for everything. ... All of a sudden you lost your job, and
you can't pay for rent, who are you going to go to? Your family. A lot of foster youth
don't have that," Grano said...Supervisor Dave Cortese spearheaded the initiative after
meeting with local philanthropist Gisele Huff, who is also the president of the nonprofit
organization The Gerald Huff Fund for Humanity.

..The program was approved for $900,000 in funding from the county's general
fund and will be used for monthly stipends as well as an in-depth evaluation of the pilot
program. .."There is overrepresentation of people of color and why is that?..Clearly they
have been disadvantaged from the start by a system that is sort of rigged against them,
..This is a way to make amends for that, not as a charity, but to try to compensate for
some of the setbacks they have experienced along the way," Cortese said. "These are
kids who have done nothing wrong, have managed through the system at this point and
are basically the children of the county so we are the surrogate parents, we have the
responsibility."

UBI FOR FOSTER YOUTH PILOT IN SANTA CLARA COUNTY IS EXTENDED
June 23, 2021 (https://sd15.senate.ca.gov/news/ubi-foster-youth-pilot-)
This week, the Santa Clara County Board of Supervisors approved extending their
first-of-its-kind pilot program that provides universal basic income to transition age
foster youth. The pilot program, created at the request of Senator Cortese in 2020, has
been extended for an additional six months with an added investment of $500,000 from
the County.

"Our pilot program in Santa Clara County is yielding clear results and inspiring
a growing number of similar direct cash assistance initiatives across the nation. Foster
youth in this program are reporting they are able to use these funds to sustain their basic
needs and to improve their credit score," said Senator Cortese.

A recent report on the County's pilot program included the following: ..respondents
reported that the funding has allowed them to cover basic expenses and some savings. Many hope
to save enough during the pilot to maintain stability after the pilot ends."

Comments
Foster Youths have no family to turn to when they reach 25 and county assistance stops.
Senator Cortese is examplary, stepping in with a stipend of $1,000/month for a year.
This is like Paine's idea of giving everyone, at the age of 21, the sum of fifteen pounds.
Respondents reported using the fund to sustain basic needs, improve their credit score.
Not many starting life have family support; a national UBI for everyone is only fair.

USA. California, Stockton. Aid in cash (2019 - 2020)

A California city gave some residents $500 a month, no strings attached By Sigal Samuel Oct 2019 *(vox.com/future-perfect/)*

The number of participants is *small*: 125 people (out of an est. 311,000 Stockton residents) who live below the median income line (~$46,000), of whom nearly half are working full- or part-time. Each recipient was given $500 per month on a debit card. However 40% was withdrawn as cash. Eight month into the 18-month experiment with Basic Income (BI), provisional data show recipients spent almost 40% BI on food, 24% on merchandise, 11% on bills and 9% on car repairs and gas. "This information is a useful corrective to the myth that people become poor because they're irrational agents." However the researchers main goal of measuring the BI effects on recipients physical and mental health, await the release of more data.

Stockton's Basic-Income Experiment Pays Off

byAnnie Lowrey. March 2021 (theatlantic.com/ideas/archive/)

Two years on, using donated funds the industrial city of Stockton launched a small demo program giving cash of $500 a month for 18 months to each recipient, with no strings attached. The 125 individuals who were randomly selected, lived in the neighborhood and had an average income lower than the city median of $46,000 a year. Data collected from these individuals was analyzed and compared with non-recipients as control. "The families receiving the $500 a month tended to spend the money on essentials, including food, home goods, utilities, and gas. (Less than 1 percent went to cigarettes and alcohol.) The cash also doubled the households' capacity to pay unexpected bills, and allowed recipient families to pay down their debts. Individuals getting the cash were also better able to help their families and friends, providing financial stability to the broader community." "In the Stockton study, the share of participants with a full-time job rose 12 percentage points, versus five percentage points in the control group."

"Finally, the cash recipients were healthier, happier, and less anxious than their counterparts in the control group. *Cash is a better way to cure some forms of depression and anxiety than Prozac,*" says Michael Tubbs, a former mayor of Stockton, who spearheaded the project. "So many of the illnesses we see in our community are a result of toxic stress and elevated cortisol levels and anxiety, directly attributed to income volatility and not having enough to cover your basic necessities." "

Comments:

Program gave 125 earners of < median-income, $500/mth.for 18 months on a debit card. Recipients used the cash mainly for food /utilities, only <1% on cigarettes and alcohol. Recipients were happier, healthier, less anxious than controls, better able to help others. *"Cash is a better way to cure some forms of depression and anxiety than Prozac,"..*

USA. Cherokee Indians, Casino (1996 -)

USA, small-scale basic income (wikipedia.org Sep. 2021. UBI around the world)
Native American nations have been distributing dividends to their members. Since 1996, the Eastern Band of Cherokee Indians based in North Carolina has been paid several thousand dollars twice a year from the profits of the Harrah's Casino. A study of the effects on children found significant declines in poverty, behavioral problems, crime, substance abuse and psychiatric problems, and increases in on-time graduation. The effects were primarily found among those who were youngest when the payments began and among those who were lifted out of poverty rather than those who were already well-off (Jane Costello, a Duke University researcher).

Cherokee banks brace for rush when casino checks go out
Caitlin Bowling Dec. 2012 (https://mokymountainnews.com/news/)
Bi-annual casino windfall: Half the casino profits go to support tribal programs. The other half is split among the tribe's 14,000 enrolled members. They received a check worth $3,912 before taxes. The children's money is kept in a trust fund until they come of age. The per capita distribution has been increasing steadily since 2009.

Crystal Hicks from Painttown said her money "goes toward bills and Christmas gifts." Steven Welch of Birdtown said his money will go toward bills. *The checks aren't a huge windfall* as many tribal members use them to make ends meet. Paul Ensley Jr. said his money goes for child support and to cover bills. For those under 18, they receive all the accrued money in a lump sum once they graduate high school or turn 21. School in Cherokee has incorporated personal financial management in its curriculum.

The argument for a basic income
John D Sutter, CNN March 2015 (///edition.cnn.com/opinion/)
Talked his way around town to meet people. Kaitlin Blaylock debt-free at 23, used the money to go to grad school. James Sander II spent on his two boys and the auto repair business. "I don't have to worry if I'm able to put food on the table or clothes on their backs." Lori Sander saved the money to send her son on a school trip to Europe. These folks' anecdotes show their thankfulness for the opportunities given them by the casino checks. Jane Costello, a Duke University researcher, had studied the effects of these payments on 1,420 Cherokee-area children over the course of 20 years. The money amounting to 30% of poor family income improved parenting quality. Kids lifted out of poverty saw behavioural problems decrease 40% and reduced crime rate by 22%.

Comments:
Since 1996, the casino checks are 'universal', cash paying out to adults and children.
This small-scale basic income (30% of poor family income) improves parenting.
Kids out of poverty saw a 40% reduction in behavioral problems and 22% lesser crime.
Adults are less worried about putting food on the table and clothes on their backs.
Indeed, a little money can go a long way in relieving stress in under-privileged families.
This is a true UBI showing benefits obviously and convincely.

USA. Dolly Parton (2016)

Dolly Parton Telethon Raises $9M for Tennessee Wildfire Victims
NBC News (//nbcnews.com/pop-culture/celebrity/dolly-parton-telethon-)

Dolly Parton accepts the Willie Nelson Lifetime Achievement Award at Country Music Awards on Nov. 2 in Nashville, Tennessee.Charles Sykes / Charles Sykes/Invision/AP
Dec. 15, 2016, 10:33 PM +08 / Updated Dec. 15, 2016, 10:33 PM +08
By The Associated Press

NASHVILLE, Tenn. — Dolly Parton says a star-studded telethon for those affected by recent wildfires in her native Tennessee has brought in about $9 million.
Parton headlined the Tuesday night event that was broadcast on several cable networks and live streamed online. Parton says in a statement that all donations have yet to be counted, but the total stands at around $9 million. The total is expected to rise in the coming days as mail donations are counted and the telethon is rebroadcast.
The money goes to the Dollywood Foundation's My People Fund. It will provide $1,000 each month for six months to families who lost their primary residence in the fires.
The fires in Tennessee's Sevier County spread to more than 2,500 structures and killed 14 people. Two juveniles were charged with aggravated arson last week, and more charges are possible, police said.

Comments:
Dolly Parton helped to provide $1,000 per month for six month to all victim-families.
Natural disasters like earthquakes, torrential rains, and wildfires may strike suddenly.
Not every county is lucky Sevier County, which has a celebrity in their midst to help.
A UBI in place is basic support under such dire circumstances for the majority of us.

USA. Mississippi, Jackson. Cash assistance (2019)

$1,000 a month, no strings attached
Robert Samuels August 31, 2019 (//washingtonpost.com/politics/ -no-string-attached/)

JACKSON, Miss. — A nonprofit organization was looking to give 20 African American single mothers living in public housing $1,000 each month for a year. They'd be able to use the money in any way they pleased.

"My mothers need cash," said Aisha Nyandoro, who also helped to establish the Jackson-based program. They fretted over bills. They'd miss work because they couldn't repair a car, or because they couldn't afford child care. "I just need $25," Nyandoro recalled one mother telling her. The woman's child had qualified for a citywide science fair, but she didn't have enough cash to pay for registration.
The requirements accompanying public assistance such as food stamps and housing vouchers left her clients "pigeonholed," without the flexibility to craft budgets based on their specific situations, Nyandoro said.

Of the 110 women eligible to be a part of the program, only 38 applied.
The 20 women selected for the experiment in November 2018 earned an average of $12,000 a year at the time. Fifteen of the women were working. Twelve had reported being so short on cash that they had used an emergency lender in the preceding six months.

The women started receiving the checks in December. Some of the women talked about their gift-filled Christmases and sported new hairstyles. Some said they took a sick day for the first time. They began paying off overdue electricity bills and high-interest loans.

At the end of six months, none of the women reported using an emergency lender. Nearly all said they had enough money to buy school supplies, when fewer than half had said that before. They reported cooking more balanced meals, visiting the doctor and attending church more often.

"The beauty of all of this has just been how folks are light," Nyandoro said. "They aren't walking around with the heaviness of life that, unfortunately, so many times low-income folks have to carry."

Comments:
Individuals' needs are different, and cash gives flexibility to spend where it is needed.
The Jackson program shows unconditional cash solved problems for the recipients.
"The beauty of all of this has just been how folks are light," Nyandoro said.
The BI of $1K/mth for a year lifted the 'heaviness' of life for these 20 poor families.
Indeed the vast majority of us low-income folks are living from paycheck to paycheck.
Paradise is created on Earth when cash assistance lifts us from the 'heaviness' of life.

USA. New Jersey (2021)

A forgotten past repeats itself as Newark's attempt to create economic equity
by Alison Lefkovitz July 2021 (///www.njcom/opinion/)

"This spring, 30 people in Newark began receiving a $12,000 income over the next two years, with no strings attached as to how the individual spends it. The program is part of Newark's universal basic income (UBI) pilot, created to provide housing security for some of the city's poorest residents."

"In the late 1960s, Lyndon B. Johnson's Office of Economic Opportunity launched a pilot program in Trenton, Passaic, Paterson and Jersey City that granted some participating families of four $4,352 a year (approximately $30,000 today). Like today's workers unemployed by the pandemic, many workers in the late 1960s suddenly lost their jobs. The pilot targeted these underemployed populations and alleviated one of the greatest concerns about UBIs: even with the program, most workers accepted new or better jobs whenever possible."

" The success of the pilot helped inspire Richard Nixon to propose a guaranteed annual income plan to Congress. The Family Assistance Plan did not heed all of the lessons of Johnson's pilot. Instead, it proposed giving families with children only about $2,400 a year (about $15,000 today). The plan also incorporated a work requirement for all but mothers of children under the age of 3. The National Welfare Rights Organization rejected those assumptions about work and welfare. First, the organization saw the proposed payout for the UBI as impossible to survive on. What the Family Assistance Plan proposed was lower than welfare payouts in all but five states. Welfare rights activists demanded "$5,500 or Fight." The Family Assistance Plan failed in Congress in 1972."

"Newark's pilot deliberately echoes not Nixon, but the plan proposed by the welfare rights organization. Newark's plan shares its demands for dignity for those who receive universal basic income payments by targeting program candidates using only income and housing insecurity. It explicitly rejects eligibility criteria, work requirements and restrictions on how funds are used. Newark's pilot resembles the Family Assistance Plan only in how modestly it has keyed its basic income payments — at $6,000. That is substantially lower than the pilot program from the 1960s or even what the Family Assistance Plan proposed when adjusted for inflation. It is not enough to sustain life in the contemporary United States."

Comments:

In the 1960s, Johnson's Family Grant ($30K/yr equiv.) recipients worked, accepted jobs.
In 1972, Nixon's Family Plan of $15K/yr (equiv.) was too meager, failed in Congress.
Now Newark's offer of $6K/yr to individuals is not enough, ie. past lessons not learned.
However, Newark's UBI pilot is still a step in the right direction of economic equity.

USA. Oregon, Sherman County. Wind dividend (2002 -)

Sherman County, Oregon has used wind power to provide a $590 dividend per household every year since 2002
Sierra Dawn McClain, Capital Press. August, 2019 (//basicincometoday.com/sherman-)

When the boom in wind power began 17 years ago in Sherman County, Ore., leaders there came up with an idea. Instead of the county simply pocketing property taxes collected from the big wind generators that were sprouting across the countryside, they would share a portion of the money with citizens. Every head of household who has lived in the county at least a year now receives $590 annually. The idea was to reimburse residents whose views were impeded by wind turbines.

The rest of the money has gone to build a courthouse, school, library, Oregon State University Extension facility and a new covered arena at the fairgrounds. For a county that has only about 1,800 people, this was a stroke of genius.

The idea was patterned after the Alaska Permanent Fund, which was created in 1976 by a constitutional amendment that allowed the state to set aside 25% of its revenue from oil pumped from the state-owned Prudhoe Bay oil field. That money was deposited in a diversified investment account. Politicians cannot spend it for anything without a vote of the people. Earnings from the fund are divided up and sent to every man, woman and child in the form of a dividend check. Last year, each check was for $1,600. This year's dividend hasn't yet been decided. The value of the Permanent Fund nowadays is north of $60 billion.

We think the folks in Sherman County and Alaska are onto something. Particularly when publicly owned natural resources are involved, citizens deserve some of the revenue. We fully understand that politicians may be unlikely to cede their power over the money, but they should remember: It's not their money.

The outcome of paying dividends to citizens is extraordinary. It gives them a direct interest in government. Instead of constantly being hounded for more taxes, they actually receive a direct benefit from the government. Also, those dividends help drive the economy. Natural resources — wind, oil, timber, natural gas or minerals — should be treated as the property of the citizens.

Comments:
Sherman County has been collecting property taxes from big wind generators
Households who stay at least a year in the County get a dividend of $590/yr since 2002.
Indeed, land and natural resources should be treated as the property of the citizens.
Scientific innovations are also social property, and the huge profits ought be shared
Yet conniving governments allow individuals and corporations to siphon off billions
Who is to be blamed when conniving politicians remain in power year in year out ?
Therefore to get action, all voters must unite under the banner, "no UBI, no Votes".

USA. Pennsylvania, Covid relief-cash (2020 -)

UBI for Pa.?: Reps. Fiedler, Lee propose sending $250 to every state resident
John Micek May 5,2020 (///www.penncapital-star-com/commentary/ubi-)
"If you liked that stimulus check you just received (or are about to receive) from Washington D.C. as part of the massive, $2 trillion CARES Act, then the chances are pretty good you'll want to give a listen to a plan that's being floated by two state House Democrats. Reps. Elizabeth Fiedler, of Philadelphia, and Summer Lee, of Allegheny County, circulated a memo looking for co-sponsors for their plan to give every Pennsylvania adult, aged 18 and older, $250 each to spend on groceries or household bills or some other pertinent expense... With another coronavirus relief package emerging in Washington, Fiedler told the Capital-Star that she and Lee envision their program running as long as the flow of federal cash continues in Pennsylvania."

Fighting Poverty With Cash
Dave Zeitlin 20 Apr 2021 (///thepenngazette.com/fighting-poverty-with-cash)
"Recently, President Joe Biden's $1.9 trillion American Rescue Plan showed how much further policymakers are willing to go to fight poverty through stimulus payments and child tax credit expansions. "But really, this is something that activists and researchers have been working on for decades,"... Chris Hughes argued in the New York Times early in the pandemic last May that *"a guaranteed income should be permanent American policy, not just an emergency measure to help with this crisis."*... Currently about 40 mayors, from American cities both big and small, have joined MGI, which together with the School of Social Policy & Practice in October established the Center for Guaranteed Income Research."

Should Harrisburg provide guaranteed income to some residents?
Charles Thompson April 29, 2021 (www.pennlive.com/news/)
"Harrisburg Mayor Eric Papenfuse, with the help of a mighty $48.8 million breeze blowing in from Washington, D.C., is calling for the establishment of a guaranteed income program in Harrisburg to help the city's poorest residents and attack generational poverty... Papenfuse's Democratic primary rivals, meanwhile, are leaning in different directions for the federal funds. Otto Banks and Dave Schankweiler say the city could get more bang for the buck by investing in housing, job readiness programs and small business assistance programs. City Council President Wanda Williams prioritized infrastructure investment. ...A U.S. Treasury spokeswoman told PennLive Wednesday that program guidelines for spending the American Rescue Plan money are still being finalized, so she could not say whether they will allow such a guaranteed income program."

Comments:
The Covid-19 pandemic lockdowns created havoc with the economy and job losses.
The US government has rushed up with 2 trillions in aids for businesses and the jobless.
State reps. plan to give all Pennsylvania adults $250 unconditionally to spend as wished.
Mayor with $48.8M from Washington wants to do the same for Harrisburg's poorest.
But others wish to invest in housing, infrastructure, aid programs for small businesses.
How much of the trillions of Covid relief-cash gets to citizens is anybody's guess!

USA. Washington, Seattle-Denver. NIT (1970 - 1972)

Overview of the Final Report of the Seattle-Denver Income Maintenance Experiment
ASPE Report Apr 30, 1983 (///aspe.hhs.gov/reports/overview-)
"SIME/DIME was launched in Seattle, Washington, in 1970 and extended in 1972 to a second site in Denver, Colorado. The prime contractors for SIME/DIME were the States of Washington and Colorado, which subcontracted with SIR International for the design, operation, and research evaluation of the experiment. SRI International, in turn, subcontracted with Mathematica Policy Research (MPR) for the administration of the cash transfer or negative income tax (NIT) treatment and all the field data collection from both experimental and control groups. For the administration of the job counseling/training subsidy treatment, SRI subcontracted with the Seattle Central Community College and the Community College of Denver. The experiment involved almost 5,000 families." ...

"In all the experiments, more than one version of the negative income tax treatment was tested. ... — making the results useful for predicting response to a wide range of cash transfer plans. Table 1 shows the plans tested: three guarantee levels and four tax rates, combined in such a way as to produce 11 negative income tax plans in all. The three guarantee levels for a family of four in 1971 dollars were $3,800, $4,800, and $5,600. The dollar guarantee levels varied with family size (as does the poverty line) with larger families qualifying for higher guarantee levels under a given NIT plan. ... SIME/DIME tested two constant tax rates: 50% and 70%... SIME/DIME also tested two declining tax rate schedules. These rates were 80% and 70%, respectively, for the first $1,000 of non-experimental income and then declined by 5 percentage points for each additional $1,000 of non-experimental income."...

"Given the magnitude of these findings, it is unlikely that any national NIT program would be neutral with respect to marital stability. Although the effects of a national NIT program are unlikely to be as dramatic as the experimental effects, the potential for such effects must not be ignored."

Do income maintenance programs break up marriages? A reevaluation
Glen G. Cain and D.A. Wissoker 1987-1988 (///irp.wisc.edu/publications/focus/pdfs/)
We conclude that the data from SIME-DIME on marital stability provide no justification for opposing income maintenance to intact couples with children, as has been claimed by some interpreters (but not by the original investigators) of SIME-DIME.

Comments:
This early negative income tax (NIT) program tried to answer too many questions !
And a design too complex, involving multiple subcontractors and sub-subcontractor, ..
Its negative findings on marital stability are not convincing and are strongly disputed.
It is also subjected to abuse by mis-reporting of income or hours worked and earnings.
The NIT program is more costly to administer than unconditional UBI payments.

UBI Studies

Summary

Brazil. Quatinga Velho (2008-)
Only R30 (4.4% of min.salary) cash in aid, can improve life, raise hope for the future.
Cash aid creates demand for food /basic needs; some recipients start small businesses.
Importantly they observed no increased use of alcohol or illicit drugs.

Brazil. Marica (2019-)
About 52,000 residents receive over half the minimum salary, 130 reais/person/mth.
It pays with 'Mumbucas' card, a local currency to be used locally, and is tractable.
Marica's basic income has proven its worth in the corona crisis (Jens Glüsing, 2021).

Canadian. Mincome (1974-1979)
An average family in Dauphin was guaranteed an annual income of 16K C$.
Mason (2017) said Hum and Simpson found little impact on work attitude of recipients.
Forget (2011) found improved population health and education in Manitoba health data.
***Cox (2020) reported banks lending, small businesses started, prosperity while it last*ed.**

Canada. Ontario (2017-2019)
The Ontario trial guaranteed US$12,180 yearly, enrolled 4,000 subjects for 3 years.
New government killed it in 17 months. Survey of 217 subjects showed positive results.
Participants reported better mental wellbeing, reduced use of public health services.
Basic Income for better education /health, with savings in public health services.

China. Macau (2017-)
Government pledged to make the Wealth Partaking Scheme (WPS) an annual affair.
It is not enough as a basic income at about 10% of a cleaner-worker's annual earnings.
Macau's small UBI is universal, hopefully the beginning of better things to come.

Finland. Experimental UBI (2017 - 2018)
Finland legislated BI experiment, subsistence UBI at 560 euros/month for 2 year.
Unconditional-recipients fare better than benefits-recipients, better health, more trust.
We safely predict more positive results if the trial can be extended to a longer term.

India. Cash transfers project (2011 -)
The grant amount accounted for 20-39% of the monthly income of these poor families.
Recipient villages showed better children nutrition /school attendance /less illnesses.
No more use of alcohol but more savings, more life-stocks, even started new businesses.
Indian villages show compelling evidence that UBI works, even in tribal communities.

Iran. Subsidy with c seeash (2012 -)
Subsidies changed to cash transfers that amount to 29% of the nation's median income.
Economists found small businesses like housekeepers /teachers /deliverymen flourished.
People didn't work less and Geier says other countries can emulate Iran's success.
Fuel subsidies benefit the rich more; cash is fairer with a positive impact on everyone.

Kenya. Give Directly (2017 - 2019)
Day 1, monthly, mobile phones of 21,000 adults in hundreds of villages ding in unison.
Cash (US$22) equal to half the income for a 2-adult household, appears in their account.
Even in poor Kenya villages, cash transfer to recipients can be so easy at little cost!

Kenya. Trials (2017 - 2019)
Not much but 75 cents/day is sufficient to cover food, health and schooling basic needs.
Recipients eat better, less likely to get sick, and even start a business in good time.
Even a small Basic Income supplement for 2 years measurably improved things.

Mongolia. Resource cash dividend (2010 - 2012)
Mongolians as co-owners of the country share in its mineral wealth directly and equally.
The Human Development Fund paid monthly to every citizen MNT 21,000 bwt 2010-2.
Government's spirit of sharing the country's wealth with citizems is commendable.

Namibia. Basic Income Grant (2008 -2009)
BIG is N$100-/pax/mth (~8% av. income) to all residents of the settlement <60 of age.
Residents empowered to form committee, started small businesses, dress-making/brick..
Improved child nutrition/schooling, reduced crime by 42%, women dependency on men.
Calculation shows the cost of a nationwide BIG would be 95 mil.USD, ~3% of the GDP.
UBI in Namibia is feasible, the missing component is the lack of political will.

Netherland. Discussion only, Never tried
The Netherlands has long discussed UBI since the 1970s, but has never tried it.
Chuka Nwanazia comprehensively summarizes the pros and cons aspects of UBI.
Concludes: With the world spending so much on wars, paying for UBI is a breeze.

Norway. Social Security System
The Norwegian social security system is popular but is supported by high taxation.
Robotics and A.I. will make manpower redundant, reducing the employment tax base.
Guaranteeing a Basic Income seems the only viable alternative in future development.
Support for UBI is gaining momentum with pilot studies announced across the world.

South Korea. Youth Basic Income (2019)
Youth Basic Income is cash, paid universally to all 24-years-olds, quarterly for a year.
It is "local currency" in a credit card, to be spent in the province, but no McDonald's.
The $880 is small but helps youths quit temporary jobs to focus on self-improvement.

South Korean. Aging Population (2019 -)
Gyeonggi Local Currency, like unconditional UBI cash, is used through a debit card.
The system provides 4x$221 for youth dividend, ~$442 for each newborn for incentive.
Concerns: subsidies stimulate inflation, negatively impact labor in an aging population.
UBI, besides alleviating poverty, can be an incentive for childbirth and aid for youth.

Spain. Pandemic UBI (2020 -)
Subsistence cash of 462 to 1,015 euros are given monthly to spend as they choose.
Supporting 850,000 households nationwide, it is the world's biggest economic trial.
Spain shows the way forward, giving aid in cash to the poorest, the most vulnerable.
Covid Pandemic sped up implementation of the concept of Universal Basic Income.

Switzerland. $2800, proposed UBI (2013)
A living UBI of $2800/mth. is possible only in the future when Robotics /A.I. matured.
However, survival UBI of $1000/mth. is more reasonable, feasible to finance presently.
Thomas Paine argues that a survival UBI is the birthright of every man born to the land.
Yes, the government should pay a survival UBI, the birthright of every citizen.

Switzerland. Rejects plan (2016)
To pay monthly SFr2,500 for an adult, SFr625 for a child is prohibitively expensive.
Likely voters may accept a subsistence UBI of $1,000 per month as proposed in the US.
The Swiss rejection is for fear of high inflation and huge increase in taxation.
A subsistence UBI is a birthright; a living UBI of $2500 only encourages dependency.

USA. Alaska Oil Dividend (1982 -)
The Alaska Permanent Fund Dividend payouts on average, about $1200 USD annually.
This is about 1/10 of what is needed for survival in the states, i.e.1000 USD per month.
Nevertheless most Alaskans are most happy to have it, and have marched to defend it.
Some extra cash or UBI is always welcome by most citizens but the 'privileged' few.

USA. California, Santa Clara County. FosterYouth
Foster Youths have no family to turn to when they reach 25 and county assistance stops.
Senator Cortese is examplary, stepping in with a stipend of $1,000/month for a year.
Respondents reported using the fund to sustain basic needs, improve their credit score.
Not many starting life have family support; a national UBI for everyone is only fair.

USA. California, Stockton. Aid in cash (2019 - 2020)
Program gave 125 earners of < median-income, $500/mth.for 18 months on a debit card.
Recipients used the cash mainly for food /utilities, only <1% on cigarettes and alcohol.
Recipients were happier, healthier, less anxious than controls, better able to help others.
"Cash is a better way to cure some forms of depression and anxiety than Prozac,"..

USA. Cherokee Indians, Casino (1996 -)
This BI (30% of poor family income) is universal, cash pay to both adults and children.
Kids out of poverty saw a 40% reduction in behavioral problems and 22% lesser crime.
Adults are less worried about putting food on the table and clothes on their backs.
A little money can go a long way in relieving stress in under-privileged families.

USA. Dolly Parton (2016)
Dolly Parton helped to provide $1,000 per month for six month to all victim-families.
Natural disasters like earthquakes, torrential rains, and wildfires may strike suddenly.
Not every county is lucky Sevier County, which has a celebrity in their midst to help.
A UBI in place is basic support under such dire circumstances for the majority of us.

USA. Mississippi, Jackson. Cash assistance (2019)
Individuals' needs are different, and cash gives flexibility to spend where it is needed.
The BI of $1K/mth for a year lifted the 'heaviness' of life for these 20 poor families.
Indeed the vast majority of us low-income folks are living from paycheck to paycheck.
'Paradise' on Earth when cash assistance lifts us from the 'heaviness' of life.

USA. New Jersey (2021)
In 1972, Nixon's Family Plan of $15K/yr (equiv.) was too meager, failed in Congress.
Now Newark's offer of $6K/yr to individuals is not enough, ie. past lessons not learned.
But Newark's UBI pilot is still a step in the right direction of economic equity.

USA. Oregon, Sherman County. Wind dividend (2002 -)
Households who stay at least a year in the County get a dividend of $590/yr since 2002.
Scientific innovations are also social property, and the huge profits ought be shared
Who is to be blamed when conniving politicians remain in power year in year out ?
Therefore to get action, all voters must unite under the banner, "no UBI, no Votes".

USA. Pennsylvania, Covid relief-cash (2020 -)
State reps. plan to give all Pennsylvania adults $250 unconditionally to spend as wished.
Mayor with $48.8M from Washington wants to do the same for Harrisburg's poorest.
But others wish to invest in housing, infrastructure, aid programs for small businesses.
How much of the trillions of Covid relief-cash gets to citizens is anybody's guess!

USA. Washington, Seattle-Denver. NIT (1970 - 1972)
This early negative income tax (NIT) program tried to answer too many questions !
With a design too complex, involving multiple subcontractors and sub-subcontractor, ..
Its negative findings on marital stability are not convincing and are strongly disputed.
The NIT program is more costly to administer than unconditional UBI payments.

UBI Studies

Conclusions:

Brazil Quatinga Velho with R30 (4.4% of min.salary) cash, improves life, raises hope.
Brazil Marica paying R130 on 'Mumbucas' card proves its worth in the corona crisis.
The Canadian Mincome project giving out C$16k brought prosperity while it lasted.
Canada.Ontario trial with US$12k/yr for 17 months saw better education/mental health.
Macau's small UBI, 10% of a cleaner's earnings, hopefully is the start of better things.
Finland, aid with 560 euros/mth, recipients had better health/trust than benefits-controls.
India's cash transfers (30% of min.income) improved nutrition/education/less illnesses.
Iran's replacing subsidies with cash is fairer with the same positive impact on everyone.
Kenya's trials with *only 75 cents/day*, for only 2 years did measurably improved things.
Poor villagers received the cash easily /instantly on their handphones monthly on day 1.
And Mongolia's *spirit of sharing* the country's wealth with citizens is commendable.
Poor Namibia shows empirical evidence that UBI works, so why not anywhere else !
Netherland's Nwanazia: "with so much spent on wars, paying for UBI is a breeze."
Norway's Social Security System is based on high taxation, and Robotics killing jobs.
UBI seems to be the solution and fundings may be from the huge profits of Robotics.
Korean youths are happier with improved quality of life, more trust in politics and law.
The $880 is small but helps youths quit temporary jobs to focus on self-improvement.
South Korea's aging population is aided with an incentive for childbirth, $442/newborn.
Spain, in line with a UBI, wishes to make the Covid pandemic cash payout permanent.
Swiss reject the living UBI of $2800/mth. as they have a good welfare system in place.
A living UBI of $2800 only encourages dependency, but subsistence UBI is a birthright.
Alaskan oil dividend is extra cash welcome by all Alaskans, though av. only ~$1000/yr.
Santa Clara Foster youths' adulthood at 25 are aided with a stipend, $1k/mth. for a year.
Stockton's Aid in cash made recipients happier, healthier and less anxious than controls.
Yes, "Cash is a better way to cure some forms of depression and anxiety than Prozac,"..
Cherokee Indians' casino dividend saw kids out of poverty, better behaved, lesser crime.
Added 30% income, the little money goes a long way relieving stress in poor families.
Having Dolly Parton a celebrity in their midst, few counties are like lucky Sevier.
Thus for most of us, only a UBI in place is our basic support under all circumstances.
Mississippi.Jackson's cash assistance gives flexibility to spend wherever needed.
'Paradise' is on Earth when cash assistance lifts us from the 'heaviness' of life.

Newark's offer of $6k/yr is not enough, but a step in the direction of *economic equity.*
Sherman County's Wind Dividend from collected property tax, emulates Alaska's Oil Dividend.
Therefore to get action, other counties may unite under the banner, "no UBI, no Votes".
Pennsylvania's state reps. plan to give out cash unconditionally, OR invest in housing, ...
Of the trillions of Covid relief-cash, how much truly gets to citizens is anybody's guess!
Seattle-Denver's Negative Income Tax program in 1970 is rather complex for action !
Indeed a NIT program is more costly to administer than unconditional UBI payments.

In short:
UBI Trials (Cash in Aid) consistently show positive results in poor and rich countries.
UBI is effective as R30 can improve life, raising hope in Brazil, Quatinga Velho.
UBI is effective, an extra 30% min.income improves nutrition/education/health in India.
Casino dividend reduces poverty /crime rate and Cherokee Indian kids behaved better.
UBI is easy, Namibian villagers receive cash instantly when their handphones 'ding'.
UBI is flexible, recipients show better health/trust than benefits-controls in Finland expt.
UBI is fairer, with the same impact on everyone when Iran replaced subsidies with cash.
UBI is prosperity, small businesses flourish while the Mincome project lasts in Canada.
UBI is the future solution, when Robots kill jobs, the high tax base for Norway's SSS.
UBi is all positive, with minimal alcohol/drugs abuse and little impact on employment.
UBI-life of $2800/mth, the Swiss reject as too expensive, fearing dependency /inflation.
UBI-subsist $1000/mth; Seems reasonable for economic equity, birthright of all citizens.
UBI is viable, robots /scientific advances do create huge profits, enough for everyone.
Quotables:
Netherland's Nwanazia: "with so much spent on wars, paying for UBI is a breeze."
"Cash is a better way to cure some forms of depression and anxiety than Prozac,"..
UBI for Democratic nations, citizens unite under the banner, "no UBI, no Votes".

Discussions

Paradise on Earth with the UBI

127   **Discussion** (35 topics)

World of Miseries

The small selfish ruling elite has been bullying the hapless multitudes since the dawn of history.
Laozi calls them 'heads' of robbers in his book of 5 thousand words, the *Daodejing*. (道德經).

09 服文采	Cloth in finery (Lords and Kings)
10 帶利剑	Carry sharp swords
11 厌饮食	Over-indulge in food and wine
12 财货有余	Wealth and goods possession in excess
13 是谓盗夸	They are chiefs of robbers (ch.53 *Daodejing*. Jingwei, 2012)

Liezi says the elite class who want ever more are 'Termites', (ch.7.16, Jingwei 2021).

01 杨朱曰：	Yangzhu Said:
02 "丰屋美服，	"Luxurious House Beautiful Clothes,
03 厚味姣色，	Rich Taste (food) Pretty Color (sex)
04 有此四者，	Having These 4 Things,
05 何求于外？	What Else To Request ?
06 有此而求外者，	People Having These And still Request More,
07 无厌之性。	Always Greedy This Character.
08 无厌之性，	Wanting Ever-more This Character,
09 阴阳之蠹也。	The Termites of Yin Yang (Nature) that's.

And Thomas Paine was pained at the misery of the masses that capitalists had exploited.
"...The most affluent and the most miserable of the human race are to be found in the
countries that are called civilized... Poverty therefore, is a thing created by that which is
called civilized life." (*Agrarian Justice*. Paine, 1737-1809)

Today, born into poverty, vulnerable millions are jailed for petty crimes.
Millions are Homelessness worldwide, and billions are living as squatters in slums.
Millions more live in cramped quarters of Hong Kong, victims of vested interest.
Even in the States, millions of households live in daily stress with a housing burden.
South Africa still suffers extreme inequality with a fifth of its people in abject poverty.
China has eliminated abject poverty, but 600 m people still earn < 1,000 yuan monthly.
Elders of South Korea are in relative poverty, the US has 40 m in poverty amidst plenty!
War destruction and displacement, alarmingly increase suicide rate of children, in Syria.
Suicide in South Korea is highest among OECD, and among the unemployed in the EU.
Suicide is also a major national public health issue in the USA, 48,344 recorded in 2018.
Likely the prevalence of World Miseries is much more than what visibly meets the eye.
Like for every sucide reported, there are 10 times more people who have attempted.

The average family just needed a few hundred dollars for an occasional emergence.
A Korean elder recycling trash said, "I just need a bit more money every month".
A UBI of $100/mth or less can still be a huge relief to many in our World of Miseries.

Capitalism, the Evil of Modern Societies

Simply put, Capitalism has generated the Poverty that we observe worldwide to this day.
"...for if we examine the case minutely it will be found that the accumulation of personal property is, in many instances, the effect of paying too little for the labor that produced it; the consequence of which is, that the working hand perishes in old age, and the employer abounds in affluence." (*Agrarian Justice. Thomas Paine, 1817*)

Capitalism creates Inequality
Wealth per adult, world's mean value ($79,952) is 10x more than World's median value.
That is, 50% of citizens are worth <1/10 of the average person (Credit Suisse, 2021).
In the States, top 1% wealth share rose to 39% in 2014 (World Inequality Report, 2018)
In socialist Russia and China, the top 1% wealth share doubled to 30% and 43%, 2015.

Capitalism is Selfish
The crisis of Wall Street in 2008 was due to overblown subprime home mortgage debt.
The high-profile corporate meltdowns of China Evergrande, HNA Group of Hainan, ..
Exposing these companies' high risk exposures from endless debt-fueled acquisitions.
Selfish pseudo-entrepreneurs shamelessly taking billions of 'profits' in the boardrooms.
Even stealing from Welfare, capitalizes as Bronx Homeless Shelter /CORE Services, ..
Welfare diversion to capitalist programs like overnight camps/sex education, ineffective.

Capitalism Corrupts
As capitalists with vested interests influence the democratic process with huge funding.
Automation raises efficiency generating immense profits but also makes many jobless.
Capitalism encourages the 'Winner-take-all' culture, making Billionaires/Homelessness.
And the government conniving, 99% of the Internal Revenue Code teaches tax evasion !
Odd Taxation bias has Amazon paying no tax, Warren Buffett paying less than secretary.

Comments:
Indeed, Capitalism has created this quote: "The rugged face of society, checkered with the extremes of affluence and want, proves that some extraordinary violence has been committed upon it, and calls on justice for redress. The great mass of the poor in all countries are becoming a hereditary race, and it is next to impossible for them to get out of that state of themselves. It ought also to be observed that this mass increases in all countries that are called *civilized*." (*Agrarian Justice.* Thomas Paine, 1817)

  To help the masses, Paine also proposes "To create a National Fund, .. to pay every person, when arrived at the age of twenty-one years, the sum of fifteen pounds sterling .. And also the sum of ten pounds per annum, during life, to every person now living, of the age of fifty years, and to all others as they shall arrive at that age."
Paine's plan of a 'UBI' to relieve inequality /poverty is indeed pragmatic and simple.

UBI Studies: All Positivity

Facts and figures are from the precised articles in the previous section on UBI Studies.

Studies clearly show UBI alleviating poverty even with very small amounts of cash.
Brazil Quatinga recipients use the cash to improve life with basic needs, no drug abuse.
Indian recipient villages showed better child nutrition/school attendance/less illnesses.
Kenyan recipients ate better, less likely to get sick and even started small businesses.
Cherokee Indians saw 40% reduction in kids' behavioral problems and 22% less crime.

UBI cash deliveries can be instantaneously completed, almost at no cost !
Brazil Marica recipients automatically received the cash pay to their 'Mumbucas' card.
Kenyan recipients received cash on day 1 of each month when their handphones 'ding'.

UBI is fairer with cash, and has the same impact on everyone.
Iran's subsidies changed to cash transfer, up to 29% of the nation's median income.
Economists found people didn't work less, small businesses like deliverymen flourish.

UBI the little extra cash that make everybody happy
Alaskan residents happily received an average of $1,000/yr Oil Dividend since 1982.
Likewise, Sherman County has given each family $590/yr Wind Dividend since 2002.

UBI is the urgent cash needed in an emergency
Not every county has a Dolly Parton in their midst to help in a sudden crisis.
UBI cash guarantee is also a daily relief for those living from paycheck to paycheck.

UBI is a birthright, sharing the country's resources and wealth
Mongolians as co-owners of the country share in its mineral wealth directly, equally.

UBI assists emerging youths first entry into society
Korean Youth Basic Income encourages 24-year-olds, help focus on self-improvement.
Santa Clara helps foster youths at 25 to sustain their basic needs on first leaving home.

UBI for promoting childbirth
Korea's aging population is aided with an incentive for childbirth, $442/new born.
Comments
Even a little UBI cash significantly alleviates poverty in the villages across the world.
But consistently show better nutrition/education/mental health, reduced illnesses/crime.
In the city, UBI helps the aged, the youths and the average families meeting ends meet.
Also these studies saw no abuse of UBI cash, like alcoholism /reduced employment.
Besides, UBI can help with another major problem of humankind, the aging population.
In short, UBI cash is the panacea of relief to the majority living under constant stress.

UBI is Birthright

Simply, Paine establishes the Birthright of every one to the shared property of the soil.
"...that the earth, in its natural uncultivated state, was the common property of the human race. In that state every man would have been born to property. He would have been a joint life proprietor with the rest in the property of the soil, and in all its natural productions, vegetable and animal." (*Agrarian Justice.* Paine, 1817)

The so-called 'Civilization' has robbed many of their Birthright to a decent living.
"...The most affluent and the most miserable of the human race are to be found in the countries that are called *civilized*... Poverty therefore, is a thing created by that which is called *civilized* life. It exists not in the natural state. ..The life of an Indian is a continual holiday, compared with the poor of Europe;" (*Agrarian Justice.* Paine, 1817)

The UN has affirmed that everyone has the Right to an adequate standard of living.
The Universal Declaration of Human Rights, proclaimed by the United Nations General Assembly in Paris on 10 December 1948 (General Assembly resolution 217A).
Article 25
1. Everyone has the right to a standard of living adequate for the health and well-being of himself and of his family, including food, clothing, housing, and medical care and necessary social services, and the right to security in the event of unemployment, sickness, disability, widowhood, old age or other lack of livelihood in circumstances beyond his control."
2. Motherhood and childhood are entitled to special care and assistance. All children, whether born in or out of wedlock, shall enjoy the same social protection.

Birthright to defend a nation is birthright to a shared Universal Basic Income (UBI)
Recently when war broke out between Russia and Ukraine, the latter government decreed restricting all adult males from leaving to help to defend and die for the country. It is fair to say, "where there is duty, there is privilege". Therefore in Peacetime, all nations should honor their citizens with a survival Universal Basic Income.
Comments:
Children of the rich are born to inherit their forebares's properties and possessions.
Thus everyone born to the motherland has birthrights to the soil and resources therein.
In our 'uncivilized' world, the minority rich have denied the majority their fair share!
Even in rich nations like the USA, many workers are living from paycheck to paycheck.
Millions more are living in abject poverty, especially in sub-saharan countries in Africa.
Universal Basic Income (UBI) is direct, guaranteed cash in the hands of everyone alike.
Studies show people can do better with cash money than bureaucrats in welfare services.
There is no need to tax and rob the rich (so to speak) to finance a UBI for every one.
The huge wealth created by technologies, let it not be 'stolen' but harnessed for a UBI.
Give the money directly to the people and they will do the rest; it is that simple!

UBI in Human Rights

Universal Declaration of Human Rights

https://www.un.org/en/about-us/universal-declaration-of-human-rights

The Universal Declaration of Human Rights (UDHR) is a milestone document in the history of human rights. Drafted by representatives with different legal and cultural backgrounds from all regions of the world, the Declaration was proclaimed by the United Nations General Assembly in Paris on 10 December 1948 (General Assembly resolution 217 A) as a common standard of achievements for all peoples and all nations.

..Article 1

All human beings are born free and equal in dignity and rights. They are endowed with reason and conscience and should act towards one another in a spirit of brotherhood.

..Article 3

Everyone has the right to life, liberty and security of person.

..Article 4

No one shall be held in slavery or servitude; slavery and the slave trade shall be prohibited in all their forms.

..Article 27

1. Everyone has the right freely to participate in the cultural life of the community, to enjoy the arts and *to share in scientific advancement and its benefits.*

2. Everyone has the right to the protection of the moral and material interests resulting from any scientific, literary or artistic production of which he is the author.

..Article 29

1. *Everyone has duties to the community* in which alone the free and full development of his personality is possible.

2. In the exercise of his rights and freedoms, everyone shall be subject only to such limitations as are determined by law solely for the purpose of securing due recognition *and respect for the rights and freedoms of others* and of meeting the just requirements of morality, public order and the general welfare in a democratic society.

3. These rights and freedoms may in no case be exercised contrary to the purposes and principles of the United Nations.

Comments:

Art.1: All human beings are born free and equal in dignity and rights (*i.e. land rights*).

Art.27.1: Everyone... to share in scientific advancement and its benefits.

Art.29: Everyone has duties to the community..respect for the rights, freedoms of others.

Land rights and benefits from scientific advancement are revenue supports for a UBI.

The Human Right to Guarantee UBI ought to be added into the UDHR as article 31 !

UBI is Justice

(*Agrarian Justice*, 1817 by Thomas Paine)
".. Cultivation is at least one of the greatest natural improvements ever made by human invention. It has given to created earth a tenfold value. But the landed monopoly that began with it has produced the greatest evil. It has dispossessed more than half the inhabitants of every nation of their natural inheritance, without providing for them, as ought to have been done, an indemnification for that loss, and has thereby created a species of poverty and wretchedness that did not exist before ..In advocating the case of the persons thus dispossessed, it is a right, and not a charity, that I am pleading for. Every proprietor of cultivated land owes to the community a ground-rent. ..To create a National Fund, out of which there shall be paid to *every person*, when arrived at the age of twenty-one years, the sum of fifteen pounds sterling, as a compensation in part, for the loss of his or her natural inheritance, by the introduction of the system of landed property: And also, the sum of ten pounds per annum, during life, to every person now living, of the age of fifty years, and to all others as they shall arrive at that age. "
"...It is not charity but a right, not bounty *but justice,* that I am pleading for. The present state of civilization is as odious as it is unjust. It is absolutely the opposite of what it should be, and it is necessary that a revolution should be made in it. The contrast of affluence and wretchedness continually meeting and offending the eye, is like dead and living bodies chained together .."
".. The rugged face of society, chequered with the extremes of affluence and want, proves that some extraordinary violence has been committed upon it, and calls on *justice* for redress. The great mass of the poor in all countries are become an hereditary race, and it is next to impossible for them to get out of that state of themselves. It ought also to be observed that this mass increases in all countries that are called civilized."

(*From Wikipedia, 11 Dec 2021 (https://en.wikipedia.org/wiki/Gross_domestic_product)*
"..GDP does not take into account the value of household and other unpaid work. Some, including Martha Nussbaum, argue that this value should be included in measuring GDP, as household labor is largely a substitute for goods and services that would otherwise be purchased for value. Even under conservative estimates, *the value* of *unpaid labor in Australia has been calculated to be over 50% of the country's GDP.* A later study analyzed this value in other countries, with results ranging from a low of about 15% in Canada (using conservative estimates) to high of nearly 70% in the United Kingdom (using more liberal estimates). For the United States, the value was estimated to be between about 20% on the low end to nearly 50% on the high end, depending on the methodology being used."

Comments

In 1817, Thomas Paine eloquently presented the concept of a Universal Basic Income (UBI) as *Justice* to redress the atrocities committed upon the masses by land-owners. Today, Martha Nussbaum and others argue that household labor is largely unpaid labor. Studies have calculated the value ranging between 15% to 70% of the country's GDP.
Ample reason to pay a UBI, at least to do Justice to women at home raising kids.

UBI for A Healthy Population

UBI pilot studies find recipients mentally relieved, healthier with less hospital visits.

Families in Dauphin were guaranteed an annual income of C$16K from 1974 - 1979. Analyzing the health administration data routinely collected in the province of Manitoba for the same period, researchers found ".. significant reduction in hospitalization, especially admissions for mental health, accidents and injuries, .." *(Forget, 2011)*

Ontario BI pilot study guaranteed C$17K/yr for singles, was aborted after 17 months. Still a survey of over 200 subjects shows, "Around a third of all subjects reported reductions in visits to doctors and hospital emergency rooms. This suggests basic income may be a useful general public health strategy .." (*Haridy, 2020)*

Among those receiving unemployment benefits from Kela, 2000 were selected. They were given 560 euros/mth directly with no string attached for 2 years. ".. recipients reported better financial well-being, better mental health, better cognitive function, more confidence for the future than the control unselected group." (*Lu, 2020)*

Everyone in 8 villages received grants of 200 Rupees, none in the other 12 villages. "In 2013, preliminary findings show recipient villages showing numerous improvements in health, productivity and financial stability. There were improved children's nutrition, lower rates of illness, more school attendance." (*MPUCTP, 2015)*

"Kenyans receiving the UBI felt less hunger, with best results from the long-term group. General health including mental health improved with reduced hospital utilization thus helping to preserve hospital capacity. Peace of mind that at least one stream of income would remain steady certainly is a factor for the well-being of people .." *(Eckas, 2021)*

Stockton's BI trial selected 125 low income subjects to receive $500/mth for 18 months. ".. the cash recipients were healthier, happier, and less anxious than their counterparts in the control group. *"Cash is a better way to cure some forms of depression and anxiety than Prozac,"* says Michael Tubbs." *(Lowrey, 2021)*

Cherokee Indians receive cash twice a year from the profits of the Harrah's Casino. " The money amounting to 30% of poor family income improved parenting quality. Kids lifted out of poverty saw behavioral problems decrease 40% .." *(Sutter, 2015)*

Comments:
Projects above listed and in the Studies section invariable find recipients healthier. They are mentally relieved with the certainty of a basic income for their basic needs. They are ill less often with fewer visits to doctors and hospital admission for accidents. ***Haridy (2020) suggests basic income may be a useful general public health strategy.***

UBI for Crime Reduction

Many pilot projects in the UBI Studies section show distinct linkage to Crime reduction.

Since 1996, the Eastern Band of Cherokee Indians based in North Carolina has been paid several thousand dollars twice a year from the profits of the Harrah's Casino. A study of the effects on children found significant declines in poverty, behavioral problems, crime, substance abuse and psychiatric problems, and increases in on-time graduation. "Jane Costello, a Duke University researcher, had studied the effects of these payments on 1,420 Cherokee-area children over the course of 20 years. The money amounting to 30% of poor family income improved parenting quality. Kids lifted out of poverty saw behavioral problems decrease 40% and reduced crime rate by 22%." (Sutter, 2015)

The Basic Income Grant (BIG) pilot project was run in the Namibian settlement of about 1,000 people in the Otjievero-Omitara area over 2 years, from Jan. 2008 to Dec.2009. The grant was N$100 per person per month (8% of the average income, around US$12), cash paid unconditionally to all residents below the age of 60 and registered living there in July 2007, regardless of social or economic status.
Initially, Otjievero-Omitara was a hopeless area of unemployment, hunger and poverty.
Findings 12 months after implementation of Basic Income Grant (BIG) project were:
a. BIG empowered formation of a local committee to advise residents on use of grants.
b. Start of small businesses such as dress-making, bakery and brick-making.
c. Contributed to creation of a local market by increasing household buying power.
d. Resulted in a huge reduction of child malnutrition.
e. Schooling-going children double with parents willing to pay fees (90%) and uniforms.
f. Residents could afford the settlement's clinic that charged N$4 per visit.
g. Reduced household debt and increased savings, reflected in having more lifestocks.
h. Reduced crime significantly as reports to the local police station down by 42%.
i. Reduced dependency of women on men, reflected in less transactional sex activity.
j. The criticism that BIG leads to alcoholism is not supported by the empirical evidence.
(Claudia & Haarmann, 2020. The Pilot Project - an executive summary. BIG Coalition.)

Comments:
Besides the host of benefits that UBI grants bring, they importantly reduced crime rates.
UBI grants at 30% of Cherokeee Indian family income saw crime rate reduced by 22%.
And UBI at only 8% of average income in Namibian settlement reduced crime by 42%.
This is very encouraging empirical evidence that also points to potential savings.
A safer environment is savings from having a smaller police force /number of prisons.

UBI is Education and Hope for the Future

More school Attendance for children in the Indian villages is more hope for the future.
"The Madhya Pradesh Unconditional Cash Transfers Project (MPUCTP): ..In 2013, preliminary findings show recipient villages showing numerous improvements in health, productivity and financial stability. There were improved children's nutrition, lower rates of illness, *more school attendance*." *(Wikipedia, Aug.2021)*

UBI in Kenya encouraged adult people to get an education, invest in their future.
"UBI recipients can afford to eat better, rest when they need it and are less likely to get sick. UBI encourages people to get an education, invest in their future." *(Piper, 2020)*

Namibia, Otjievero-Omitara was a hopeless area of unemployment, hunger and poverty.
"Findings 12 months after implementation of Basic Income Grant (BIG) project were:
d. Resulted in a huge reduction of child malnutrition.
e. Schooling-going children double with parents willing to pay fees (90%) and uniforms.
f. Residents could afford the settlement's clinic that charged N\$4 per visit." *Claudia & Haarmann, 2020)*

In Manitoba Canada, just guaranteed an Annual Income can improve education.
"This research did not use the Mincome data directly, but revisited the outcome of the study with analysis of the health administration data routinely collected in the province of Manitoba between 1974 and 1979. They found significant reduction in hospitalization, especially admissions for mental health, accidents and injuries, and a greater proportion of students finishing high school." *(Forget, 2011)*

Canada Ontario's Basic Income allows adults to up-skill for future employment.
"Only 17 percent of those in the pilot leave employment and most significantly, nearly half of those subjects returned to school or university to up-skill for future employment. A 35-year-old man describes how the basic income allowed him to complete a training course which resulted in him getting a security guard license." *(Haridy, 2020)*

And Casino's small-scale basic income for Cherokee Indians improves graduation.
"A study of the effects on children found significant declines in poverty, behavioral problems, crime, substance abuse and psychiatric problems, and increases in on-time graduation." *(wikipedia.org Sep. 2021. UBI around the world)*

Comments:
Worldwide, Basic Income experiments commonly reported improvement in education. Children now eat better and parents are willing to pay fees and uniforms for schooling. The extra dollars also allow adults to leave jobs temporarily for training for better work.
Even a small-scale Basic Income supports Education, raising Hope for the Future.

UBI is Liberation Long Overdue

Long ago, Laozi (c.580BC) scolded the ruling elite as head of robbers. (Jingwei, 2012)

06朝甚除	Palace steps very high (grand building)
07田甚芜	Crop fields very overgrown (with grass)
08仓甚虚	The granary nearly empty
09服文采	Cloth in finery (Lords and Kings)
10带利剑	Carry sharp swords
11厌饮食	Over-indulge in food and wine
12财货有余	Wealth and goods possession in excess
13是谓盗夸	They are chiefs of robbers
14非道也哉！	Not in accord with Dao indeed *(Daodejing, ch. 53)*

Yangzhu (c.395-335BC) in the Leizi called the elite termites of nature. (Jingwei, 2021)

01 杨朱曰：	Yangzhu Said:
02 "丰屋美服,	"Luxurious House Beautiful Clothes,
03 厚味姣色,	Rich Taste (food) Pretty Color (sex)
04 有此四者,	Having These 4 Things,
05 何求于外？	What Else To Request ?
06 有此而求外者,	People Having These And still Request More,
07 无厌之性。	Never Dislike (always greedy) This Character.
08 无厌之性,	Never Dislike (wanting ever more) This Character,
09 阴阳之蠹也。	The Termites of Yin Yang (Nature)that's. *(Liezi, ch.7.16)*

And Thomas Paine (1737-1809) has called out the despicable nature of the most affluent in his Agrarian Justice.

"The present state of *civilization* is as odious as it is unjust. It is absolutely the opposite of what it should be, and it is necessary that a revolution should be made in it. The contrast of affluence and wretchedness continually meeting and offending the eye, is like dead and living bodies chained together…" *(Paine, 1817)*

Paine has proposed a UBI plan, easy to implement and is the exact Panacea we needed!

"The plan here proposed will reach the whole. It will immediately relieve and take out of view three classes of wretchedness--the blind, the lame, and the aged poor; and it will furnish the rising generation with means to prevent their becoming poor;" *(Agrarian Justice, 1817)*

Comments:

Today, poverty is still endemic in the world as revealed in the World of Miseries section.

The Homeless, estimated at 100m people worldwide, a billion more living as squatters.

They are citizens living in cramped quarters in Hong Kong, victims of vested interest.

Also the millions of households, daily stressed with a housing burden in the U.S.A.

South Africa still suffers extreme inequality with a fifth of its people in abject poverty.

Suicide is the fourth highest cause of death in South Korea, highest amongst the OECD.

Suicide is also a major national public health issue in the USA, 48,344 recorded in 2018.

Indeed, liberation by UBI is long overdue.

UBI Bears No Stigma

Society is prejudiced, the unfortunate are people responsible for their own misfortune.
The affected are so ashamed of themselves, often they reject what little help was offered.
"..According to Japanese laws, begging is not allowed in the country and may constitute a criminal offense. Together with this situation of illegality, is the socially extended prejudice that considers homeless people to be solely responsible for their misfortune. ..and no solutions being provided for a situation which, given that social stigma, even the homeless considered to be shameful. To such an extent that many of those affected would reject what little help was offered as they considered it to be offensive."
(Eduardo, 2021)

This stigmatization of those in need of assistance seems 'universal' worldwide.
Even in first world countries such as the USA, says the UN Special Rapporteur.
"GENEVA (4 June 2018) – The United States' principal strategy for dealing with extreme poverty is to criminalize and stigmatize those in need of assistance, .."For one of the world's wealthiest countries to have 40 million people living in poverty and over five million living in 'Third World' conditions is cruel and inhuman," the UN Special Rapporteur on extreme poverty and human rights, Philip Alston, said in a new report."
(UN expert, 2019)

Public assistance recipients are perceived as less hardworking or worthy than others.
And they often try to hide their participation to avoid further stigmatization.
"STIGMA OF PUBLIC ASSISTANCE: Though public assistance programs are funded by public dollars, participation in these programs has always been stigmatized, creating animosity between people of different socioeconomic classes. From the perspective of people who have wealth and privilege, people receiving public assistance may be perceived as less hardworking or worthy than others. Because of this, individuals receiving assistance often try to hide their participation to avoid further stigmatization."
(Overview, 2021)

In contrast, a UBI policy is guaranteed to reach everyone alike, regardless of status.
Thus there is no question of a stigma in receiving support from a UBI program.
"If every person received the same basic income "floor" regardless of income, class, race, location of residence, or other status, the stigma of receiving support could be eliminated." *(Overview, 2021)*

Comments:
It is very unkind to assume that those in need of assistance are less worthy than others.
Forty years ago, my generation was fortunate to buy a 5-room HDB flat for 30 SGD.
In contrast, today my children's generation needs to fork out >300 SGD for the same.
Also, the enormous wealth generated by automation has been 'hijacked' by billionaires.
So, it is time for a modest UBI to level the playing field for everyone, with no Stigma.

World Population shrinkage

Total Fertility Rate 2022
https://worldpopulationreview.com/country-rankings/total-fertility-rate
.. According to World Bank data, the global fertility rate was 2.4 children per woman in 2019. This rate is approximately half of what it was in 1950 (4.7), and more economically developed countries such as Australia, most of Europe, and South Korea, tend to have lower rates than do less-developed or low-income countries. Three main factors have been credited for a decrease in the global fertility rate: fewer deaths in childhood, greater access to contraception, and more women are getting an education and seeking to establish their careers before—and sometimes instead of—having a family. The population replacement rate, which is the fertility rate needed to maintain a society's population size, is 2.1 children per woman. Countries with fertility rates below this number may experience an overall older demographic and a decrease in population size over time. Lower fertility rates and the resulting population contraction can be seen as beneficial in some countries, especially those experiencing overpopulation, by reducing the strain on infrastructure and social programs. However, lower fertility rates can also lead to challenges, such as a workforce that lacks the new workers it needs to replace those who are retiring, or too few workers paying into social programs (such as Social Security in the U.S.) that support those who cannot work or have retired.

..Fertility rates in Africa: The vast majority of the countries with the highest fertility rates are in Africa. Collectively, the countries of Sub-Saharan Africa have the highest average fertility rate in the world at 4.6. Niger tops the list at 6.8 children per woman, ..While it is true that many African countries are experiencing declining fertility rates ..these reductions reflect a global trend as opposed to a regional one.
..Fertility rates in Asia: South Korea has the lowest fertility rate globally at 0.9 children per woman, ..The two most populous countries in the world, China (1.7) and India (2.2) have fertility rates on the lower-middle part of the scale. ..figures are impacted by government policies ..China, for instance, maintained a "one-child policy" from roughly 1980 until 2016, but passed a law in August 2021 formally declaring married couples could have as many as three children.
..Fertility rate in Europe: is relatively low overall, with no countries above 2.0, and has declined in recent years—which is, as stated previously, a global trend. Several factors are credited for driving this trend, including socioeconomic incentives to delay childbearing, a decline in the desired number of children, a lack of child care, and changing gender roles.
Comments:
The global trend is declining fertility rates in all other countries, rich and poor alike.
All European countries have fertility rate below 2.1 the population replacement rate.
South Korea at 1 is lowest, and Japan at 1.4 recently reported more deaths than births !
UBI may be helpful in reversing this trend as Financial burden is the main reason.

UBI Benefits Children Especially

"The project started in 2008, organized by the non-profit organization ReCivitas.
It provided R30 monthly (4.4% of minimum salary, 2013), just sufficient to help people satisfy the most basic material needs. Even with such a small amount of money, when people's most basic needs are met, the positive impacts are huge. Children especially enjoy the benefits and the results indicate that the BI contributed to sustainable development in Quatinga Velho." *(wikipedia.org Sep. 2021. UBI around the world)*

"The Madhya Pradesh Unconditional Cash Transfers Project (MPUCTP): ..In 2013, preliminary findings show recipient villages showing numerous improvements in health, productivity and financial stability. There were improved children's nutrition, lower rates of illness, more school attendance. *(Wikipedia, Aug.2021)*

The Basic Income Grant (BIG) pilot project was run in the Namibian settlement.
"Initially, Otjievero-Omitara was a hopeless area of unemployment, hunger and poverty.
Findings 12 months after implementation of Basic Income Grant (BIG) project were:
d. Resulted in a huge reduction of child malnutrition.
e. Schooling-going children double with parents willing to pay fees (90%) and uniforms.
(Claudia & Haarmann - BIG Coalition, 2020.)

"..Since 1996, the Eastern Band of Cherokee Indians based in North Carolina has been paid several thousand dollars twice a year from the profits of the Harrah's Casino. A study of the effects on children found significant declines in poverty, behavioral problems, crime, substance abuse and psychiatric problems, and increases in on-time graduation." *(wikipedia.org Sep. 2021. USA, small-scale basic income)*

Single mothers are particularly targeted with assistance for their child.
"A nonprofit organization was looking to give 20 African American single mothers living in public housing $1,000 each month for a year. They'd be able to use the money in any way they pleased. ..At the end of six months, none of the women reported using an emergency lender. Nearly all said they had enough money to buy school supplies, when fewer than half had said that before. They reported cooking more balanced meals, visiting the doctor and attending church more often. *(Samuels, 2019)*

And Switzerland's plan of a guaranteed basic income for all, includes children.
"The proposal: an unconditional monthly income for all adults, whether working or not.
Supporters suggested a monthly income of SFr2,500 for an adult, SFr625 for a child.
(BBC News, 5 June 2016. Switzerland's voters reject basic income plan)
Comments:
Children are the priority of parents, and UBI positively affects their future development.
UBI benefits children in particular, and raises hope for their future.

Youth Basic Income

Young people emerging into the work market for the first time deserve UBI support.

Aware of the vulnerability of youth, Paine suggested giving them 15 pounds at age 21.
"..To create a National Fund, out of which there shall be paid to *every person*, when
arrived at the age of twenty-one years, the sum of fifteen pounds sterling, as a
compensation in part, for the loss of his or her natural inheritance, by the introduction of
the system of landed property: And also, the sum of ten pounds per annum, during life,
to every person now living, of the age of fifty years, and to all others as they shall arrive
at that age." *(Paine, 1817)*

South Korea had one of the highest youth unemployment rates at 10.4% in 2019.
"The largest UBI trial in Asia to date, the mayor of Seongnam in Gyeonggi Province
initiated the Youth Basic Income in 2018. At 24, most young South Koreans graduate
from university. Many need to take additional courses to develop skills or qualification
to get a job. The 175,000 24-year-olds in Gyeonggi, each receive an equivalent of $220
in a locally negotiable currency per quarter via a credit card for a single year. The
amount is small, but the program is popular with young people and local businesses.
With the money, they quit their temporary job to focus on self-improvement."*(Li, 2021)*

Santa Clara County rolls out a UBI program for youth transitioning out of foster care.
"..provides a monthly stipend of $1,000 for a year to former foster youth ages 24 and
over who are too old to receive foster assistance...Foster youth stop receiving assistance
from the county at 25, .."When you turn 25 you are alone, no one is helping you. You
have to work for everything. ... All of a sudden you lost your job, and you can't pay for
rent, who are you going to go to? Your family. A lot of foster youth don't have that,"
Grano said...Supervisor Dave Cortese spearheaded the initiative after meeting with local
philanthropist Gisele Huff, who is also the president of the nonprofit organization The
Gerald Huff Fund for Humanity."(*Bay City News Service Jul28, 2020)*
Comments:
Korea's Youth Basic Income, paid universally to all 24-years-olds, quarterly for a year.
It is "local currency" in a credit card, to be spent in the province, but no McDonald's.
The 175,000 recipients are happier and their willingness to work has not diminished.
Quality of lives improved and they had more trust in politics, law and fellow citizens.
Foster Youths have no family to turn to when they reach 25 and county assistance stops.
Senator Cortese is examplary, stepping in with a stipend of $1,000/month for a year.
Respondents reported using the fund to sustain basic needs, improve their credit score.
This is like Paine's idea of giving everyone, at the age of 21, the sum of fifteen pounds.
Not many starting life have family support; a national UBI for everyone is only fair.

The Aged Deserves UBI Support for a Graceful Closure

It is our responsibility collectively to enable the aged to have a gracious closure in life.

*And so it is written in the Rites of Zhou (*周礼 *.*礼運*) some 2,500 years ago:*

使老有所終	Enabling **the Old** to Have Provision for Closure
壯有所用	the Strong Have Provision for Employment
幼有所長	the Youngs have Provision for Growth
矜寡孤獨廢疾者	Weak,Widowed,Single,Lonely,Abandoned,Sick
皆有所養	All Have Provision for Care *(Jingwei, 2019)*

More recently, Paine (1871) proposed a UBI plan to address the plight of the aged poor. "The plan here proposed will reach the whole. It will immediately relieve and take out of view three classes of wretchedness--the blind, the lame, and **the aged poor**; and it will furnish the rising generation with means to prevent their becoming poor; and it will do this without deranging or interfering with any national measures."

The over caring culture in the East often causes old people to be trapped in poverty. "..Ironically, part of the reason for their plight may be the cost of supporting their own offspring. "While they were still working," says Shin, "many elderly people were unable to put aside enough savings for later in life because they spent too much on their children's education." ..A woman in her late 70s says she can't afford to feed herself on her pension. "I come here for free meals," says the woman, who declines to give her name. "My children can't help me because they are struggling financially themselves. *I don't want much, but a bit more money every month would be a great help." (McCurry, 2017. South Korea's inequality paradox: long life, good health and ..)*

Around the world, old folks too feeble to help themselves often ended up in tragedy. "..For 2009–2011, 44% of all suicides occurred among those aged 65 or above and 79% among rural residents." (*Wikipedia, 10 November 2021. Suicide in China)*

 The 70 year-old said, "And just a bit more money every month would be a great help." "..A woman in her late 70s says she can't afford to feed herself on her pension. "I come here for free meals," says the woman, who declines to give her name. "My children can't help me because they are struggling financially themselves. I don't want much, but a bit more money every month would be a great help." *(McCurry, 2017. South Korea's inequality paradox: long life, good health and ..)*

Comments:
"I don't want much, but a bit more money every month would be a great help.*"*
Only a UBI can reach everyone without fail, and just a modest UBI is needed.
Can we deny anyone in distress a modest UBI that is an 'inherited' right.

Is it Doubly Criminal to deny Women the UBI ?

Thomas Paine says it is criminal to deny people UBI, the compensation for loss of natural inheritance.

"To create a National Fund, out of which there shall be paid to *every person*, when arrived at the age of twenty-one years, the sum of fifteen pounds sterling, as a compensation in part, for the loss of his or her natural inheritance, by the introduction of the system of landed property: And also, the sum of ten pounds per annum, during life, to every person now living, of the age of fifty years, and to all others as they shall arrive at that age. ..The fault, however, is not in the present possessors. No complaint is intended, or ought to be alleged against them, unless they adopt the crime by opposing justice." *(Paine, 1817)*

Thus women are doubly discriminated against, raising families with no-pay /no UBI.
"There is money for saving corporations in the pandemic, there is money to pay for UBI. **Women working at home giving care, the value of unpaid work is estimated >50% GDP.**" *(Nwanazia, 2021)*

UBI projects benefiting women in the villages always benefited the children first.
"The Madhya Pradesh Unconditional Cash Transfers Project (MPUCTP): .. In 2013, preliminary findings show recipient villages showing numerous improvements in health, productivity and financial stability. There were improved children's nutrition, lower rates of illness, more school attendance." *(Wikipedia, Aug.2021)*

Children aside, women needed UBI themselves to reduce their dependence on men.
"Namibia: 12 months after implementation of Basic Income Grant (BIG) project:
d. Resulted in a huge reduction of child malnutrition.
e. Schooling-going children double with parents willing to pay fees (90%) and uniforms.
f. Residents could afford the settlement's clinic that charged N$4 per visit.
i. Reduced dependency of women on men, reflected in less transactional sex activity."
(Claudia & Haarmann - BIG Coalition, 2020)

And UBI cash to single moms in Jackson literally makes them 'walk on air' like Liezi !
"The beauty of all of this has just been how folks are light," Nyandoro said. "They aren't walking around with the heaviness of life that, unfortunately, so many times low-income folks have to carry." *(Samuels, 2019)*

Comments:
Ancient Laozi has poetically appreciated the supportive role of women. (Jingwei, 2012)
守其雌　　　　　　　　　Hold the female (support position)
为天下谿　　　　　　　　Be the world's creek (small stream) (ch.28)
Yes indeed for so many reasons, is it Doubly Criminal to deny Women their UBI.

It is Criminal to Oppose UBI

In the 19th century, Paine was abhorred by the misery he saw of the human race.
"...The most affluent and the most miserable of the human race are to be found in the countries that are called civilized... Poverty therefore, is a thing created by that which is called civilized life." *(Paine, 1817)*

He declares that every man born to the land is a joint life proprietor with the rest.
"...that the earth, in its natural uncultivated state, was the common property of the human race. In that state every man would have been born to property. He would have been a joint life proprietor with the rest in the property of the soil, and in all its natural productions, vegetable and animal." *(Paine, 1817)*

He observed that it was the landlords who monopolized the land depriving the masses.
"But the landed monopoly that began with it has produced the greatest evil. It has dispossessed more than half the inhabitants of every nation of their natural inheritance, without providing for them, as ought to have been done, an indemnification for that loss, and has thereby created a species of poverty and wretchedness that did not exist before"
"...for if we examine the case minutely it will be found that the accumulation of personal property is, in many instances, the effect of paying too little for the labor that produced it; the consequence of which is, that the working hand perishes in old age, and the employer abounds in affluence." *(Paine, 1817)*

He advocates that every person has a right to be compensated with a UBI payment.
"..To create a National Fund, out of which there shall be paid to *every person*, when arrived at the age of twenty-one years, the sum of fifteen pounds sterling, as a compensation in part, for the loss of his or her natural inheritance, by the introduction of the system of landed property: And also, the sum of ten pounds per annum, during life, to every person now living, of the age of fifty years, and to all others as they shall arrive at that age." *(Paine, 1817)*

UBI reaches everyone with instant eradication of poverty, hope for future generations.
"The plan here proposed will reach the whole. It will immediately relieve and take out of view three classes of wretchedness--the blind, the lame, and the aged poor; and it will furnish the rising generation with means to prevent their becoming poor; and it will do this without deranging or interfering with any national measures." *(Paine, 1817)*

And that anyone opposing such payment is committing a crime against justice.
"..The fault, however, is not in the present possessors. No complaint is intended, or ought to be alleged against them, unless they adopt the crime by opposing justice. The fault is in the system, and it has stolen imperceptibly upon the world, aided afterwards by the agrarian law of the sword." *(Paine, 1817)*

Comments:
The extreme inequality between the rich and the poor that Paine saw still exists today.
Every man is a joint life proprietor with the rest, in the property of the soil inclusively.
His proposed UBI payment is indeed justice, to reach everybody directly and simply
Thus it is criminal for anyone to oppose Universal Basic Income payment.

Does UBI mean People Work Less ?

"The Manitoba Basic Annual Income Experiment, a $17-million Guaranteed Annual Income (GAI) social experiment in Manitoba, started 1974. The main purpose was to assess if GAI is a disincentive for work by its recipients. It was aborted 1979 and no final Mincome report was issued. .. Several studies emerged between 1984 and 1991. Importantly Derek Hum and Wayne Simpson found little impact on the work behavior of recipients." *(Mason, 2017)*.

"In 2010, Iran cut oil and bread subsidies and replaced them with a guaranteed citizens cash payment equivalent to 29% of the nation's median income. Now 6 years on, economists found no evidence that people work less with a universal basic income. Instead people in the service industry work more expanding their small businesses, or finding better employment. And young people in their twenties only worked a little less because they were enrolled for higher education. "*(Ihaza, 2017)*

"The Self-Employed Women's Association (SEWA) recently completed a large pilot project on Basic Income in India. .. Importantly, the study also found that grant recipients worked more than people in the control villages and that they were three times more likely to start a new business." *(Vanderborght, 2013)*

"The referendum: a guaranteed basic income for all, was rejected by 77% Swiss voters. The proposal: an unconditional monthly income for all adults, whether working or not. Supporters suggested a monthly income of SFr2,500 for an adult, SFr625 for a child. Che Wagner from Basic Income Switzerland argued, it is not money for not working. "In Switzerland over 50% of the total work that is done is unpaid. It's care work, it's at home, it's in different communities, so that work would be more valued with a basic income." *(BBC News, 5 June 2016)*

".. the mayor of Seongnam in Gyeonggi Province initiated the Youth Basic Income in 2018. ..The recipients are happier and the willingness to work among UBI beneficiaries has not wane as some have feared" *(Li, 2021)*

"In the Stockton study, the share of participants with a full-time job rose 12 percentage points, versus five percentage points in the control group." *(Lowrey. 2021)*

Comments:
One argument against UBI is: people work less, adversely affecting the labor market. However most studies found recipients active, enterprising starting small businesses. ***So far, no study on UBI has definitively reported recipients working less.***

Do People abuse the use of UBI ?

"For 3 years now, Recivitas has run a privately funded basic income for a small impoverished rural community. The project pays 30 Brazilian Reals (~US$15) per month to people of Quatinga Velho, São Paulo, Brazil. .. Coordinators noted no increase in alcohol consumption, or illicit drugs." *(Widerquist, June 2012)*

"The Ontario Basic Income Experiment: presented a model where participants were guaranteed either 16,989 CAD (US$12,180) per year if they were single, or 24,027 CAD (US$17,230) per year for a couple. ..Around half of the subjects reported decreased use of alcohol and tobacco, while 79 percent reported better physical well-being and 83 percent reported better mental well-being…" *(Haridy, 2020)*

"The Self-Employed Women's Association (SEWA) recently completed a large pilot project on Basic Income in India. ..Researchers found no increase in alcohol consumption in the treatment villages." *(Vanderborght, Sep.2013)*

"Initially, Otjievero-Omitara was a hopeless area of unemployment, hunger and poverty. Findings 12 months after implementation of Basic Income Grant (BIG) project were: j. The criticism that BIG leads to alcoholism is not supported by the empirical evidence. *(Claudia & Haarmann - BIG Coalition, 2020)*

"Since 1996, the Eastern Band of Cherokee Indians based in North Carolina has been paid several thousand dollars twice a year from the profits of the Harrah's Casino. A study of the effects on children found significant declines in poverty, behavioral problems, crime, substance abuse and psychiatric problems, and increases in on-time graduation." *(wikipedia.org Sep. 2021. UBI around the world)*

"Two years on, using donated funds the industrial city of Stockton launched a small demo program giving cash of $500 a month for 18 months to each recipient, with no strings attached. "The families receiving the $500 a month tended to spend the money on essentials, including food, home goods, utilities, and gas. (Less than 1 percent went to cigarettes and alcohol.)" *(Lowrey. March 2021)*

Comments:
There is no empirical evidence that poor people abuse the use of UBI on drugs/alcohol.
In rural Brazil, people use the small amount of money to meet their most basic needs.
In India, households use their cash wisely, even investing in more life-stocks.
Residents in Stockton spent 40% BI on food, 24% on merchandise, 11% on bills, ..
Cherokee Indians use their small windfall to improve life like going on school trips, ..
Therefore it is a myth that the recipients become poor because they're irrational

UBI: Hope, Business and Prosperity for the Poor

Projects in the UBI Studies section often reveal Hope and Prosperity of recipients.

ReCivitas provided R30/mth to the impoverished community in Quatinga Velho, Brazil. ".. cash aid creates market demand for food and other needs that could be met by entrepreneurs. Some recipients will use the money to start small businesses .." *(Widerquist, 2013)*

Canada's Mincome guaranteed an annual income of $16K to families in Dauphin, 1974. "Her husband was suddenly able to get a loan to open a local record store, with banks being more willing to lend money to small businesses because of the guaranteed payments." *(Cox, 2020)*

SEWA recently completed a large pilot project on Basic Income in India. "Importantly, the study also found that grant recipients worked more than people in the control villages and that they were three times more likely to start a new business." *(Vanderborght, 2013)*

In 2010, Iran replaced subsidies with a guaranteed cash up to 29% of median income. ".. economists found no evidence that people work less ..people in the service industry work more expanding their small businesses, or finding better employment. *(Ihaza, 2017)*

Kenya 2017, some 6,000 recipients in a 12-year trial received 75 cents a day, not much but enough for people to be less food-insecure and more likely to start a business. "UBI lets people start businesses in a good time. UBI makes people more resilient when business is bad like in a lockdown, they can still eat." *(Piper, 2020)*

Namibia. Basic Income Grant (2008 -2009) was N$100/person/month (8% av. income). Initially, Otjievero-Omitara was a hopeless area of unemployment, hunger and poverty. Findings 12 months after implementation of Basic Income Grant (BIG) project were: "b. Start of small businesses such as dress-making, bakery and brick-making." *(Claudia & Haarmann, 2020)*

Comments:
Basic Income cash (8-29% of poor family income) creates demand for food/other needs. People feeling less food-insecure are ready to start small businesses to help themselves. Local banks are more willing to support when there is guaranteed income, albeit small. BI projects raise a flourish of activities in the local market, stimulating the economy. ***Basic Income often instills a sense of 'hope and prosperity' in the local community.***

Economy of a UBI

Small UBI payments not only improve life quality but also stimulate the local economy.

Villages given Basic Income saw three times more new businesses than control villages.
"The Self-Employed Women's Association (SEWA) recently completed a large pilot project on Basic Income in India. ..Researchers found no increase in alcohol consumption in the treatment villages. Importantly, the study also found that grant recipients worked more than people in the control villages and that they were three times more likely to start a new business." *(Vanderborght, 2013)*

Even with 30 Brazilian Reals, some recipients use the money to start new businesses.
".. Also cash aid creates market demand for food and other needs that could be met by entrepreneurs. Some recipients will use the money to start small businesses or pay school fees." *(Widerquist, 2013)*

Canada's Mincome experiment has results, small businesses sprung up over the 4 years.
".. with banks being more willing to lend money to small businesses because of the guaranteed payments. ..But when the experiment ended in 1979, the improvements which had been seen in health and education soon returned to how things had been in 1974. Taylor remembers how many of the small businesses that had sprung up over the preceding four years began to vanish." *(Cox, 2020)*

Labor leader Andy Stern believes raising the floor with a UBI can renew the economy.
"In "Raising the Floor: How a Universal Basic Income Can Renew Our Economy and Rebuild the American Dream" (2016), the labor leader Andy Stern nominates U.B.I. as the right response to technological unemployment..." *(Matthews, 2017)*

In 2010, Iran cut oil and bread subsidies and replaced them with a cash payment.
"Now 6 years on, economists found no evidence that people work less with a universal basic income. Instead people in the service industry work more expanding their small businesses, or finding better employment." *(Ihaza, May 2017)*

Participants of the trial were given 2,250 Kenyan shillings on the first of every month.
"..Each text alert means a chance to invest in their own lives or their businesses with the security that they can still put food on the table. And that, they say, is priceless."
(Arnold, 2018)

Comments:
As Andrew Yang says, giving people UBI cash will result in a trickle-up economy.
With the guaranteed cash monthly, people are willing to spend to improve life quality.
To meet the demand, more shops like bakeries, cafes and beauty salons will spring up.
The local market is stimulated and the trickle-up economy will help increase the GDP.

UBI is Affordable

Basic Income has produced positive results worldwide, hence is the logical next step.
".. Conditional cash transfers like Brazil's Bolsa Familia or Mexico's Oportunidades already play an important role in poverty alleviation. Basic income is the logical next step. And let's not fall prey to the myth that, in poor countries or rich ones, a basic income is unaffordable, .." *(Matthews, 2017)*

Technological advances do generate an abundance of resources to pay for a UBI.
"One reason we think it may work is that technological improvements should generate an abundance of resources," wrote Y Combinator president Sam Altman in a blog post. "Although basic income seems fiscally challenging today, in a world where technology replaces existing jobs and basic income becomes necessary, technological improvements should generate an abundance of resources and the cost of living should fall dramatically." *(Gunn, 2019)*

Alarmingly, incompetent governments the world over allow inequality to rise !
.. However, because of high and rising inequality within countries, the top 1% richest individuals in the world captured twice as much growth as the bottom 50% individuals since 1980. *(World Inequality Report, 2018)*

Financing Basic Income is a political issue; it depends on government's will to do so.
"The level of taxation needed to pay for a basic income is, of course, an important issue. But the sustainable level of taxation in any country is not mainly an economic issue. It is a political issue that depends on the administrative capacity to extract taxes and the political will to do so." (*Wright, 2017)*

With money for saving corporations/sponsoring wars, paying for UBI can be a breeze.
"UBI can be financed with the abolition of tax cuts, tax credit, increased VAT rate, ... There is money for saving corporations in the pandemic, there is money to pay for UBI. During the coronavirus lockdown, governments met the challenge with 'free money'. With so much spent on sponsoring wars, paying for such an endeavor is a breeze."
(Nwanazia, 2021)

But we ought to be mindful of robbing the rich for the poor ending in 'common poverty'.
"Chinese economists were quick to move to ease fears that China's drive for common prosperity signals aggressive policies are afoot that will seize money from the rich to close the country's yawning wealth gap. "Robbing the rich to give to the poor" would only result in "common poverty," said Zhang Jun, .." *(Mullen, 2021)*
Comments:
Indeed, we cannot rob the rich to give to the poor resulting in 'common poverty'.
Neither can we rob the poor to give to the rich by stopping all aid-programs for a UBI.
Automation creates abundance for billionaires, also affordable UBI for 99% others.

UBI Funding

Paine (1817) proposed to collect a ground-rent from every proprietor of cultivated land. As a National Fund to pay every person a UBI for loss of his or her natural inheritance.
"Every proprietor of cultivated land, owes to the community a ground-rent...To create a National Fund, out of which there shall be paid to *every person*, when arrived at the age of twenty-one years, the sum of fifteen pounds sterling, as a compensation in part, for the loss of his or her natural inheritance, by the introduction of the system of landed property: And also, the sum of ten pounds per annum, during life, to every person now living, of the age of fifty years, and to all others as they shall arrive at that age."

Silicon Valley Leaders Think A.I. will one day fund free cash handouts.
"In as little as 10 years, AI could generate enough wealth to pay every adult in the U.S. $13,500 a year, Altman said in his 2,933 word piece called "Moore's Law for Everything" My work at OpenAI reminds me every day about the magnitude of the socioeconomic change that is coming sooner than most people believe," said Altman, the former president of renowned start-up accelerator Y-Combinator earlier this month. "Software that can think and learn will do more and more of the work that people now do." "We could do something called the American Equity Fund," wrote Altman. "The American Equity Fund would be capitalized by taxing companies above a certain valuation 2.5% of their market value each year, payable in shares transferred to the fund, and by taxing 2.5% of the value of all privately-held land, payable in dollars."
He added: "All citizens over 18 would get an annual distribution, in dollars and company shares, into their accounts. People would be entrusted to use the money however they needed or wanted — for better education, healthcare, housing, starting a company, whatever." *(Shead, 2021)*

The potential is even greater in countries with great mineral or natural resource wealth.
"In 2011, Iran introduced basic income providing about 29% of the median household income on average... Thus Oil rich countries in Africa like Nigeria, Angola and Equatorial Guinea can follow Iran's example in this regard. Say, a quarter or a third of revenues are to be distributed as a basic income, you could probably wipe out extreme poverty altogether." *(Matthews, 2017)*

Nwanazia (2021): Salient points on funding a Universal Basic Income UBI).
"UBI can be financed with the abolition of tax cuts, tax credit, increased VAT rate, ... There is money for saving corporations in the pandemic, there is money to pay for UBI. With so much spent on sponsoring wars, paying for such an endeavor (UBI)is a breeze."
Comments:
Motherland has sufficient resources to bequeath every person with a subsistent UBI.
With A.I. creating so much more resources, funding UBI should be a 'breeze' today.
Bad governments have money for saving corporations and money for sponsoring wars !
The majority of us want UBI, hence should make our voice heard at the ballot box.

UBI Implementation is Simplicity

Wright's idea of UBI is indeed quite simple, without touching existing welfare services.
"The idea of an unconditional basic income (UBI) is quite simple: every legal resident in a country receives a monthly stipend sufficient to live above the poverty line. Let's call this the 'no frills culturally respectable standard of living'. The grant is unconditional on the performance of any labour or other form of contribution, and it is universal – everyone receives the grant, rich and poor alike. Grants go to individuals, not families. Parents are the custodians of under-age children's grants which may be smaller. Universalistic programmes such as public education and healthcare, that provide services to people rather than cash, continue alongside UBI, but most other redistributive transfers are eliminated since the UBI provides everyone with a decent subsistence. ...The net increase in cost represented by UBI is not large. Special needs subsidies of various sorts continue – for example, for people with disabilities. Minimum wage rules are relaxed, since all earnings in effect generate discretionary income."
 (Wright, Erik Olin. 2017)

In poorest Kenya, mobile phones can deliver cash to thousands of people, effortlessly.
"Along the shores of Lake Victoria in western Kenya, mobile phones in several hundred villages ding in unison on the first of every month. For more than 21,000 adults, the sound means one thing: 2,250 Kenyan shillings appearing in their bank accounts. The cash equals one-quarter to half of the average income for a two-adult household in Bomet County, one of the poorest in Kenya." *(Arnold, 2018)*

In contrast, documentation/surveillance of benefit programs is highly cost ineffective.
"For the past five decades, the U.S. relied on a patchwork of public assistance programs, such as SNAP, WIC, and Temporary Assistance for Needy Families (TANF). Each program has their own unique eligibility criteria.The government focus on documentation and surveillance as part of these benefit programs is highly inefficient. Outdated systems and technology also lead to increased labor costs and reduced efficiency in administering programs. For participants, these programs demand a significant amount of time, effort, and documentation,.." *(Drexel.edu, 2021)*

Also not implemented as UBI, welfare money has been much abused and wasted !
"In the United States, the federal Temporary Assistance for Needy Families program—often known simply as "welfare"—is administered by the 50 states, which have considerable leeway in how to spend the money. ..But depending on which state you live in, TANF may provide barely any cash assistance at all." *(Parolin, 2019)*
Comments:
Mobile phone technology transfers UBI cash to every person instantly almost at no cost. Whereas welfare money is costly to administer as benefits, open to abuse and wastage.
Distributing UBI cash is simplicity itself; and trust that people are good in self-help.

UBI Relief for Covid Lockdown !

The Covid-19 pandemic had seen nationwide lockdowns, causing millions of job loss. The masses of citizens are at risk, and governments need immediate relief plans.

"Spain's government has started what might just be remembered as the world's biggest economics experiment. On 15 June, it launched a website offering monthly payments of up to €1,015 (US$1,145) to the nation's poorest families. The programme, which will support 850,000 households, is the largest test yet of an idea called universal basic income (UBI) — in which people are given a cash payment each month to spend however they choose." *(Arnold, 2020)*

"Recently, President Joe Biden's $1.9 trillion American Rescue Plan showed how much further policymakers are willing to go to fight poverty through stimulus payments and child tax credit expansions. "But really, this is something that activists and researchers have been working on for decades,"... Chris Hughes argued in the New York Times early in the pandemic last May that *"a guaranteed income should be permanent American policy, not just an emergency measure to help with this crisis."(Zeitlin, 2021)*

"The Macau SAR Government has brought forward its Wealth Partaking Scheme in 2021 due the impact of COVID-19 on the people's livelihoods." *Newsdesk, April 2021. IAG (inside asian gaming)*

The basic income experiment helped Kenyans weather the Covid-19 crisis.
"UBI recipients can afford to eat better, rest when they need it and are less likely to get sick. UBI encourages people to get an education, invest in their future. UBI lets people start businesses in a good time. UBI makes people more resilient when business is bad like in a lockdown, they can still eat. UBI doesn't fix everything, it just makes things a little easier." *(Piper Sep. 2020)*

"..With the outbreak of COVID-19 during the winter of 2019-2020, Mongolian citizens were promised a cheque of up to 96,480 tugrugs (USD 34), ..Mongolians who were born before April 11th 2014 are shareholders of a company called Erdenes Tavan Tolgoi (ETT).. these cash payments are dividends distributed by the company to its shareholders." *(Yorgun, 2020)*

Comments:
To alleviate the impact of COVID-19, people are given cash to spend as they choose.
Spain launched a UBI payment of up to €1,015/mth for the nation's poorest families.
Joe Biden signed a $1.9 trillion American Rescue Plan to aid citizens and businesses.
The Macau SAR Government brought forward its Wealth Partaking Scheme in 2021.
Already in place, a UBI experiment helped Kenyans weather the Covid-19 crisis.
UBI cash for Covid-19 relief has been proven to be swift and efficient, worldwide.

UBI is Dao

Ch. 60 of Laozi's Dao De Jing seems to describe UBI as Dao, exactly !
The chapter is reproduced below for immediate reference.
Having UBI is like having Dao prevailing in the world.
People are empowered and strong to help themselves, to resist all forms of bullying.
Then the ghosts (pseudo-entrepreneurs/capitalists) are powerless to hurt the people.
The Sage (selfish government) is also powerless to hurt the people.
Daoism is government for the benefit of all people, not just for leaders and their cronies.
With Daoism prevailing, there will be harmony, peace, and prosperity in the world.
In a happy environment, the ghosts and the Sage are powerless in hurting the people.
Daoism makes governing as easy as cooking a small fish, and so will having the UBI !

From *Laozi: Quest for the Ultimate Reality.* ISBN 978.981.07.3758.0 *(Jingwei, 2012).*

Dao De Jing

六十章	**Chapter 60**
01治大国, 若烹小鲜	Governing big nation, like cooking small fish
02以道莅天下	With Dao prevailing in the world
03其鬼不神	The ghosts not powered
04非其鬼不神	Not that ghosts not powered
05其神不伤人	Their powers not hurting people
06非其神不伤人	Not that their powers not hurting people
07圣人亦不伤人	The Sage also not hurting people
08夫, 兩不相伤	Indeed, both not hurting (the people)
09故, 德交归焉	Hence, virtues interact and return indeed (to the people)

Laozi's thinking

Governing a big nation is like cooking a small fish. L1
It is this easy, provided that the principles of Dao are established. L2
When Dao prevails in the world, everyone is taken care of and gets a fair share in all things.
The people are not burdened with high taxes, conscription for conquests or building palaces.
There is prosperity and happiness over the land and everybody is contented.
Hence, evil elements, and their powers will not be effective in hurting the people. L3-5
Besides them, the Sage also will not hurt the people. L6,7
Indeed, both do not hurt the people. L8
Hence, their virtues interact and return to benefit the people. L9

Comment

Daoism makes governing easy as cooking a small fish (ch. 60)

Daoism is government for the benefits of people, not for the benefits of leaders and their cronies.
With Daoism prevailing, there will be harmony, peace, and prosperity in the world.
In such a happy environment, the ghosts and the Sage are powerless in hurting the people.
Governing a big nation is as easy as cooking a small fish when Daoism prevails over the land.
Laozi urges the use of Daoism for effective and easy government in the world.

Have UBI will 'Ride on Wind'

Robert Samuels (2019) wrote: *$1,000 a month, no strings attached*
"JACKSON, Miss. —A nonprofit organization was looking to give 20 African American single mothers living in public housing $1,000 each month for a year. They'd be able to use the money in any way they pleased.

.. At the end of six months, none of the women reported using an emergency lender. Nearly all said they had enough money to buy school supplies, when fewer than half had said that before. They reported cooking more balanced meals, visiting the doctor and attending church more often.

"The beauty of all of this has just been how folks are light," Nyandoro said. "They aren't walking around with the heaviness of life that, unfortunately, so many times low-income folks have to carry."

This is reminiscent of the story of Liezi 'Riding on wind'. (Jingwei, 2021).
Chapter 2.3   Return Riding On Wind
It was said that Liezi had attained 'Dao' from Laoshangshi, and had returned 'Riding on Wind'.
Yinsheng had this delusional wish to learn the art of 'Riding on Wind', so went to stay with Liezi.
He left in anger when Liezi refused to teach him anything, only to return a few months later.
Liezi scolded him for being ignoble to this extent and sat him down to listen to his experience.
In 3 years, not dare think of right/wrong, not dare speak of good/evil, the teacher gave a glance.
In 5 years, never think of right/wrong, never speak of good/evil, the teacher only gave a smile.
In 7 years, all thoughts no right/wrong, speaks no good/evil, the teacher allowed to share his mat.
In 9 years, inside and outside all immersed in 'Dao', no more concept of right/wrong, good/evil,

So, it is all about meditating on Right and Wrong, Good and Evil. And for 9 years, not easy !
Relieved of these concepts of self and of others, we shall feel absolutely free in mind and body.
The feeling of 'Riding on Wind' is real, for when happy and carefree, the spring is in every step.
Liezi is certainly not delusional that 'Riding On Wind' is a reality, for he also says:
竟不知风乘我邪？   Somehow Not Know If the Wind is Riding on Me ? L53
我乘风乎？   Or am I Riding on Wind ? L54
Unselfish we can think no wrong, speak no evil, and the world can 'Ride on Wind' together.

Comments:
Liezi was first introduced by Zhuangzi, described as having the ability to 'ride on wind'.
Liezi himself denied this supernatural, saying he does not know if wind is riding on him.
He had merely meditated for 9 years, thinking no right/wrong, speaking no good/evil.
That is, he is a-walking light, liberated from the heavy burden of right/wrong, good/evil.
"Like the folks are light, aren't walking around with the heaviness of life".
As Nyandoro said, ".. unfortunately, so many times low-income folks have to carry."

So, for us all to also 'ride on wind' today, simply implement a universal Basic Income.

Yijing: Is UBI a Good Idea ?

For centuries, *Yijing* has been used in China for divination and prediction of outcome.
It is listed among the 100 most influential books ever written (Seymour-Smith 1998).
I have studied the ancient text directly, and in 2019 self-published my findings:
Yijing: Wisdom of 4 Sages (a complete translation and appreciation of Yijing)
ISBN 978-981-14-0204-3.

When consulted, Yijing does not give a definitive Yes or No answer.
Images of the trigrams and hexagrams thrown up, can conjure up fun scenarios.
Interactions of the liners, passive Sixers and active Niners, give live to imagination.

Documented here is probable the first real-life *Yijing* consultation on UBI:
Question: Is UBI a Good Idea !
18 coins were mixed, thrown down on the table and arranged randomly in 6 rows of 3.
Results:

Tail	Head	Head	TopSixer
Head	Tail	Head	Sixer5
Tail	Head	Head	Sixer4
Head	Tail	Tail	Niner3
Tail	Tail	Tail	Sixer2 c (changeable to Niner2)
Tail	Head	Tail	FirstNiner

TopSixer	— —		TopSixer	— —
Sixer5	— —		Sixer5	— —
Sixer4	— —	changes	Sixer4	— —
Niner3	———	to	Niner3	———
Sixer2	— — c		Niner2	———
FirstNiner	———		FirstNiner	———
(Hex.36)	Enlighten-hurt		(Hex.11)	Interaction

Enlighten-Hurt (Hexagram 36): Fire Trigram below and Earth Trigram above
image: Fire beneath Earth, is like the Sun going into Earth, being obscured cover-up.
signification: UBI (fire, enlightenment) is enlightenment obscured, not yet active i.e. !
Interaction (Hexagram 11): Heaven Trigram below and Earth Trigram above.
image: Heaven (light) rises and Earth (heavy) settles down crossing paths, Interaction.
signification: UBI like Heaven will rise above Earth, benefiting all humankind.
Divination Verdict:
UBI obscured in the subconscious will rise above the conscious to benefit the world.
Interation is auspicious and will bring prosperity.

Comments:
It seems consistent that Yijing can be consulted for an opinion on any matters.
Yijing's coverage is broad enough to raise interesting Hexagrams for all consultations.
There are 64x64=4096 possible combinations of Hexagram and Conversion pairs!
Yijing has not failed us, giving us the interesting image of a dormant UBI rising.

Does China need UBI after Poverty Alleviation ?

Recently China has declared full success in eliminating extreme poverty in the country.
"China's fight against poverty entered a critical stage after the 18th CPC National Congress in 2012. At the end of 2020, through eight years of hard work, China achieved the goal of eliminating extreme poverty – a key goal for the new era of building socialism with Chinese characteristics. The 98.99 million people in rural areas who were living below the current poverty threshold all shook off poverty; all the 128,000 impoverished villages and 832 designated poor counties got rid of poverty. China has eliminated poverty over entire regions and eradicated extreme poverty." *(White paper, China. 2021)*

However there are 600 million citizens still earning barely 1,000 yuan per month.
"..Chinese Premier Li Keqiang said China still had 600 million people whose monthly income was barely 1,000 yuan ($154). ..by any measure China has made huge strides to lift millions out of the toughest standards of living over the last few decades."
(*Goodman, 2021*)

With a Gini index of 0.49, inequality remains unbearably high in China.
"China's Gini coefficient – a measure of inequality from 0 to 1, with 0 being perfect equality – has hovered between 0.46 and 0.49 over the past two decades. A level of 0.40 is usually regarded as a red line for inequality." (*Mullen, 2021*)
"Wealth inequality among individuals has increased at different speeds across countries since 1980." "The rise in wealth inequality has nonetheless been very large in the United States, where the top 1% wealth share rose from 22% in 1980 to 39% in 2014." "The top 1% wealth share doubled in both China and Russia between 1995 and 2015, from 15% to 30% and from 22% to 43%, respectively." *(World Inequality Report. 2018)*

China has set the year 2035 as the target date to achieve common prosperity.
"President Xi pledged last year to make "more substantial progress on common prosperity for all" by 2035, and a pilot programme in Zhejiang province is designed to narrow the income gap there by 2025." (*Mullen, 2021*)

Comments:
China has eradicated poverty, and now embarks on achieving common prosperity.
With a Gini Index of 0.49, China is set to tackle the serious problem of inequality.
The UBI is cash, guaranteed to reach everyone, simply and directly reducing inequality.
China is rich now, having successfully embraced great advances in digital technology.
But the huge profit gain has somehow enriched only a small number of people.
Yes, China needs UBI to eradicate inequality after lifting its people out of poverty.

Political Will Lacking for UBI Implementation

UBI has potentially profound ramifications for global inequalities.
"Poverty is eliminated, the labour contract becomes more nearly voluntary, and the power relations between workers and employers become less unequal since workers have the option of exit. The possibility of people forming cooperative associations to produce goods and services to serve human needs outside the market increases."
(*Wright, 2017*)

UBI can solve global inequalities, but depend on the political will for implementation.
"The level of taxation needed to pay for a basic income is, of course, an important issue. But the sustainable level of taxation in any country is not mainly an economic issue. It is a political issue that depends on the administrative capacity to extract taxes and the political will to do so." (*Wright, 2017*)

This is clearly seen in Namibia - UBI success and institutional failure -
"In conclusion, the pilot project had a dramatic overall positive effect on the selected community. The Basic Income Grant Coalition calculated that the cost for nationwide implementation of unconditional universal basic income for all would be N\$ 1.2 – 1.6 billion (USD 71 – 95 million) per year, equivalent to 2.2 – 3% of Namibia's GDP (2019 – 12.37 USD Billion). In short, UBI in Namibia was and is feasible. The missing component then and now remains the lack of political will to apply the project on a national level." *(Petrova, 2020)*

Nwanazia (2021) in the Netherlands similarly high-lighted the lack of political will.
"UBI can be financed with the abolition of tax cuts, tax credit, increased VAT rate, ... There is money for saving corporations in the pandemic, there is money to pay for UBI. With so much spent on sponsoring wars, paying for such an endeavor is a breeze."

In contrast, Silicon Valley Leaders are very optimistic that A.I. will one day fund UBI.
"In as little as 10 years, AI could generate enough wealth to pay every adult in the U.S. \$13,500 a year, Altman said in his 2,933 word piece called 'Moore's Law for Everything" ..Software that can think and learn will do more and more of the work that people now do. ..We could do something called the American Equity Fund .. would be capitalized by taxing companies above a certain valuation 2.5% of their market value each year, ..and by taxing 2.5% of the value of all privately-held land, payable in dollars." *(Shead, 2021)*

Comments:
Studies the world over show that even very small UBI does improve life for recipients. Political Will is lacking because of the cost, like 3 trillions needed annually in the USA. Starting small, \$100/mth instead of \$1,000/mth, reduces the cost to a mere 0.3 trillion.
At least with an extra \$1,200/yr millions are helped to pay their \$500 emergency bills

UBI Revolution and Evolution

*Indeed, the state of civilization is so wretched that a **revolution** should be made in it !*
"The present state of *civilization* is as odious as it is unjust. It is absolutely the opposite
of what it should be, and it is necessary that **a revolution should be made in it**. The
contrast of affluence and wretchedness continually meeting and offending the eye, is
like dead and living bodies chained together... I care not how affluent some may be,
provided that none be miserable in consequence of it." *(Paine, 1817)*

And paying people for no work, UBI is a revolutionary idea even to learned professors !
"Con 3: UBI removes the incentive to work, adversely affecting the economy and
leading to a labor and skills shortage...However "if we pay people, unconditionally, to
do nothing… they will do nothing" and this leads to a less effective economy, says
Charles Wyplosz PhD, Professor of International Economics at the Graduate Institute in
Geneva (Switzerland)." (*ProCon.org, 2021*)

The full subsistent UBI of $10k/yr is too costly, then may consider $5k/yr for a start.
"The Cost: There are over 300 million Americans today. Suppose UBI provided
everyone with $10,000 a year. That would cost more than $3 trillion a year.
This single figure equals more than three-fourths of the entire yearly federal budget. It's
also equal to close to 100 percent of all tax revenue the federal government collects...
Or, consider UBI that gives everyone $5,000 a year. That would provide income equal
to about two-fifths of the poverty line for an individual (which is a projected $12,700 in
2016) and less than the poverty line for a family of four ($24,800)." *(Greenstein, 2019)*

Alaska Permanent Fund Dividend (apfc.org) is popular, paying only $1k to $2k per year.
"All Alaskan citizens are eligible for the same annual amount of APFD, (young and old,
natives and non-natives) who have resided in the state for a year or more, except for
those who have been incarcerated for felonies of the state. ..The first annual individual
payout of PFD in 1982 was $1000 USD. The lowest individual dividend payout was
$331.29 in 1984 and the highest was $2,072 in 2015. ..And, seemingly unnoticed, it has
provided unconditional cash assistance to needy Alaskans .." (wikipedia.org).

In poor villages, a meager grant (8% of the average income) shows positive results.
"The Basic Income Grant (BIG) pilot project was run in the Namibian settlement of
about 1,000 people in the Otjievero-Omitara area ..The grant was N$100 per person per
month (8% of the average income, around US$12), cash paid unconditionally to all
residents .. Besides improving child nutrition and school attendance, the project
produced many economic activities in the community.." *(Wikipedia, 2021)*
Comments:
Paying people an unconditional Universal Basic Income is indeed a **revolutionary** idea.
Because of the high cost, UBI may be allowed to evolve from say $100 to $1,000/mth.
Even $100/mth will allow needy people to pay two emergency bills of $500 in a year.
Start a small UBI now and allow its evolution with support from A.I. progression.

The Hapless Majority: Stand UP

For milleniums, the hapless Majority has been victimized by the Minority ruling class.

01民之饥	The people's hunger *(Laozi, ch.75)*
02以其上食税之多	Because their rulers tax too much
03是以，饥	Hence, the hunger
09服文采	Cloth in finery (Lords and Kings) *(Laozi, ch.53)*
10帶利剑	Carry sharp swords
11厌饮食	Over-indulge in food and wine
12财货有余	Wealth and goods possession in excess
13是谓盗夸	They are chiefs of robbers *(Jingwei, 2012)*

Paine observed the wretchedness of the Majority (denied of their natural inheritance).
"Cultivation is at least one of the greatest natural improvements ever made by human invention. It has given to created earth a tenfold value. But the landed monopoly that began with it has produced the greatest evil. It has dispossessed more than half the inhabitants of every nation of their natural inheritance, without providing for them, as ought to have been done, an indemnification for that loss, and has thereby created a species of poverty and wretchedness that did not exist before.." *(Paine, 1817)*

And the hapless Majority remains helpless till this day, denied its Birthright to a UBI.
"In 2005, an estimated 100 million people worldwide were homeless and as many as one billion people (one in 6.5 at the time) lived as squatters, refugees or in temporary shelter, all lacking adequate housing. Historically in the Western countries, the majority of homeless have been men (50–80%), with single males in particular ..When compared to the general population, people who are homeless experience higher rates of adverse physical and mental health outcomes. Chronic disease severity, respiratory conditions, rates of mental health illnesses and substance use are all often greater in homeless populations than the general population. Homelessness is also associated with a high risk of suicide attempts." *(Wikipedia, Nov. 2021)*

While the poor get poorer, and the rich get richer by the day.
"Wealth inequality among individuals has increased at different speeds across countries since 1980. ..The rise in wealth inequality has nonetheless been very large in the United States, where the top 1% wealth share rose from 22% in 1980 to 39% in 2014. ..The top 1% wealth share doubled in both China and Russia between 1995 and 2015, from 15% to 30% and from 22% to 43%, respectively." *(World Inequality Report. 2018)*

Comments:
Since the time of Laozi (c.580 BC), the hapless Majority has been bullied non-stop.
It is time for the hapless Majority to Stand Up, to demand a rightful UBI for everyone.
To vote out of office the politicians/governments that do not provide a subsistent UBI.

Characteristics of UBI Truly

*Paine's UBI is truly **universal**, paying **every person** at 21 years 15 pounds sterling once. And **every person** from the age of 50 years the sum of 10 pounds per annum, **for life**.*
"To create a National Fund, out of which there shall be paid to *every person*, when arrived at the age of twenty-one years, the sum of fifteen pounds sterling, as a compensation in part, for the loss of his or her natural inheritance, by the introduction of the system of landed property: And also, the sum of ten pounds per annum, during life, to every person now living, of the age of fifty years, and to all others as they shall arrive at that age." *(Paine, 1817)*

*Thus Iran is among the first countries to introduce a **Universal** Basic Income.*
"For years Iran had been subsidizing its citizens for petrol, fuel and other supplies that benefit the rich more. In 2010 such subsidies were replaced with a cash payment equivalent to 40 USD **per person** monthly. Thus Iran is among the first countries to introduce a national basic income." *(Wikipedia, Aug 2021)*

*The BIG excluded those above the age of 60, hence **Not Universal** Basic Income.*
"The Basic Income Grant (BIG) pilot project was run in the Namibian settlement of about 1,000 people in the Otjievero-Omitara area over 2 years, from Jan. 2008 to Dec.2009. The grant was N$100 per person per month (8% of the average income, around US$12), cash paid unconditionally to all residents below the age of 60 and registered living there in July 2007, regardless of social or economic status."
(wikipedia, Aug. 2021. Universal basic income around the world.)

*Spain's programme is limited to the poorest families, also **Not Universal** Basic Income.*
"Spain's government has started what might just be remembered as the world's biggest economics experiment. On 15 June, it launched a website offering monthly payments of up to €1,015 (US$1,145) to the nation's poorest families. The programme, which will support 850,000 households, is the largest test yet of an idea called universal basic income (UBI) — in which people are given a cash payment each month to spend however they choose." *(Arnold, 2020)*

*All pilot studies worldwide are **Not UBI truly**, but they are nevertheless more effective.*
Evidence amassed UBI is more effective than traditional forms of social security.
UBI is an unconditional income, money you are entitled to, regardless of your status.
Difference between UBI and a benefit is that there are conditions attached to a benefit.
(Nwanazia, 2021)

Comments:
Many studies, purportedly on Universal Basic Income have been done worldwide.
But none are truly UBI, i.e. *universal, unconditional, monthly cash income, for life.*
As UBI has been proven positive, nations should start implementing UBI Truly.

UBI: from Apes to Humanity

Laozi (c.580- BC) has called the ruling class Robber Chiefs, for over taxing the people.

01民之饥　　　　　　　　The people's hunger *(Laozi, ch.75)*

02以其上食稅之多　　　　Because their rulers tax too much

03是以，饥　　　　　　　Hence, the hunger

09服文采　　　　　　　　Cloth in finery (Lords and Kings) *(Laozi, ch.53)*

10帶利剑　　　　　　　　Carry sharp swords

11厌饮食　　　　　　　　Over-indulge in food and wine

12财货有余　　　　　　　Wealth and goods possession in excess

13是谓盗夸　　　　　　　They are chiefs of robbers *(Jingwei, 2012)*

Liezi (c.450- BC) called the ruling elite nature's termites, for greed/ever wanting more.

02 "丰屋美服，　　　　　"Luxurious House Beautiful Clothes, *(Liezi, ch.7.16)*

03 厚味姣色，　　　　　　Rich Taste (food) Pretty Color (sex)

04 有此四者，　　　　　　Having These 4 Things,

05 何求于外？　　　　　　What Else To Request ?

06 有此而求外者，　　　　People Having These And still Request More,

07 无厌之性。　　　　　　Never Dislike (always greedy) This Character.

08 无厌之性，　　　　　　Never Dislike (wanting ever more) This Character,

09 阴阳之蠹也。　　　　　The Termites of Yin Yang (Nature) that's. *(Jingwei, 2021)*

Paine (1817) is totally disgusted in his description of the state of civilization in his time.
"The present state of *civilization* is as odious as it is unjust. It is absolutely the opposite of what it should be, and it is necessary that a revolution should be made in it. The contrast of affluence and wretchedness continually meeting and offending the eye, is like dead and living bodies chained together... I care not how affluent some may be, provided that none be miserable in consequence of it."

Nwanazia (2021) discussed Universal Basic Income in the Netherlands: would it work ?
"The rich get richer, the poor get poorer, this is unsustainable and unchecked capitalism. UBI helps eradicate poverty, giving us a much fairer, better, more sustainable world."

Technological advances can generate an abundance of resources to pay for a UBI.
"One reason we think it may work is that technological improvements should generate an abundance of resources," wrote Y Combinator president Sam Altman in a blog post. "Although basic income seems fiscally challenging today, in a world where technology replaces existing jobs and basic income becomes necessary, .." *(Gunn, 2019)*

Comments:

Since ancient times, the greedy ruling elite never stopped exploiting the commoners.

UBI is the only policy guaranteed to reach everyone, unlike any other welfare schemes.

Automation destroys jobs, but also creates abundance of wealth for all Humanity.

With a UBI, unlike birds/animals, humans no longer need to worry about the next meal.

We graduate from apes to humans; hence book title, UBI: from Apes to Humanity.

A Proposed UBI Index

"There's a saying in business that 'what gets measured gets managed for.' We need to start measuring different things." *(Yang, 2018. pp.200)*

A UBI is the natural inheritance from the motherland for every citizen, man and woman. It must be the responsibility of the national government to deliver a UBI to its citizens. And so far to date, no nation on earth has managed a UBI for its people, except Iran !

Google it: What is the median income of the US 2022?
"The average personal income in the United States is $63,214, with the median income across the country being $44,225. Real wages averaged $67,521 in 2022, and average household incomes averaged to $87,864.
Average Family Income by State 2022 - World Population Review
https://worldpopulationreview.com › state-rankings › aver…"

Google it: What is the 2022 US poverty level?
For individuals   2021 income number $12,880
                       2022 income number $13,590
Federal Poverty Level (FPL) - Glossary - HealthCare.gov
https://www.healthcare.gov › glossary › federal-poverty...

Recently in his presidential campaign, Yang proposed giving every American a $1,000/mth with no string attached. This guaranteed UBI cash raises every American above the poverty line. Thus in this situation, we may propose a UBI Index of 100%. The UBI Index is: UBI cash given out, expressed as % of the national poverty level. When only $800/mth is received by every citizen, then a UBI Index of 80% is achieved. When only $500/mth is received by each citizen, then a UBI Index of 50% is achieved. Directly each citizen knows whether government has delivered by the cash received.

Where is the poverty line in Kenya?
The overall rural and urban poverty lines are, respectively, 3,252 and 5,995 Kenya shillings (Kshs) per month per person (in adult equivalent terms) and include minimum provisions for both food and non- food expenditures. *(Poverty & Equity Brief - World Bank DataBank https://databank.worldbank.org › data › poverty)*
Kenya paying 3,252 Kshs/mth to citizens raises every Kenyan above the poverty line. Likewise Kenya has achieved a UBI Index of 100%.
Comments:
A birthright, subsistent UBI is a natural inheritance of humans from the motherland. All governments should initiate a UBI for citizens, maybe starting at 10% UBI Index. Even a $100/mth UBI allows the average US citizen to pay two $500 emergency bills. ***Yearly the UBI Index will show which nations have improved life for their citizens.***

In Conclusions

*In our World of Miseries, a $100/mth UBI is still a relief to many to pay the $500 emergency bill.
The World of Capitalism is Selfish /Corrupt, creating Inequality /Poverty that we observe today.
Studies show, even a small UBI is a panacea of relief, recipients are happier/healthier/trustful.*

***UBI is BirthRight,** "as joint life proprietor with the rest in the property of the soil"(Paine,18171)
UBI ought to be added into the Universal Declaration of Human Rights as new article 31.
UBI is Justice, paying women for unpaid work at home, caring work that amounts to 50% GDP.
UBI for a Healthy Population, may be a useful general public health strategy. (Haridy, 2020)
UBI for Crime Reduction, a safer environment is savings from a smaller police force, less prisons.
UBI is Education /Hope for the future, as studies report children having more school attendance.
UBI is Liberation long overdue as the majority remains oppressed since Laozi's (c.580 BC) time.
UBI for everyone, bears no Stigma; those in need of assistance are not less worthy than others.*

*UBI may reverse population shrinkage, as financial burden is the main reason for low birth rate.
UBI benefits children more as they are the priority for parents, positively affecting their future.
Youth Basic Income is timely and fair as they start out in life, for not many have family support.
Also the Aged deserves support for a graceful closure, and a modest UBI is their Inherent Right.
It's doubly criminal to deny women, for UBI is her Right, for unpaid caring-work done at home.
It is criminal to oppose UBI as Paine said, "..unless they adopt the crime of opposing justice."*

*No UBI pilot reported recipients working less, rather they are more like starting small businesses.
No empirical evidence that poor people Abuse the use of UBI on drugs/alcohol; they are rational.*

*UBI projects raise a flourish of local market activities, and hope/business/prosperity for the poor.
UBI Economy is a trickle-up economy that stimulates the local market, helps increase the GDP.
UBI is affordable, A.I. can generate abundance for billionaires, a subsistent UBI for 99% others.
UBI funding is a breeze as governments have money saving corporations, money sponsoring wars
UBI implementation is simple, as mobile phone technology transferring cash is done in an instant.
Governmental UBI cash for Covid-19 relief has been proven to be swift and efficient, worldwide.*

*UBI is Dao in Laozi's Daoism, given to the people, making governing easy as cooking small fish.
UBI is like 'Ride on Wind' with Liezi; "like the folks are light, aren't ..with the heaviness of life."
On the UBI idea, Yijing has not failed, giving us the interesting image of a dormant UBI rising.
China does need a UBI after poverty alleviation, it makes the goal of common prosperity easier.*

*Political Will is lacking for UBI; still the Alaskans are happy with a very small UBI (~$100/mth).
UBI is a Revolutionary idea, best allowed to evolve, say from $100 to $1,000/mth over 10 years.
The hapless Majority must stand up to demand the rightful UBI from government, else no votes.
Characteristics of UBI Truly: Universal for everyone/unconditional/monthly cash income/for life.
UBI: from Apes to Humanity; humans no longer need worry over the next meal like birds/animals.*

***A UBI Index is proposed, UBI cash as % of the national poverty level, paid out monthly.
UBI Index to guide implementation, to show which nations have improved life for its citizens.***

Just Imagine

In the morning, I used to walk to the basketball courts at a distance for exercise.
I never fail to see early birds foraging busily on grass patches all along the way.
Often squabbling over a larger piece of edible found that cannot be swallowed whole.
When nobody needs to have anxiety over the next meal, like the birds !
Then we may graduate from being truly clothed apes into truly human beings !

Just Imagine a world when everyone can enjoy a guaranteed survival UBI !
A guaranteed minimum UBI will turn the world into a paradise on earth !
The unfortunate homeless folks will not need to worry over the next meal.
Then they have the time and energy to plan and work for their own salvation.
Unpaid housewives will have a little extra to feed / clothe their children better.
Healthier children will produce more laughter in their play and happiness at home.
Young people can use their UBI in savings for a good education and better future.
Instead of early abortion from school or landed with a debt burden after graduation.
Many hard working salaried people are living from paychecks to paychecks.
Some extra cash for contingency will greatly relieve them of their constant stress.
With some spare cash, retirees can be more enterprising to start small businesses.
Or indulge in new hobbies and stay healthier, lessening demand on the health system.
Those born sick and handicapped are helpless but too have the same birthright to a UBI.
May this resource be returned to them so that they may compensate their caregivers.

Just Imagine a world when everyone can enjoy a guaranteed survival UBI !
People are less stressed resulting in fewer visits to hospitals' emergency units.
People have less quarrels at home resulting in less break-up families.
Less desperate people who rob for just a few dollars even in cities of first-world nations.
Less desperate people willing to borrow from loan-sharks, getting into debt-trap scams.
It will give hope and support to the weak who are more prone to suicidal thoughts.
It will strengthen the underprivileged and make them more resistant to scams.
It supports the unscrupulous who feel less need to scheme and scam the innocent.

So far, many UBI studies the worldover have demonstrated its many potential benefits.
Prevent the trillions that unlawfully accumulated with the devious privileged few.
Just spread and give the people a little extra and trust them to work to help themselves.
The power of the masses when awakened and released can build a paradise on earth.
Then the planet may graduate from a planet of Apes to a planet of Humanity !

Looking Forward

Laozi (c.580 BC) has called the ruling class 'Chiefs of robbers' some 2500 years ago.

09 服文采	Cloth in finery (Lords and Kings)
10 帶利剑	Carry sharp swords
11 厌饮食	Over-indulge in food and wine
12 财货有余	Wealth and goods possession in excess
13 是谓盗夸	They are chiefs of robbers *(ch.53, Jingwei 2012)*

Liezi (c.450- BC) says the elite class who want ever more are 'Termites of Society'.

02 "丰屋美服,	"Luxurious House Beautiful Clothes,
03 厚味姣色,	Rich Taste (food) Pretty Color (sex)
04 有此四者,	Having These 4 Things,
05 何求于外？	What Else To Request ?
06 有此而求外者,	People Having These And still Request More,
07 无厌之性。	Always Greedy This Character.
08 无厌之性,	Wanting Ever-more This Character,
09 阴阳之蠹也。	The Termites of Yin Yang (Nature). *(ch.7.16, Jingwei 2021)*

Paine (1817) is no less critical and disgusted of the 'affluent possessor of property'.
"...The superstitious awe, the enslaving reverence, that formerly surrounded affluence, is passing away in all countries and leaving the possessor of property to the convulsion of accidents. When wealth and splendour, instead of fascinating the multitude, excite emotions of disgust;.."

Paine's solution: property be placed on national protection for the general mass.
"...when the more riches a man acquires, the better it shall be for the general mass; it is then that antipathies will cease, and property be placed on the permanent basis of national interest and protection." *(Paine, 1817)*

In short:
The abundance of wealth generated by A.I./automation is common property.
It is Government duty to harness it for distribution to the general mass as UBI.
Before pseudo-capitalists hijacked this common resource for personal possession.
Then there is No question of taxing the rich to support the poor.
The Hapless Majority should unite to vote in governments supportive of UBI.
Remember, UBI is not charity, but an inherent Right of everyone on earth.

Bibliography

Clearly, Thomas (1993). *I Ching*. Shambhala, Boston & London. ISBN 978-0-87773-661-5.

Coutinho, Steve (not dated). *Liezi*. Internet Encyclopedia of Philosophy. (site visited, June 2020)

Dawkins, Richard (2006). *The God Delusion*. ISBN 9780618918249.

Graham, A.C. (1990). *The Book of Lieh-tzu*. Columbia University Press. ISBN 0-231-07236-8.

Hawking, S.W., Mlodinow L. (2010). *The Grand Design*. A Bantam Book, London. ISBN 9780553819229

Jingwei (2012). *Laozi: Quest for the Ultimate Reality*. Self-publication. Print-on-demand, Lightning Source, UK. ISBN 978-981-07-3758-0.

Jingwei (2018). *Yijing: Wisdom of 4 Sages*. Self-publication. Print-on-demand by Lightning Source, UK, ISBN 978-981-14-0204-3.

Jingwei (2021). Liezi: *World of Delusions. Self-publication.* Print-on-demand by Lightning Source, UK, ISBN 978-981-14-8572-5.

New Encyclopedia Britannica (1988). *Lieh-tzu*. Vol. 28 , 5th ed., Encyclopedia Britannica Inc. Chicago USA.

Paine, Thomas (1817). *Agrarian Justice*. W.T. Sherwin Printed. London.

Pearson, Margaret J. (2011). *The Original I Ching*. North Clarendon, U.S.A., Tuttle Publishing. ISBN 978-0-8048-4181-8.

Stein, Jess (1984). *Random House College Dictionary*. Revised Edition. Random House, USA. ISBN 0-394-43600-8.

Seymour-Smith, Martin (1998). *The 100 most influential books ever written: the history of thoughts from ancient times to today*. Secaucus, N.J. : Carol Publ. Group. ISBN 978-0806520001.

The Bible Societies (1976). *Good News Bible*. Collins. UK. Bible Society. ISBN 0-564-00311-5.

Wong, Eva (2001). *Lieh-Tzu: A Taoist Guide to Practical Living*. Boston: Shambhala. ISBN 1-57062-899-8.

Yang, Andrew (2018). *The War on Normal People*. Hachette Books, New York Boston. ISBN 978-0-316-41421-0.

References

World of Miseries (articles)

World Population Review, (2021). Crime Rate By Country 2021. (*https://worldpopulationreview.com/country-rankings/crime-rate-by-country*

Prison
From Wikipedia, the free encyclopedia (///en.wikipedia.org/ wiki/Prison)

Homelessness
Wikipedia, last edited on 17 November 2021 (///en.wikipedia.org/wiki/Homelessness)

Homelessness in Canada
Wikipedia, 28 November 2021 (///en.wikipedia.org/wiki/Homelessness_in_Canada)

Homelessness in China
Wikipedia. 6 September 2021 (///en.wikipedia.org/wiki/Homelessness_in_China)

Homelessness in Finland
From Wikipedia, 22 Nov. 2021 (///en.wikipedia.org/wiki/Homelessness_in_Finland)

What's stopping Hong Kong from fixing its housing crisis?
Zhou Wenmin and Wang Duan. Caixin Global. 09 Jul 2021(thinkchina.sg/whats-)

Homelessness in India
From Wikipedia, 2 August 2021 (///en.wikipedia.org/wiki/Homelessness_in_India)

HOMELESSNESS IN JAPAN: THE COUNTRY WITH THE SMALLEST PERCENTAGE OF HOMELESS PEOPLE
Eduardo Bravo, AUGUST 03, 2021 (///tomorrow.city/a/homelessness-in-japan)

State of Homelessness: 2021 Edition
(///endhomelessness.org/homelessness-in-america/homelessness-statistics/)
Has China lifted 100 million people out of poverty?
By Jack Goodman. 28 February 2021 (https://www.bbc.com/news/56213271)

1 in 5 South Africans Are Living in Extreme Poverty: UN Report
- Khanyi Mlaba December 23, 2020 (///www.globalcitizen.org/en/content/)

South Korea's inequality paradox: long life, good health and ...
Justin McCurry in Seoul, Wed 2 Aug 2017 (///www.theguardian.com › inequality ›)

https://en.wikipedia.org/wiki/Syria
Since March 2011, Syria has been embroiled in a multi-sided civil war, with a number

"Contempt for the poor in US drives cruel policies,"
says UN expert. Sep, 2019 (https:web.archive.org/web/)

Poverty Rate By Country 2021
(https://worldpopulationreview.com/country-rankings/poverty-rate-by-country)

Syrian children turn to suicide, self-harm to escape horrors of war: report
By Lin Taylor, MARCH 7, 2017 (///www.reuters.com/article/us-mideast-)

North West Syria: Number of suicide attempts and deaths rise sharply
Source: Save the Children 29 Apr 2021 (///reliefweb.int/report/syrian-arab-republic/)

Suicide in China
From Wikipedia, 10 November 2021, (///en.wikipedia.org/wiki/Suicide_in_China#)

Health at a Glance: Europe 2020 : State of Health in the EU Cycle
OECD/EU (2018), (///www.oecd-ilibrary.org/sites/89109c81-en/)

Latvia and Lithuania begin to tackle a chronic scourge: suicide
By Gordon F. Sander, 11 Feb. 2020 (///www.csmonitor.com/World/Europe/)

Suicide crisis soars in South Africa
Charlotte Motsoari. 5 Oct 2021 (///mg.co.za/opinion/2021-10-05-suicide-)

Suicide in South Korea
From Wikipedia, the free encyclopedia (///en.wikipedia.org/wiki/Suicide_)

Suicide in the United States
From Wikipedia, 6 November 2021 (///en.wikipedia.org/wiki/Suicide_in_United_States)

Suicide Rate By Country 2021
© 2021 World Population Review (///worldpopulationreview.com/country-rankings/)

References (Discussions)

Arnold, Carrie. May 2018. *Money for nothing: the truth about universal basic income* (//nature.com/articles/d41586-018-05259-x)

Arnold, Carrie. July 2020. *Pandemic speeds largest test yet of universal basic income* (https://www.nature.com/articles/d41586-020-01993-3)

Arnold, Carrie. July 2020. *Pandemic speeds largest test yet of universal basic income* (https://www.nature.com/articles/d41586-020-01993-3)

Bay City News Service Jul 28, 2020. *Santa Clara County rolls out UBI program for youth transitioning out of foster care.* (//paloaltoonline.com/news)

BBC News, 5 June 2016. **Switzerland's voters reject basic income plan** (//bbc.com/news/world-europe)

Bravo Eduardo, AUG 2021. Homelessness in Japan. The country with the smallest percentage of homeless people. (//tomorrow.city/a/homelessness-in-japan)

Claudia & Haarmann - BIG Coalition, 2020. *The Pilot Project - an executive summary* (http://www.bignam.org/BIG_pilot.html)

Cox, David. Jun.2020. *Canada's forgotten universal basic income experiment.* BBC worklife. (//www.bbc.com/worklife/article/20200624-)

Drexel.edu, 2021. Universal Basic Income: Key to reducing food insecurity and improving health - Overview 2021 (//drexel.edu/hunger-free-centre/research/briefs-)

Eckas, Andrew. 2021. *Examining Universal Basic Income in Kenya* (//borgenproject.org/UBI-in-kenya/).

Forget, EL. 2011. *The Town with No Poverty: The Health Effects of a Canadian Guaranteed Annual Income Field Experiment.* Canadian Public Policy vol. 37.

Goodman, Jack. February 2021. *Has China lifted 100 million people out of poverty?* (https://www.bbc.com/news/56213271)

Greenstein, Robert June 2019. *Commentary: Universal Basic Income May Sound Attractive But, If It Occurred, Would Likelier Increase Poverty Than Reduce It* (//cbpp.org/research/poverty-and-opportunity/)

Gunn, Dwyer. Feb.2019. *A Universal Basic Income might hurt poor people more than help.* (//psmag.com/economics/a-universal-basic-income-)

Haridy, Rich. 2020. *Canada's canceled basic income trial produces positive results* (//newatlas.com/good-thinking/canada-basic-income-).

Hyun-ju, Ock. August 2020. *Gyeonggi Province sets example for universal basic income* (koreaherald.com)

Ihaza, Jeff. May 2017. (the online.com/post/1613/Iran-introduces-basic-income).

Jingwei, 2012. *Laozi: Quest for the Ultimate Reality (an appreciation of the Dao De Jing).* self-published. ISBN 978-981-07-3758-0.

Jingwei, 2019. *Yijing: Wisdom of 4 Sages (a complete translation and appreciation of Yijing).* self-published. ISBN 978-981-14-0204-3.

Jingwei, 2021. *Liezi (列子): World of Delusions (A complete translation and analysis of Liezi).* self-published. ISBN 978.981.14.8572.5

 Kottasova, Ivana and Wattles, Jackie. June 2016. *Switzerland rejects plan to pay every citizen at least $2,500 a month* (//money.cnn.com/).

Li, Fan. July 2021. *Is Universal Basic Income the Key to Happiness in Asia?* (StanfordSocialInnovationReview, https://ssir.org).

Lowrey, Annie. 2021. *Stockton's Basic-Income Experiment Pays Off* (theatlantic.com/ideas/archive/).

Lu, Donna. 2020. *Universal basic income seems to improve employment and well-being* (//newscientist.com/article/2242837-).

Mason, G. 2017. *Revisiting Manitoba's basic-income experiment.* Winnipeg FreePress.

Matthews, Dylan. Jul. 2017. *A basic income really could end poverty forever But to become a reality, it needs to get detailed and stop being oversold.* (//vox.com/policy-and-politics- automation)

McCurry, Justin in Seoul, Wed 2 Aug 2017. *South Korea's inequality paradox: long life, good health and ...* (//www.theguardian.com › inequality ›)

MPUCTP, 2015. *Executive Summary.pdf* (sewabharat.org). The Madhya Pradesh Unconditional Cash Transfers Project.

Mullen, Andrew. Aug. 2021. *What is China's common-prosperity strategy that calls for an even distribution of wealth?* (scmp.com/economy/china-economy/article/3146271/)

Newsdesk, April 2021. *IAG (inside asian gaming)*

Nwanazia, Chuka. 2021. *Universal basic income in the Netherlands: would it work?* (//dutchreview.com/culture/ubi-in-the-netherlands-)

Overview, 2021. *Universal Basic Income: Key to reducing food insecurity and improving health.* (//drexel.edu/hunger-free-centre/research/briefs-and-reports/UBI)

Paine, Thomas. 1817. *Agrarian Justice* (http://piketty.pse.ens.fr/files/Paine1795.pdf) grundskyld.dk Digital edition 1999 by www.grundskyld.dk

Parolin, Zach. June 2019. *Welfare Money is Paying for a Lot of Things Besides Welfare Columbia University* (theatlantic.com/ideas/archive/..)

Petrova, Gery. 2020. *Namibia - UBI success and institutional failure* (BIEN website. basicincome.org/news/2020/07)

Piper, Kelsey. 2020. *How a basic income experiment helped these Kenyans weather the Covid-19 crisis* (vox.com/future-perfect/).

ProCon.org (Author). Feb. 2021. *Universal Basic Income - Top 3 Pros and Cons* (www.procon.org/headline/universal-basic-income-)

Samuels, Robert. 2019. *$1,000 a month, no strings attached* (//washingtonpost.com/politics/ -no-string-attached/)

Seymour-Smith, Martin. 1998. *The 100 most influential books ever written: the history of thoughts from ancient times to today.* Secaucus, N.J.: Carol Publ.Group. ISBN 978-0806520001.

Shead, Sam. Mar 2021. *Silicon Valley Leaders Think A.I. will one day fund free cash handouts.* (//.cnbc.com/openai-ceo-sam-altman-)

Sutter, John D. 2015. *The argument for a basic income* (//edition.cnn.com/opinion/).

UN expert says (Alston, Philip). Sep. 2019. *"Contempt for the poor in US drives cruel policies,"* (https:web.archive.org/web/).

Vanderborght,Yannick. Sep. 2013. posted in BIEN News (basicincome.org/news).

Widerquist, Karl. June 2012. *Brazil: Basic Income in Quatinga Velho celebrates 3-years of operation* (//basicincome.org/news/)

Widerquist, Karl. 2013. *Google gives $2.5 Million to a Direct Cash Transfer Charity* (//basicincome.org/news/).

The Madhya Pradesh Unconditional Cash Transfers Project (MPUCTP)

White paper, China.Xinhua. April 6, 2021. *Poverty Alleviation: China's Experience and Contribution.* (//english.scio.gov.cn/whitepapers/2021-04/06/content_77380652_4.)

Wikipedia, Aug.2021. *Universal basic income around the world.* (https://en.wikipedia.org. Aug 2021)

Wikipedia, Sep. 2021. *UBI around the world. USA, small-scale basic income*

Wikipedia.org, Sep. 2021. *UBI around the world, Quatinga Velho.*

Wikipedia, Aug. 2021. *Universal basic income in India*

Wikipedia, Nov. 2021. *Homelessness.* (//en.wikipedia.org/wiki/Homelessness)

Wikipedia, 10 November 202. *Suicide in China* (//en.wikipedia.org/wiki/Suicide_in_China#)

World Inequality Report. 2018 Executive Summary Coordinated by: Facundo Alvaredo, et al. (//wir2018.wid.world/files/...)

Wright, Erik Olin. Feb 2017. *Can universal basic income solve global inequalities?* (//en.unesco.org/inclusivepolicylab/news/)

Yang, Andrew. 2018. *The war on normal people.* Hachette Books, USA. ISBN: 978-0-316-41421-0.

Yorgun, Meric. Sep 15, 2020. *Mongolia's resource-to-cash transfers* (//basicincome.org/news/)

Zeitlin, Dave. 20 Apr 2021. *Fighting Poverty With Cash* (//thepenngazette.com/fighting-poverty-with-cash)

173   Appendices

Glossary

BI   Basic Income

GDP   Gross domestic product is the standard measure of the value added created through the production of goods and services in a country during a certain period.

Gini Index   Gini Index or Gini ratio, is the most commonly used measure of income distribution—simply put, the higher the Gini coefficient, the greater the gap between the incomes of a country's richest and poorest people.

GST   Goods and Service Tax

Income, average   Average income, a measure of total income including wage, investment benefit, and other capital gains divided by total number of people in the population including non-working residents. Average wages can differ from median wages; for example, the Social Security Administration estimated that the 2020 average wage in the United States was $53,383, while the 2020 median wage was $34,612.

Income, median   The median income is the income amount that divides a population into two equal groups, half having an income above that amount, and half having an income below that amount.

MMT   Modern Money Theory is a heterodox macroeconomic theory that describes currency as a public monopoly and unemployment as evidence that a currency monopolist is overly restricting the supply of the financial assets needed to pay taxes and satisfy savings desires.

Paine, Thomas   (1737-1809). Author of *Agrarian Justice*. 1817. W.T. Sherwin Printed. London.

Poverty line, Int'l   In September 2022 the international poverty line is being updated from $1.90 to $2.15 per person per day.

Poverty line, USA   Poverty line for an individual (which is a projected $12,700 in 2016)

UBI   Universal basic income (UBI) is a sociopolitical financial transfer policy proposal in which all citizens of a given population regularly receive a legally stipulated and equally set financial grant paid by the government without a means test. If the level is sufficient to meet a person's basic needs (i.e., at the poverty line), it is sometimes called a full basic income; if it is less than that amount, it may be called a partial basic income.

UBI Index (proposed)   Equals to UBI cash payout monthly, expressed as % of the **national poverty level**.
Example: poverty level in the US is $1,000/mth.
When UBI payout is $1,000/mth, the Index is 100%.
When UBI payout is $500/mth, the Index is 50% achieved.
Example: poverty level in rural Kenya is 3252 shillings
When monthly payout is 3252 shillings, the Index is 100%.
When monthly payout is 1626, the Index is 50% achieved.
This simple Index may be a good indicator of social wellbeing. Listing in comparison will show which countries are better able to take care of their citizens.

UBI living   UBI cash pay-out monthly to all citizens for life, equivalent to the national median income, for a decent living (The median income is the income amount that divides a population into two equal groups, half having an income above that amount, and half having an income below that amount). Example: Switzerland rejects plan to pay every citizen at least $2,500 a month, citing too expensive, high taxes and inflation. *(Kottasova and Wattles. 2016)*

UBI subsistence   UBI cash pay-out monthly to all citizens for life, equivalent to the national poverty level, to meet a person's basic needs for food and lodging, like $,1000/mth in the USA or 3252 shillings in Kenya.

Yang, Andrew   (1975 -) American businessman, attorney, candidate in the 2020 Democratic Party presidential primaries. Author of *The war on normal people*. 2018. Hachette Books, USA. ISBN: 978-0-316-41421-0.

UBI Human Rights. UN

https://www.un.org/en/about-us/universal-declaration-of-human-rights

Universal Declaration of Human Rights

The Universal Declaration of Human Rights (UDHR) is a milestone document in the history of human rights. Drafted by representatives with different legal and cultural backgrounds from all regions of the world, the Declaration was proclaimed by the United Nations General Assembly in Paris on 10 December 1948 (General Assembly resolution 217 A) as a common standard of achievements for all peoples and all nations. It sets out, for the first time, fundamental human rights to be universally protected and it has been translated into over 500 languages. The UDHR is widely recognized as having inspired, and paved the way for, the adoption of more than seventy human rights treaties, applied today on a permanent basis at global and regional levels (all containing references to it in their preambles).

Preamble

Whereas recognition of the inherent dignity and of the equal and inalienable rights of all members of the human family is the foundation of freedom, justice and peace in the world,

Whereas disregard and contempt for human rights have resulted in barbarous acts which have outraged the conscience of mankind, and the advent of a world in which human beings shall enjoy freedom of speech and belief and freedom from fear and want has been proclaimed as the highest aspiration of the common people,

Whereas it is essential, if man is not to be compelled to have recourse, as a last resort, to rebellion against tyranny and oppression, that human rights should be protected by the rule of law,

Whereas it is essential to promote the development of friendly relations between nations,

Whereas the peoples of the United Nations have in the Charter reaffirmed their faith in fundamental human rights, in the dignity and worth of the human person and in the equal rights of men and women and have determined to promote social progress and better standards of life in larger freedom,

Whereas Member States have pledged themselves to achieve, in co-operation with the United Nations, the promotion of universal respect for and observance of human rights and fundamental freedoms,

Whereas a common understanding of these rights and freedoms is of the greatest importance for the full realization of this pledge,

Now, therefore,

The General Assembly,

Proclaims this Universal Declaration of Human Rights as a common standard of achievement for all peoples and all nations, to the end that every individual and every organ of society, keeping this Declaration constantly in mind, shall strive by teaching and education to promote respect for these rights and freedoms and by progressive measures, national and international, to secure their universal and effective recognition and observance, both among the peoples of Member States themselves and among the peoples of territories under their jurisdiction.

Article 1

All human beings are born free and equal in dignity and rights. They are endowed with reason and conscience and should act towards one another in a spirit of brotherhood.

Article 2

Everyone is entitled to all the rights and freedoms set forth in this Declaration, without distinction of any kind, such as race, colour, sex, language, religion, political or other opinion, national or social origin, property, birth or other status. Furthermore, no distinction shall be made on the basis of the political, jurisdictional or international status of the country or territory to which a person belongs, whether it be independent, trust, non-self-governing or under any other limitation of sovereignty.

Article 3

Everyone has the right to life, liberty and security of person.

Article 4

No one shall be held in slavery or servitude; slavery and the slave trade shall be prohibited in all their forms.

Article 5

No one shall be subjected to torture or to cruel, inhuman or degrading treatment or punishment.

Article 6

Everyone has the right to recognition everywhere as a person before the law.

Article 7

All are equal before the law and are entitled without any discrimination to equal protection of the law. All are entitled to equal protection against any discrimination in violation of this Declaration and against any incitement to such discrimination.

Article 8

Everyone has the right to an effective remedy by the competent national tribunals for acts violating the fundamental rights granted him by the constitution or by law.

Article 9

No one shall be subjected to arbitrary arrest, detention or exile.

Article 10

Everyone is entitled in full equality to a fair and public hearing by an independent and impartial tribunal, in the determination of his rights and obligations and of any criminal charge against him.

Article 11

1. Everyone charged with a penal offence has the right to be presumed innocent until proved guilty according to law in a public trial at which he has had all the guarantees necessary for his defence.

2. No one shall be held guilty of any penal offence on account of any act or omission which did not constitute a penal offence, under national or international law, at the time when it was committed. Nor shall a heavier penalty be imposed than the one that was applicable at the time the penal offence was committed.

Article 12

No one shall be subjected to arbitrary interference with his privacy, family, home or correspondence, nor to attacks upon his honour and reputation. Everyone has the right to the protection of the law against such interference or attacks.

Article 13

1. Everyone has the right to freedom of movement and residence within the borders of each state.
2. Everyone has the right to leave any country, including his own, and to return to his country.

Article 14

1. Everyone has the right to seek and to enjoy in other countries asylum from persecution.
2. This right may not be invoked in the case of prosecutions genuinely arising from non-political crimes or from acts contrary to the purposes and principles of the United Nations.

Article 15

1. Everyone has the right to a nationality.
2. No one shall be arbitrarily deprived of his nationality nor denied the right to change his nationality.

Article 16

1. Men and women of full age, without any limitation due to race, nationality or religion, have the right to marry and to found a family. They are entitled to equal rights as to marriage, during marriage and at its dissolution.
2. Marriage shall be entered into only with the free and full consent of the intending spouses.
3. The family is the natural and fundamental group unit of society and is entitled to protection by society and the State.

Article 17

1. Everyone has the right to own property alone as well as in association with others.
2. No one shall be arbitrarily deprived of his property.

Article 18

Everyone has the right to freedom of thought, conscience and religion; this right includes freedom to change his religion or belief, and freedom, either alone or in community with others and in public or private, to manifest his religion or belief in teaching, practice, worship and observance.

Article 19

Everyone has the right to freedom of opinion and expression; this right includes freedom to hold opinions without interference and to seek, receive and impart information and ideas through any media and regardless of frontiers.

Article 20

1. Everyone has the right to freedom of peaceful assembly and association.
2. No one may be compelled to belong to an association.

Article 21

1. Everyone has the right to take part in the government of his country, directly or through freely chosen representatives.
2. Everyone has the right of equal access to public service in his country.
3. The will of the people shall be the basis of the authority of government; this will shall be expressed in periodic and genuine elections which shall be by universal and equal suffrage and shall be held by secret vote or by equivalent free voting procedures.

Article 22

Everyone, as a member of society, has the right to social security and is entitled to realization, through national effort and international co-operation and in accordance with the organization and resources of each State, of the economic, social and cultural rights indispensable for his dignity and the free development of his personality.

Article 23

1. Everyone has the right to work, to free choice of employment, to just and favourable conditions of work and to protection against unemployment.
2. Everyone, without any discrimination, has the right to equal pay for equal work.
3. Everyone who works has the right to just and favourable remuneration ensuring for himself and his family an existence worthy of human dignity, and supplemented, if necessary, by other means of social protection.
4. Everyone has the right to form and to join trade unions for the protection of his interests.

Article 24

Everyone has the right to rest and leisure, including reasonable limitation of working hours and periodic holidays with pay.

Article 25

1. Everyone has the right to a standard of living adequate for the health and well-being of himself and of his family, including food, clothing, housing and medical care and necessary social services, and the right to security in the event of unemployment, sickness, disability, widowhood, old age or other lack of livelihood in circumstances beyond his control.
2. Motherhood and childhood are entitled to special care and assistance. All children, whether born in or out of wedlock, shall enjoy the same social protection.

Article 26

1. Everyone has the right to education. Education shall be free, at least in the elementary and fundamental stages. Elementary education shall be compulsory. Technical and professional education shall be made generally available and higher education shall be equally accessible to all on the basis of merit.
2. Education shall be directed to the full development of the human personality and to the strengthening of respect for human rights and fundamental freedoms. It shall promote understanding, tolerance and friendship among all nations, racial or religious groups, and shall further the activities of the United Nations for the maintenance of peace.
3. Parents have a prior right to choose the kind of education that shall be given to their children.

Article 27

1. Everyone has the right freely to participate in the cultural life of the community, to enjoy the arts and to share in scientific advancement and its benefits.
2. Everyone has the right to the protection of the moral and material interests resulting from any scientific, literary or artistic production of which he is the author.

Article 28

Everyone is entitled to a social and international order in which the rights and freedoms set forth in this Declaration can be fully realized.

Article 29

1. Everyone has duties to the community in which alone the free and full development of his personality is possible.
2. In the exercise of his rights and freedoms, everyone shall be subject only to such limitations as are determined by law solely for the purpose of securing due recognition and respect for the rights and freedoms of others and of meeting the just requirements of morality, public order and the general welfare in a democratic society.
3. These rights and freedoms may in no case be exercised contrary to the purposes and principles of the United Nations.

Article 30

Nothing in this Declaration may be interpreted as implying for any State, group or person any right to engage in any activity or to perform any act aimed at the destruction of any of the rights and freedoms set forth herein.

Comments:

In Spite of this Declaration of Human Rights, millions worldwide are living in poverty. The bottom 90% of citizens are still subjected to bullying by the elitist top 10%.
Provision of a UBI ought to be added to this Declaration for everyone.

Acknowledgements

I like to register my highest respect for Thomas Paine, and feel privileged to quote him. I am grateful to all the authors and contributors listed and not listed in the Bibliography and references.

I am grateful to the National Library Singapore for the complimentary ISBN and CIP.

I'm thankful to Lightning Source UK. for facilitating the print-on-demand (POD) setup. And for online distribution through Ingram International.

Much effort has been exercised with the honest use of facts/figures in this monograph. My deepest apologies for any errors and omissions that remain.

*Laozi: Quest for the Ultimate Reality
(an appreciation of the Dao De Jing).*
ISBN 978-981-07-3758-0. Jingwei, 2012. (self-published)

Kirkus Reviews

Laozi: QUEST FOR THE ULTIMATE REALITY
BY JINGWEI · RELEASE DATE: OCT. 26, 2012

Jingwei offers a new translation and analysis of an ancient Chinese text.

Serving as an archivist for the imperial court of the Zhou Dynasty (circa sixth century B.C.E.), Laozi postulated that the universe was formed by Dao, the benevolent spirit of the bellows, who creates and asks nothing in return. Laozi compiled his thoughts in the Dao De Jing, encouraging readers to model their actions after the nurturing Dao: "He suggests reconciliation in response to grievance suffered, and to embrace the gentle, feminine way in life." Jingwei gives readers all 81 chapters of the Dao De Jing, in both the original Chinese and in English translation. These are followed by sections labeled "Laozi's thinking," which breaks down the text further, and "Comments," which delivers a more modern interpretation of the text. Following the 81 chapters are supplementary sections that analyze the text by theme—"On Fears and Crises"; "On Femininity Appreciated"; "On Freedom"—as well as some thoughts on the composition of the text and the intentions of Laozi. Jingwei has used a very small font for his debut book so that each chapter fits on one page. The volume's 200-page length belies the amount of material found therein. Jingwei's translation remains clear and easy to follow, and the notes further clarify the text. Chapter 61, for example, begins: "Whatever big nation, be low flowing (humble) / Be the world's female." "Laozi's thinking" reads: "For big nation, be humble; be like the mother of the world." The "Comment" reads: "Here Laozi simply urges nations to behave with humility to avoid conflicts with each other." The reiteration of each concept (in verse, then ancient note, then modern note) has an almost meditative effect on the reader, and the frequent use of metaphors from nature allows discussions of conflict and strife to be removed from any emotion-laden, real-world context. Jingwei occasionally falters in his English, though never in a way that makes his intention unclear. He states that his purpose in this translation is to bring the text to a wider audience, and in this he has succeeded.

An accessible and informative presentation of the Dao De Jing.

Yijing: Wisdom of 4 Sages
(a complete translation and appreciation of Yijing).
 ISBN 978-981-14-0204-3. Jingwei, 2019. (self-published)

Synopsis

The *Yijing* (易經) or *Book of Changes* is the best known Chinese book in the West.
There are translations and much academic interests in its teaching and philosophy.
However there is no comprehensive popular version in the shop for the general public.
This title, *"Yijing: Wisdom of 4 Sages"*, presents the ancient book in its entirety.
It includes King Wen's 64 Hexagrams that developed from Fuxi's 8 Trigrams;
King Wen's Hexagram assessments; Zhougong's 384 Liner descriptions and advice;
Together with all '10 Wings' of Kongzi's comprehensive explanations, commentaries.
Both ancient texts and English translation are arranged side by side for easy reference.
Author's analysis and comments are placed on the same page for immediate reading.

The *Yijing* Hexagrams depict 64 images of life, each with 6 Liners for societal strata.
A total of 384 human situations are covered with predictions and advice for actions.
Life is never static, *Yijing* basic tenets are Changes with inter-conversion of Hexagrams.
A total of 64x64 or 4096 combinations, covering any imaginable situation variations.
Hence Yijing has been popular for oracular consultation down the centuries.

Herein are topical discussions of what can be learned from the *Yijing* in its entirety.
Examples of consultation are also documented to illustrate enjoyment of using *Jijing*.
For teaching morals and counseling, Yijing's full potential has yet to be realized.
Kongzi says reading the *Yijing* is like getting council from our parents
        (如臨父母).
Towards this end, the general public and scholars may find this self-help manual useful.

*Liezi (*列子*): World of Delusions*
(A complete translation and analysis of Liezi).
ISBN 978.981.14.8572.5. Jingwei, 2021. (self-published)

Synopsis

Liezi (c.450-375BC), with Laozi and Zhuangzi are the pillars of philosophic Daoism.
A lesser known philosopher among the trio, we have seen little translation of his work.
He was first introduced by Zhuangzi, described as having the ability to 'ride on wind'.
After Zhuangzi, philosophical Daoism has developed into religious Daoism in China.
"*Liezi:World of Delusions*", translates the ancient *"Liezi"* in its entirety, all 8 chapters.
Includes herein are analysis of his thinking such as on destiny, freedom, life and death.

Heavenly Signs (ch.1*天瑞*): Explores Origin of the Universe, to Humanity and Nature.
Like postulating the self-Creator, achieving longevity, to timing & harvesting of nature.
Huangdi (ch.2 黄帝***):*** Explores forms of Government, exposes Sorcery, and no 'Dao'.
Like Huangdi's dream, Liezi 'ride on wind', god-like sorcerer, to catching cicada.
King Mu of Zhou (ch.3 周穆王***):*** Narratives on Illusions, Dreams, Realities, Emotions.
Like King Mu's astro-travels, woodcutter's lost deer to Yanren's emotional return.
Zhongni (Confucius, ch.4 仲尼***):***Examines what is Sagehood, Sages and Philosophies.
Like Confucius teaches flexibility, hermit Nankuazi talks to win, hedonism of Yangzhu.
Tang's Queries (ch.5 汤问***):*** Limits of Heaven and Earth, limits of Balance and skills.
Like Kuafu chased the sun, exchanging hearts to balance, Zaofu learned charioteering.
Effort or Destiny (ch.6 力命***):*** That shapes the march of events, success and failure.
Like Beigonzi thick in Virtue thin in Destiny, and Yiwu's inevitable denial of Baoshu.
Yangzhu (ch.7 杨朱***):*** Covering his thoughts on life, death, and aspects of humanity.
Like: "not to lose a hair to save the world", "not privatizing body and possessions".
Charming talks (ch.8 說符***):*** Miscellaneous narratives, revealing human delusions.
Like liberating doves, better to ban catching; disaster fell from Heaven; the axe thief.

Liezi's narratives and stories are simple, engaging, entertaining and enlightening.
*Kuafu chased sun (*夸父追日*)*, *Yugong moves mountains (*愚公移山*)*, are much read.
And Liezi's logic is simple: "Nothing creates nothing; outside of limits, no limit".
Liezi exposes sorcery, illusions and delusions, and repeatedly says there is 'No Dao'.
Liezi advises constant meditation on 'thinking no right/wrong, speaking no good/evil'.
Life is short, not be shackled with convention, to enjoy life with *no intrusion on others*.
Naturally, Liezi believes in Effort for success, leaving Destiny to account for failures !
Liezi rejects transcendence and such, saying 'Dao' cannot be acquired and possessed.
Liezi teaches natural Woral Daoism, his charming stories are all reflective of human society.
Take note of our Delusional failings, and self-cultivate for the better.

Self-Publishing

These days when one has something to say, self-publishing a book is not difficult.
Do-it-yourself all the way will cost less than SD1000/- with self-editing, self-assessment.
As a self-publisher, you have to do your own promotion of the book to readers!
However, you are your own boss and you get to keep all the publisher compensation.
To help avoid the Vanity Press, my simple experience to share is as followed:

Manuscript
Have the full script between covers all completed, format digitally in a doc.pdf for print.

Optional
Kirkus Reviews (online)
For a 250-word review in 6 weeks, UDS550 (~SD850/-).
(my first book *Laozi: Quest for the Ultimate Reality*, 206 pages in 2016)

Accounting and Corporate Regulatory Authority (ACRA)
As a self-publisher, I need to register an account with the above authority.
First registration on site cost SD68/- in 2012, subsequently yearly fee SD20/-.
Require a registered Office address (home address, $5/- annually, HDB authority)

National Library Board (NLB) Legal Deposit Office (online)
In Singapore these are complimentary services and take about a week.
First apply for an International Standard Book Number (ISBN).
Then apply for Cataloguing in Publication (CIP) -
(require to submit title page, title page verso, copyright page, table of contents, preface and introduction).

Obligation
To submit 2 printed copies of the title to the NLB Legal Deposit Office.
And henceforth established the author's copyright to the book.

Local Printer
Ultra Supplies, Queensway Shopping Centre, Singapore.
Have a book cover design for about SD100/-.
Print the First test copy with perfect binding for about SD30/- (paperback, 300 pages).
Confirmed that the book product is in order, and print more as required.

Lightning Source UK (online)
Set-up fee GBP42 (~SD84/-) for Print-on-demand (POD).
Market Distribution fee GBP7 yearly(~SD14/-) for distribution worldwide to online retailers.

Copyrights and Disclaimer

Universal Basic Income (UBI): from Apes to Humanity
by Jingwei, 2022 June
email: jjingwei11@gmail.com

Disclaimer:
Every precaution has been taken in the preparation of this monograph.
The publisher and author apologize for any errors or omissions that may remain.
The publisher and author assume no liability whatsoever for damages suffered
from its usage.

Universal Basic Income was proposed by Thomas Paine in the *Agrarian Justice* (1817).
Andrew Yang revitalized this idea in his campaign as a presidential candidate in 2019.
In our world today, great advances in technologies have generated abundance of wealth,
enough to make the majority of us wealthy and to eliminate poverty on earth. But
instead selfish governments have allowed wealth loss through cronyism, enriching only
the top 1% of the population, and the gap between the Have and the Have-nots has
widened !! The *uncivilized* state of society that Paine described has persisted to this day.
The solution has to be the simple UBI that he proposed, fair to everyone and easily
administered by any government who honestly cares for its citizens. Just put the cash
into the hands of the people and their own self-help effort is certain to make a happier
world for themselves.
UBI Index of happiness is proposed, UBI cash paid as % of the national poverty level.

Universal Basic Income (UBI): from Apes to Humanity

Introduction
World of Miseries
  25 articles reviewed
World of Capitalism
  25 articles examined
UBI pilot Studies
  29 schemes appreciated
Discussions
  35 topics on UBI
In Conclusions
Just imagine
Looking Forward
Bibliography & References

Jingwei (景維) 1945-, a research-biochemist retired in 2007, self-published since 2012.
1. *Laozi: Quest for the Ultimate Reality* (ISBN 978-981-07-3758-0), 206pp. nonfiction.
2. *Yijing: Wisdom of 4 Sages* (ISBN 978-981-14-0204-3), 2019, 311pp. nonfiction.
3. *Liezi: World of Delusions* (ISBN 978-981-14-8572-5), 2021, 350pp. nonfiction.
All books are available print-on-demand (POD) by Lightning Source UK.
Only offered on Espresso Book Machine, Amazon.com, other online stores worldwide.
Email: jjingwei11@gmail.com

Book cover:
Thousand miles of rivers and mountains landscape (Wang Ximeng, Northern Song)
千里江山圖 (王希孟, 北宋, c.1113 AD. 青綠山水, 12 m. 長卷)